HEARTBEAT

GEORGE BUSH
IN HIS OWN WORDS

COMPILED AND EDITED BY

JIM McGRATH

A LISA DREW BOOK

SCRIBNER

New York   London   Toronto   Sydney   Singapore

SCRIBNER
1230 Avenue of the Americas
New York, NY 10020

Compilation copyright © 2001 by Jim McGrath

SCRIBNER and design are trademarks of Macmillan Library Reference USA, Inc.,
used under license by Simon & Schuster, the publisher of this work.

For information about special discounts for bulk purchases,
please contact Simon & Schuster Special Sales:
1-800-465-6798 or business@simonandschuster.com

DESIGNED BY ERICH HOBBING

Text set in Adobe Garamond

Manufactured in the United States of America

1   3   5   7   9   10   8   6   4   2

Library of Congress Cataloging-in-Publication Data is available.

ISBN 0-7432-2479-5

For sweet Anna Maria,
mi hija linda,
and our hero,
Paulina.

When I left office and returned to Texas in January 1993, several friends suggested I write a memoir: . . . "The press never really understood your heartbeat—you owe it to yourself to help people figure out who you really are."

" . . . It's all about heartbeat."
> —from *All the Best, George Bush:*
> *My Life in Letters and Other Writings,*
> by George Bush

EDITOR'S NOTE

The speech excerpts, interview quotes, and statements presented in this book appear in their original form with the following two exceptions: (1) most entries were edited for length; (2) for the sake of clarity, typos were corrected.

Many of these entries were taken from the *Public Papers of the Presidents,* published by the National Archives. In 7,521 pages, this encompasses President Bush's 1,459 days in office and contains official transcripts of his 273 press conferences and exchanges with the White House press corps; 1,520 speeches, remarks, and toasts; and dozens more full-length interviews. I also reviewed several hundred postpresidential speeches and transcribed selected material from 37 taped media interviews and conferences the former President participated in in conjunction with the George Bush School of Government and Public Service at Texas A&M University.

CONTENTS

INTRODUCTION

by Barbara Bush

I first knew George Bush was the most articulate man I had ever met way back in 1941. I was sixteen, he was seventeen, and although we did not know each other, we were attending the same Christmas party. When he walked across the room and asked me if I'd like to dance, they were without a doubt the most brilliant words I had ever heard.

After fifty-six years of marriage, I haven't changed my mind. I could be accused of being prejudiced, but George is one of the funniest, wisest, most caring people I know. I know this because I have listened carefully to everything he's said all these years.

That is why I was thrilled when our friend Jim McGrath told me he was thinking of compiling a book of quotes from George's speeches. Several years ago George published a book of letters, *All the Best,* which revealed a very private side to a very public man. The letters showed that through the ups and downs of his life, George never lost his sense of humor, his sense of purpose, or his sense of honor. I felt that Jim's idea would be the perfect follow-up to the letters book, this time focusing on the spoken word.

Heartbeat is a wonderful record of how an American President led his country—and the world—during an interesting time in our history. Whether it was George speaking about the challenge of Desert Storm, or the somewhat sudden peaceful end to the Cold War, *Heartbeat* provides insight into how a President tries to both reassure and inspire.

And whether it was George's declaration "I hate broccoli" or his words explaining away the stomach flu in Japan, *Heartbeat* serves as a reminder that our Presidents are, after all, just plain people like the rest of us.

Unlike his predecessor, Ronald Reagan, George was never accused of being the Great Communicator. He was always too impatient to fine-tune his speech-giving skills, which once in a while resulted in a twisted syntax or two. (I'm sure you all remember the media teasing him that English was his second language.)

But after reading *Heartbeat,* I think you'll be reminded of an American President who felt the issues deeply, stood by his principles, never forgot the importance of honor, and never lost his sense of humor.

Best of all, *Heartbeat* is George Bush doing what he does best, speaking from the heart.

PREFACE

To the degree that one can separate a historical figure like George Bush from the high office he once held, this is *not* a political book. This book is not about defending a partisan ideology or advancing issues; rather, it is about one man's values and character as reflected in the documented words he spoke.

Put another way, this is not a book about prayer in school; but it is partly about prayer in the White House. It does not dissect arms control treaties; but in part, it does weave a vision of superpower cooperation and peace just beyond the horizon of conflict and war. It does not attempt to spin campaign results; but rather, show, in his own words, how a great and good man withstood defeat in the political arena bloodied but unbowed—his sense of honor undiminished, his sense of humor intact. Finally, this is not a book about a family dynasty; but it occasionally catalogs an insightful thought or two about a nation's enduring legacy of service.

George Bush speaks often of what he calls "heartbeat." He also periodically delves into what a friend of his, golf writer Dan Jenkins, calls "life its ownself." But *heartbeat* is a George Bush original. It is a simple word—a code word—referring to personal bedrock values. For him, *heartbeat* taps into the strong undercurrents of faith, friends, and particularly family that have molded the first sevety-seven years of his life. We hope this book, *Heartbeat,* does likewise.

Admittedly lacking the academic credentials to provide a scholarly analysis of the historic events that define the first Bush presidency, I have had the good fortune—to put it mildly—to work at the forty-first President's side since 1993. I've helped carry his briefcase, both literally and figuratively, around the world— watching, listening, and learning all the way. Like so many others, he and his wife have taught me so much.

Accordingly, my profound gratitude goes, first and foremost, to George and Barbara Bush. This book was not their idea, but both have been supportive from the start. It is a terrible irony that a writer cannot find the right words to describe what their friendship means. They, and their entire family, have been unfailingly kind to me and mine.

Which leads me to my amazing wife, Paulina—my best editor, my best friend. Her love and support are everything. Thanks and love also go to my devoted parents, Anne and James, my loyal sisters, Eileen and Kay, my bawdy brother, Michael, my wonderful in-laws, the Sepulvedas, and long-standing close friends—particularly John Middleton, who offered sound legal counsel.

Upon conceiving this idea, I first consulted Jean Becker, the Bushes' chief of staff and book-writing partner—and since 1994, my mentor and friend. Despite her obsession with deadlines, Jean's judgment is always dead-on. My colleagues at the Bush office and numerous members of the extended Bush political family also offered strong support and encouragement.

It was Lisa Drew, publisher extraordinaire, who called my bluff and commissioned me to make this concept a reality. What Lisa, a dear friend to the Bush family, does not know about the book world can't be worth knowing. She was generous with her expertise—and a joy with whom to work.

Special thanks go to Doug Menarchik, and Warren and Mary Finch at the Bush Presidential Library, for facilitating my research. My gratitude also goes to my esteemed father-in-law, Carlos Sepulveda, George Denison, Steve Kurzweil, Shara Castle, Tracy Davis, Shirley Green, Anita McBride, the Honorable Andy Card, and Rose Zamaria, who helped me prove myself at the White House, the Bush Transition, and the Office of George Bush. Finally, I remain eternally indebted to Jack Steel, who, story by story, first helped me learn the true heartbeat of the great man he knew so well. Were it not for the dirty jokes, you could even say Jack was like a grandfather to Paulina and me. We miss him still.

CHAPTER ONE

1989:
A NEW BREEZE

The President's first Oval Office guest—his beloved mother, Dorothy.
January 21, 1989.

At 12:05 P.M. on January 20, 1989, standing on the U.S. Capitol's West Front, George Herbert Walker Bush addressed the American people for the first time as the forty-first President of the United States. Declaring that a "new breeze is blowing, and a world refreshed by freedom seems reborn," the new President launched an administration that would indeed see the winds of change remake the face of Europe and Latin America within the year. The Wall fell in Berlin; the dictator Manuel Noriega fell in Panama; and the superpowers charted a new path of cooperation at the historic Malta Summit. Meanwhile, closer to home, the President announced a new war on drugs, convened an Education Summit, and confronted the Savings and Loan crisis; and Millie, the Bushes' dog, had puppies.

Commenting on his Inaugural Address the next day, President Bush dictated to his diary: "The speech went about 20 minutes, and it was well received. Congress liked it. We've got to find ways to do this compromise, 'kinder, gentler world'" (All the Best, p. 411).

FAITH, FAMILY, AND FRIENDS:
Values That Remain, Ties That Bind

We are not the sum of our possessions. They are not the measure of our lives. In our hearts we know what matters. We cannot hope only to leave our children a bigger car, a bigger bank account. We must hope to give them a sense of what it means to be a loyal friend; a loving parent; a citizen who leaves his home, his neighborhood, and town better than he found it.
Inaugural Address, U.S. Capitol West Front,
January 20, 1989

ONE NATION UNDER GOD

Never wanting to appear "holier-than-thou," as he would often say, President Bush walked a fine line throughout his Presidency between referencing his deeply held faith and "preaching" too much in public . . .

I freely acknowledge my need to hear and to heed the voice of Almighty God. I began my Inaugural Address with a prayer out of a deep sense of need and desire of God's wisdom in the decisions we face.

Remarks at the National Prayer Breakfast, Washington Hilton Hotel
International Crystal Ballroom, Washington, D.C., February 2, 1989

During their visit to China, the Bushes returned to the church where their daughter, Doro, was baptized . . .

Our family has always felt that church is the place to seek guidance and seek strength and peace. And when you are away from home, you realize how much that means. This church, in a sense, was our home away from home. It's a little different though. Today we came up with twenty motorcars in a motorcade, and I used to come to church on my bicycle, my Flying Pigeon.

Remarks at Chongmenwen Christian Church
in Beijing, China, February 26, 1989

I am convinced that faith and family can help us honor God in a most profound and personal way—daily, as human beings—by the conduct of our lives. They teach us not only to revere but to practice the Golden Rule. And they also help us reflect the internal values of decency, humility, kindness, and caring.

Remarks on the National Day of Prayer,
White House State Dining Room, May 4, 1989

The pupil-turned-President returns to his old school . . .

I can speak very briefly of my time here. I loved those years. They did, indeed, teach me the great end and real business of living. And even now its lessons of honesty, selflessness, faith in God—well, they enrich every day of our lives.

You remember, I'm the guy that said Pearl Harbor Day was on September 7. I want to clear that up—[laughter]—because it was right about here, where that guy in a red coat is standing, that I heard our country was at war on December 7, 1941. And it was over there, in Cochran Chapel, that in June of 1942, a graduate of Phillips Academy gave our commencement address—Henry Stimson. He was then secretary of war, and he observed how the American soldier should be brave without being brutal, self-reliant without boasting, becoming a part of irresistible might without losing faith in individual liberty. I never forgot those words.

For 211 years, Phillips Academy has embodied these qualities that Secretary Stimson alluded to. And it has shown we are "one nation under God." It has inculcated into its sons and daughters a sense of service to others—each day I'm reminded of this. This is the message of our years here and the message with which I close. Without God's help we can do nothing. With God's help there is nothing we cannot do, for our children and for the world.

Remarks at the Bicentennial Convocation of Phillips Academy,
Samuel Phillips Hall, in Andover, Massachusetts, November 5, 1989

MILLIE

The Bushes' dog, Mildred Kerr Bush, was the subject of much media interest throughout 1989. Here, amid questions on terrorism and aid to the Nicaraguan contras, the new President is pressed for details about their dog's pregnancy . . .

Q. How many puppies are you going to have?
The President. If I had to bet—and we've done no sonograms—I would bet six.

Q. Are you going to keep any of them?

The President. . . . I don't think so. A tremendous demand out there, Tom, enormous demand for these puppies. And I'm particularly interested in the op-ed page in one of the great newspapers the other day, where they had two English spaniel breeders saying this was the most outrageous thing they'd ever seen—the attention to having these puppies here in the White House. And then, offsetting opinion, counterpoint, came by an eighty-five-year-old woman who has written a book on English spaniels, who announced that this was one of the greatest things that had ever happened. So, it's causing a very lively debate, much like the AK-47 debate—[laughter]—a tremendous interest in this.

Q. So, you'll be happy when it's over.

The President. Yeah. It's changed my life. . . . Can I tell them what Barbara told me on the phone?

Mr. Fitzwater [Press Secretary Marlin Fitzwater]. Sure.

The President. She said, "Tonight, you're in the Lincoln bed, alone." I said, "Well, why?" She said, "Well, Millie had a very bad night last night, thrashing around, and you would be irritable." So I am being sent down the hall, which just suits the heck out of me.

Q. Who's in the doghouse? You or the dog?

The President. The dog refuses to go in the doghouse is the problem. There's a beautiful pen made for her to have this blessed event in. It's wonderful—little shelf built out so that the puppies can scurry under there and not get rolled on by the mother. I never thought we'd go through something like this again, after the six kids and eleven grandchildren. But it's a whole new thing.

Q. Is this worse?

The President. In a way, it is. In a way, it is. It's mainly because of Barbara's abiding interest in it. She can't move without the dog being two feet away from her. But it's exciting, and we're real thrilled. Millie's mother gave birth on the Farish [friend Will Farish, who gave Millie to the Bushes] bed at night. He woke up, and he heard a little squeak, and there were three pups and more arriving—right on the bed. So we're trying to avoid that. It's wonderful—[laughter]—great new dimension to our lives.

The President's news conference, aboard Air Force One
en route to Washington, D.C., from Colorado Springs,
Colorado, March 17, 1989

The biggest secret in town is that Will Farish's springer spaniel—or English spaniel—is actually Millie's boyfriend. [Laughter] Up to now we've tried to keep his name out of the press. [Laughter] I think it's okay now, though, to reveal his name—Tug Farish III. [Laughter] Just what my elitist image needs—puppies with Roman numerals after their names. [Laughter]

. . . You may have been reading that the pups are sleeping, or have been, on the *Washington Post* and the *New York Times*—[laughter]—the first time in history those papers have been used to prevent leaks. [Laughter]

Remarks at a fund-raising reception
for Senator Mitch McConnell at Lane's End Farm,
Lexington, Kentucky, May 13, 1989

Q. Can you confirm these widespread stories that your dog has been eating rats and squirrels?

The President. She's doing her part. [Laughter]

Q. Has she been eating rats and squirrels?

The President. Not eating them.

Q. Just killing them?

The President. Our dog is a fearless hunter, and what she does on her own time—that's her business.

Q. What does it tell us—that there are rats in the White House yard here?

The President. Look, I just want to keep them out of the swimming pool. One jumped in there when Barbara was swimming. And we're relying heavily on Millie to cut that down.

Q. Mr. President, thank you very much.

The President. There was a mouse in this very room you're sitting
   in. I hope that doesn't terrify you, but he was done in the
   other day, too.

> *Interview with Peter Maer of Mutual/NBC Radio,*
> *Oval Office, November 17, 1989*

Q. How's your dog doing?

The President. Oh, she's wonderful. I don't want to say this in
   front of anybody, but I had to take her into the shower the
   other day and give her a bath because she rolled in something
   bad. I mean, really bad. [Laughter] And so, Barbara, my wife,
   said, "Would you mind giving Millie a bath?" So, even when
   you're President, you've got to do some stuff that isn't too
   good or fun. But when she slept in our bed last night, she was
   very clean, and she smelled real good.

Q. How many puppies did Millie have?

The President. Millie had six puppies. She had five daughters and
   a son. And the son: he's now eight months old. . . . He's much
   bigger than Millie, and he plays with her. We had her up to
   Camp David, and they run through the woods looking for
   things, but there's some bad news. See that rabbit over there?
   Don't let him out if Millie comes to this school, okay?
   [Laughter]

> *Remarks and question-and-answer session with students*
> *at Pickard Elementary School, Room 305, in Chicago, Illinois,*
> *November 20, 1989*

A CLOSE FAMILY

**Early in 1989, after a series of tests, Mrs. Bush was diagnosed
with Graves' disease stemming from a thyroid gone bad. Here
her husband comments on the latest prescription . . .**

I'm delighted that Barbara Bush is with me today. She got a
good, clean bill of health from Walter Reed Hospital, I might add.

But I'm taking another look at her doctor. He told her, "It's okay to kiss your husband, but don't kiss the dogs." [Laughter] So, I don't know exactly what that means. [Laughter]

Remarks to participants in Project Educational Forum
at the Union High School gymnasiumin, Union, New Jersey,
April 13, 1989

The war on drugs earned President Bush the wrath of South American drug cartels, as was evidenced by this exchange with reporters about the security of the President's family . . .

Q. Mr. President, there's a report in *Newsday* today that the drug lords are threatening to kidnap one of your children if they are not granted amnesty. . . .

Q. Do you have any information about what *Newsday* says is a threat?

The President. I do not. And I have a feeling that that matter is of enough importance to me that it would have been brought to my attention. I don't mean to be complacent, but I have confidence in our intelligence community. I have confidence in the international cooperation in intelligence—sometimes I wish it were more. And I have confidence in the Secret Service and their ability to do their job. So, I don't live in fear of anything like this, but, Terry [Hunt of the Associated Press], I've not heard that, and I feel confident I would have if there had been some—what I would call hard intelligence. I can't do my job if I get deterred by rumors. . . . I think I'd know if there was something serious—

Q. But you have increased security, and your children now all have it, when they had declined it.

The President. Yes. Varying degrees. And I don't discuss it because I think one of the contradictions in an open society is, I can understand everyone's interest in knowing every detail, but I can also understand the security system's desire that every detail not be known. I think security is better that way. But that, Helen [Thomas of United Press International]—to the degree security has been stepped up in accordance with the law and the Bush kids, it is not because of a specific, hard piece of intelligence, hard threat. And I'm confident of that. My problem is, would I tell you if I weren't? But I am confident of that. And I'm confident that I gave you the right answer because I think I would have known that.

Q. You may be the last to know. I'm teasing . . .

The President. Thank you all. Any more questions on education? [Laughter]

> *Remarks on the Education Summit and a question-and-answer*
> *session with reporters, Oval Office, September 27, 1989*

On a personal note, all four of the Bush kids played it [Little League]. I coached it. And Barbara—well, back then there were tens of thousands of Texas kids in Little League. And as I've often said, she'd keep score, but there were times when I thought she was carpooling each and every one of them.

> *Remarks congratulating the Trumbull Nationals on winning*
> *the Little League World Championship, Rose Garden,*
> *October 10, 1989*

I'm very sorry that Barbara Bush is not here. She is doing a superb job as First Lady, and she is in good health. I get asked that all the time. You know, there's a magazine, that I'm sure nobody here is too familiar with, called the *National Enquirer.* [Laughter] But apparently they printed a story about her on the front page, and we have had more crazy letters and inquiries about her state of play [health]. But since some of you were nice enough earlier on at this little receiving line that Dan [Ouellette, former Bee County GOP chairman] worked out, that I would tell you she's in very good health. She feels great, and she's kinda winding down her responsibilities as a grandparent. We have our Dallas twins charging around the White House, having been up there at Camp David with us. And she will meet me in Houston, which is no consolation to her because she wanted very much to come back here. But she did ask me to extend to you her warm wishes. And I'll tell you—but I've only been married for close to forty-five years; in January, it'll be forty-five—I think Bar's doing a fantastic job for our country.

Remarks at a barbecue at the Bee County Coliseum,
Beeville, Texas, December 27, 1989

Texas Memories

Before entering politics, George Bush was one of the original pioneers in the offshore drilling industry . . .

A few years after World War II, when I got out of college, I moved out to west Texas; and a couple of years after that, the early fifties, started my own business. And it was a very small firm—not too small to teach me the economic facts of life. But we got started by risk-taking—got the business education by helping others make that company grow. And our company was a high-risk venture. There was new technology that was unproven, full of half-starts and failures in that—it was all called the offshore drilling business. And we took a gamble, and we invested in new technology, and then we succeeded in pioneering a new way to find America's energy.

And it wasn't always easy, even in the years that the company did reasonably well. I recall our despair one time . . . when one of those hurricanes swept through the Gulf of Mexico and one-third of our company's assets were invested in a brand-new drilling rig, with brand-new technology—a hurricane swept through the Gulf. And I went out with our drilling engineer and rented a little Piper . . . in the aftermath of the hurricane and looked and looked and looked. And the rig had totally vanished. People had been taken off before the storm, but the rig was gone. One-third of the investment of our company totally disappeared. But from that and other such similar events, I learned some very important lessons. When that rig went down and people lost their jobs—when we rebuilt, there was the satisfaction of seeing people go back to work. And I saw the strain of the family breadwinners, but I also saw the joy.

Remarks to the National Legislative Conference
of the Independent Insurance Agents of America,
Capitol Hilton Hotel Presidential Ballroom,
Washington, D.C., March 14, 1989

Unlike Davy Crockett, I first set out for Texas not on horseback from Tennessee but from Connecticut in a red Studebaker in June of 1948. And more than forty years later, that trip is still a vivid memory: Highway 80, neon Pearl Beer signs appearing in the desert twilight . . . and stopping at a café—I'll admit it I didn't know if chicken-fried steak was chicken fried like a steak or a steak that tasted like chicken, but I've learned.

Remarks to the Texas State Legislature,
Texas State Capitol House Chamber, April 26, 1989

On the plains of Texas, where for twelve years Barbara and I raised our children, the story is told of a pioneer tradition that said, "Plant plums for yourself, pecans for your grandchildren." A hundred years ago, some farsighted Texas settlers planted these tiny pecan seedlings, and it took hours of backbreaking work, hauling water in the hot prairie sun. But pecan trees take many years to mature, and the settlers themselves would never live to enjoy the shade or food from the tree. It was called, therefore, a grandchildren's cove. Other settlers—well, they wanted quick results, and they planted the fast, quick-growing plum trees. And for a few years they got good fruit. Soon, the soft bark split, sprouting tangled, barren plum bushes. And instead of enjoying the protection of these tall, stately pecan trees, the grandchildren who followed were saddled with the hardship of clearing a thicket.

Remarks at the South Dakota Centennial Celebration
at Sioux Falls Arena, Sioux Falls, September 18, 1989

"Anchor to Windward"

I started fishing at the age of five or so, in the cold waters along the Atlantic coast at Maine, using a lead jig with . . . a little white cloth for bait, trolling with one those old green cotton lines. And after a while, you get the hang of it, pulling in the fish—mackerel and maybe a flounder. But I became acquainted with the waters up there, and so well now that I think I know every reef, when the swells will break and where they will, the sea conditions and where you can find the seals on a given day.

Remarks at the Boy Scout National Jamboree
at Fort A. P. Hill, Bowling Green, Virginia, August 7, 1989

This is a place where we really enjoy ourselves—but more than that, kind of refurbish our souls and get our batteries all charged up and enjoy life really to the fullest. It's a point of view. You can feel it in the land and in the water here. And I know that people that are members of this chamber and other visitors that we have here with us understand exactly what I'm talking about. Barbara has told you that I've been coming here every summer since 19—well, I was born in '24. And the only one I missed was in 1944 when, like many of you, I was in the service. That's the only time we missed being here. And there is a certain magic about the place.

Our kids live in five different states—one in Cape Elizabeth and the others, four different states—and for them, this is an anchor to windward because not far from where this picture was painted my mother was born in a house still standing right there—not too far from St. Ann's Church.

Remarks at a luncheon hosted by the Chamber
of Commerce at Shawmut Inn, Kennebunkport, Maine,
August 30, 1989

FRIENDS

I used to play baseball. Knew I'd never make the big leagues, but I made a lot of friends—friends I learned to count on, both on and off the field. And we trusted each other to come through, no matter how tough it got. And I learned from that. I learned that the kind of people you make your friends can either give you strength or take it away. I'm not sure why it is, but some people just make you find the best in yourself. They can help you become a better person, help you discover more of who you are.

Nationwide Address to Students on drug abuse,
televised from the White House Library, September 12, 1989

Poking fun at Lee Atwater, Republican National Committee chairman and amateur guitarist . . .

The tunes Lee likes to play aren't always music to everyone's ears. I hear Lee asked [Republican Utah senator] Orrin Hatch, "If I bring my guitar tonight, would you have any special requests?" Orrin said, "Yes, just one. Don't play it."

Remarks at the National Hispanic Heritage Presidential Tribute Dinner,
Omni Shoreham Hotel Regency Ballroom, September 12, 1989

We're pleased that Governor [John] Sununu is with us today. Like many young Catholics, as a boy John dreamed of one day becoming pope. [Laughter] It was only after having eight kids that we got him to settle for chief of staff.

Remarks at a luncheon hosted by the Catholic Lawyers Guild
at the Park Plaza Hotel Ballroom, Boston, Massachusetts,
September 23, 1989

The friends you make here last you for the rest of your life, and I'm grateful for that. Some other things don't change. Kindness doesn't change. The education and service that is embodied in the Phillips constitution—talk about—it says both goodness and kindness come from the noblest character and lay the surest foundation of usefulness to mankind.

Remarks to the Phillips Academy Board of Trustees,
at the Borden Gymnasium, in Andover, Massachusetts,
November 5, 1989

THE VISION THING:
On Peace and the Presidency

A President is neither prince nor pope, and I don't seek a window on men's souls. In fact, I yearn for a greater tolerance, and easygoingness about each other's attitudes and way of life.
Inaugural Address, U.S. Capitol West Front,
January 20, 1989

***

When the record of our time is finally written, I hope it will be the story of the final triumph of peace and freedom throughout the globe, the story of the sunrise in the day of mankind's age-old aspirations.
Remarks aboard the USS America, Norfolk, Virginia,
January 31, 1989

THE CHALLENGE TAKEN TO HEART

His first full day on the job, January 21, the new President commented on his new life at a reception for campaign staff members . . .

When you spend the first night in the White House and then when you go to work in that Oval Office, it does sink in, but it sinks in in a wonderful way.

I opened the top drawer of my desk now—a beautiful, historical presidential desk—and there was a really lovely, warm note from my predecessor, which I think demonstrates more than the continuity. It says a lot because it said a lot about our own personal friendship, and it said a lot to me—though he, the modest, now former President, would never say it—but a lot of how I got the chance to be in this job. And so, it was emotional, and yet it had a nice steady feeling to it: that the presidency goes on. . . .

You've got plenty of problems to go around. But because of the reestablished credibility of the United States, because our word is seen as good, because our determination is not doubted, I think I have been dealt a very good hand.

Remarks to campaign staff members and political supporters,
State Department Diplomatic Reception Room, January 21, 1989

Response when asked if, as a World War II veteran, he felt uneasy appearing before the coffin of the late Emperor Hirohito, who had led Japan against the Allies in World War II . . .

I'm representing the United States of America. And we're talking about a friend, and we're talking about an ally. We're talking about a nation with whom we have constructive relationships. . . . Back in World War II, if you'd predicted that I would be here, because of the hard feeling and the symbolic nature of the problem back then of the former emperor's standing, I would have said, "No way." But here we are, and time moves on; and there is a very good lesson for civilized countries in all of this.

The President's news conference in Tokyo,
United States ambassador's residence, February 25, 1989

This nation must stand for tolerance, for pluralism, and a healthy respect for the rights of all minorities.

Remarks to members of the Anti-Defamation League of B'nai B'rith,
Old Executive Office Building, Room 450, March 14, 1989

A truly free society is within reach if, in our hearts, we abolish bias and bigotry and discrimination.

Remarks on signing the Martin Luther King Jr. Federal Holiday Commission Extension Act, White House East Room, May 17, 1989

The Chinese government's repression of the Tiananmen Square demonstrations shook the world. In this reference, President Bush reveals the value he places on personal contacts between leaders and also comments on one of the most indelible images of his presidency . . .

I have a special affection for the Chinese people. I've kept up my relationship with various leaders there. I've been back to China five times since Barbara and I left in 1975. And she's been back six times. And it is with a saddened heart that I, joining many of you, watched the proceedings in Tiananmen Square.

I was so moved today by the bravery of that individual that stood alone in front of the tanks rolling down the main avenue there. And I heard some speculation on the television on what it is that gives a young man the strength, gives him the courage, to stand up in front of a column of tanks right there in front of the world. And I'll tell you, it was very moving, because all of us have seen the bravery and the determination of the students and the workers, seen their commitment to peaceful protest. And that image, I think, is going to be with us for a long time. And all I can say to him, wherever he might be, or to people around the world is: We are and we must stand with him. And that's the way it is, and that's the way it's going to be.

Remarks at the annual meeting of the Business Roundtable, J. W. Marriott Hotel Capitol Ballroom, June 5, 1989

The condition of our inner cities isn't a matter of charts and graphs and these cold statistics. It's more than an exercise in sociology or public policy. It's a question of how people live their

lives, a question of human dignity; and it's a challenge that I take
to heart.

Remarks at the Urban League Conference,
Washington Convention Center, August 8, 1989

———

I think America is waking up, and we are beginning to condemn
that which, let's face it, we've condoned.

Remarks at the South Dakota Centennial Celebration
at the Sioux Falls Arena, Sioux Falls, September 18, 1989

SECURING THE PEACE

This is a time for America to reach out and take the lead, not
merely react. And this is a time for America to move forward
confidently and cautiously, not retreat. As the freest and fairest
and the most powerful democracy on the earth, we must continue to shine as a beacon of liberty, beacon of justice, for all the
people of the world.

Remarks at the swearing-in ceremony for James A. Baker III
as secretary of state, White House East Room, January 27, 1989

———

**On February 9, suffering from laryngitis, President Bush trav-
eled to Capitol Hill to outline his administration's goals before
a Joint Session of Congress, in the House Chamber. "Even the
President worries about getting the jitters," he would later
write (*ATB*, p. 413). But as he noted in his diary of that night:
"My voice held out, although I had to drink some water; but I
felt in command and in control, no nervousness . . ."**

Securing a more peaceful world is perhaps the most important
priority I'd like to address tonight. You know, we meet at a time
of extraordinary hope. Never before in this century have our values of freedom, democracy, and economic opportunity been
such a powerful and intellectual force around the globe. Never

before has our leadership been so crucial, because while America has its eyes on the future, the world has its eyes on America.

———————

Veterans share a special bond. We've seen the face of war; we know its terrible costs. Americans will never knowingly choose conflict. But we know, as well, that we must be ready and willing to respond when our interests and our ideals come under threat.

Let me be clear. I prefer the diplomatic approach. Nations can and should explore every avenue toward working out their differences without resorting to force or military intimidation, but I'm also a realist. I know there is no substitute for a nation's ability to defend its ideals and interests. And too often we hear that we face a stark choice in coping with conflict. We can pursue a diplomatic situation, or we can seek resolution through military means. One, we're told, is incompatible with the other.

Well, this doesn't square with real-world experience. Diplomacy and military capability are complementary; they're not contradictory. Creative diplomacy can help us avert conflict. Negotiations stand the greatest chance of success when they proceed from a position of strength. The fundamental lesson of this decade is simply this: strength secures the peace. America will continue to be a force for peace and stability in the world provided we stay strong.

Remarks at the annual conference of the Veterans of Foreign Wars, Sheraton Washington Hotel Ballroom, March 6, 1989

———————

Yes, we're a prosperous country, and we are at peace. But such quiet moments often become pivotal in the nation's history. The choices we make now are going to determine whether the door to the next American century is closing or opening wide, for all who dare to dream.

Remarks to the National Association of Manufacturers, Mayflower Hotel Grand Ballroom, March 23, 1989

———————

No peace can succeed in a political vacuum.

Remarks following discussions with Prime Minister
Yitzhak Shamir of Israel, at the White House South Portico,
April 6, 1989

As you know, I've just had an audience with His Holiness Pope John Paul II. He was so generous with his time and so generous with his thinking and imparted to me once again his views on world peace and his views on how perhaps we can all work together in that regard. He has devoted his whole life to serving God, and the things that we focused on in this meeting were broad questions of peace and freedom and justice as they apply, or might be applied, all around the world. So, it's a talk that I'll long remember.

Remarks to students at the American Seminary in Vatican City,
Sala Clementina, May 27, 1989

Democracy has captured the spirit of our time. Like all forms of government, though it may be defended, democracy can never be imposed. We believe in democracy—for without a doubt, though democracy may be a dream deferred for many, it remains, in my view, the destiny of man.

Remarks to the Polish National Assembly,
Parliament Building Main Chamber, Warsaw, July 10, 1989

"EUROPE WHOLE AND FREE"

Throughout the spring of 1989, the Bush administration conducted a thorough review of U.S. foreign policy—particularly as it related to Central and Eastern Europe. The first of four major speeches outlining the administration's new strategy was set for Hamtramck, Michigan—a community outside Detroit with strong ethnic ties to Eastern Europe, particularly Poland. Of that speech, President Bush would later write: "The Hamtramck speech was one instance when I was involved from the outset. I worked on the content, and on my delivery, at Camp David the weekend before I was supposed to give it. There were a number of points I wished to make and several issues to avoid. . . . Hamtramck decked itself out in festival manner, with American flags in every window, and smaller ones in what seemed every hand. . . . This was small town ethnic America at its best . . ." (*A World Transformed*, pp. 51–52).

Unknown to the President at the time, an assassin was in the back of the audience but was deterred from getting too close by the Secret Service's metal detectors. He was later apprehended. Meanwhile, the President began setting forth his strategy to engage the world . . .

The West can now be bold in proposing a vision of the European future. We dream of the day when there will be no barriers to the free movement of peoples, goods, and ideas. We dream of the day when Eastern European peoples will be free to choose their system of government and to vote for the party of their choice in regular, free, contested elections. And we dream of the day when Eastern European countries will be free to choose their own peaceful course in the world, including closer ties with Western Europe.

Remarks to citizens at Hamtramck City Hall,
Hamtramck, Michigan, April 17, 1989

The United States now has as its goal much more than simply containing Soviet expansionism. We seek the integration of the Soviet Union into the community of nations. And as the Soviet Union itself moves toward greater openness and democratization, as they meet the challenge of responsible international behavior, we will match their steps with steps of our own. Ultimately, our objective is to welcome the Soviet Union back into the world order. . . .

Forty-three years ago, a young lieutenant by the name of Albert Kotzebue, the class of 1945 at Texas A&M, was the first American solider to shake hands with the Soviets at the bank of the Elbe River. Once again, we are ready to extend our hand. Once again, we are ready for a hand in return.

Remarks at Texas A&M University
Commencement Ceremony, G. Rollie White Coliseum,
College Station, May 12, 1989

While an ideological earthquake is shaking asunder the very Communist foundations, the West is being tested by complacency. We must never forget that twice in this century American blood has been shed over conflicts that began in Europe. And we share the fervent desire of Europeans to relegate war forever to the province of distant memory. But that is why the Atlantic alliance is so central to our foreign policy. And that's why America remains committed to the alliance and the strategy which has preserved freedom in Europe. We must never forget that to keep the peace in Europe is to keep the peace in America.

Remarks at the Boston University commencement ceremony,
Dickerson Field, Massachusetts, May 21, 1989

For too long, unnatural and inhuman barriers have divided the East from the West. And we hope to overcome that division, to see a Europe that is truly free, united, and at peace.

Remarks upon departure for Europe, Andrews Air Force Base,
May 26, 1989

Of course, leadership has a constant companion: responsibility. And our responsibility is to look ahead and grasp the promise of the future. I said recently that we're at the end of one era and the beginning of another. And I noted that in regard to the Soviet Union, our policy is to move beyond containment. For forty years, the seeds of democracy in Eastern Europe lay dormant, buried under the frozen tundra of the Cold War. And for forty years, the world has waited for the Cold War to end. And decade after decade, time after time, the flowering human spirit withered from the chill of conflict and oppression; and again, the world waited. But the passion for freedom cannot be denied forever. The world has waited long enough. The time is right. Let Europe be whole and free.

Remarks at the Rheingoldhalle to the citizens of Mainz,
Federal Republic of Germany, May 31, 1989

On July 11, President and Mrs. Bush traveled to Gdansk, where they had lunch at the home of Lech and Danuta Walesa before the two men addressed the biggest crowd Walesa said he had ever seen outside the Lenin Shipyard—the birthplace of the Solidarity movement. President Bush later wrote: "At the end of the day, I had the heady sense that I was witnessing history being made on the spot . . ."

A new century is almost upon us. It is alive with possibilities. And in your quest for a better future for yourselves and for those wonderful children that I saw coming in from the airport—in that quest America stands shoulder to shoulder with the Polish people in solidarity. Americans and Poles know that nothing can stop an idea whose time has come. The dream is a Poland reborn, and the dream is alive.

Remarks at the Solidarity Workers Monument,
outside the Lenin Shipyard, Gdansk, Poland, July 11, 1989

News of the fall of the Berlin Wall reached President Bush in the Oval Office midafternoon on November 9; and while reports of what was transpiring were still unconfirmed, a decision was made to hold an impromptu press conference in the Oval Office rather than holding a more formal press briefing. President Bush would later reflect: "It was an awkward and uncomfortable conference. The press wanted me to give a summation of this historic moment. Of course, I was thankful about the events in Berlin, but as I answered questions my mind kept racing over a possible Soviet crackdown, turning all the happiness to tragedy. My answers were cautious . . ." (*AWT,* p. 149).

Q. Mr. President, do you think now that East Germany appears to be moving in the direction of Poland and Hungary that the rest of the Eastern Bloc can continue to resist this? I'm thinking of Czechoslovakia, Bulgaria, Romania—will they be next?

The President. No, I don't think anyone can resist it, in Europe or in the Western Hemisphere.

Q. Did you ever imagine—

The President. That's one of the great things about dynamic change in Central America: it's moving in our direction.

Q. Did you ever imagine anything like this happening?

Q. On your watch?

The President. We've imagined it, but I can't say I foresaw this development at this stage. Now, I didn't foresee it, but imagining it—yes. When I talk about a Europe whole and free, we're talking about this kind of freedom to come and go, this kind of staying with and living by the Helsinki Final Act, which gives the people the right to come and go.

Q. In what you just said, that this is a sort of great victory for our side in the East-West battle, but you don't seem elated. And I'm wondering if you're thinking of the problems.

The President. I am not an emotional kind of guy.

Q. Well, how elated are you?

The President. I'm very pleased. And I've been very pleased with a lot of other developments. And, as I've told you, I think the United States part of this, with us not related to this development today particularly, is being handled in a proper fashion. And we'll have some that'll suggest more flamboyant courses of action for this country, and we're, I think, handling this properly with allies, staying in close touch in this dynamic change— try to help as developments take place, try to enhance reform, both political and economic.

And so, the fact that I'm not bubbling over—maybe

it's getting along towards evening, because I feel very good about it.

Remarks and a question-and-answer session with reporters
on the relaxation of East German border controls,
Oval Office, November 9, 1989

What is happening in Berlin and on our television screens is astounding. World War II, fought for freedom, ironically left the world divided between the free and the unfree; and most of us alive today were born into that sundered world. And now almost fifty years have passed, and some have wondered all these years why we stayed in Berlin. And let me tell you! We stayed because we knew, we just knew—all Americans—that this day would come. And now a century that was born in war and revolution may bequeath a legacy of peace unthinkable only a few years ago.

Remarks on presenting the Presidential Medal of Freedom
to Lech Walesa and the Presidential Citizen's Medal
to Lane Kirkland (President of the AFL-CIO),
White House East Room, November 13, 1989

Some historians point to the Malta Summit as the beginning of the end of the Cold War. It was also known as the Seasick Summit because of high winds that buffeted the harbor-bound U.S. and USSR ships . . .

Frankly, I'd like to get Chairman Gorbachev to get an idea of what U.S. navy food is like. [Laughter] Maybe not—[laughter]—what I'm trying to do is ease tensions.

Remarks to the crew and guests on the USS Forrestal
in Malta, December 1, 1989

President Bush would later comment on "Malta's positive effect upon my personal relationship with Gorbachev, which I

thought was symbolized in our joint press conference—the first ever in U.S.-Soviet relations. The talks had shown a friendly openness between us and a genuine willingness to listen to each other's proposals . . ." Quoting from that historic press conference . . .

For forty years, the Western alliance has stood together in the cause of freedom. And now, with reform under way in the Soviet Union, we stand at the threshold of a brand-new era of U.S.-Soviet relations. And it is within our grasp to contribute, each in our own way, to overcoming the division of Europe and ending the military confrontation there.

Remarks of the President and Soviet Chairman Mikhail Gorbachev
and a question-and-answer session with reporters on the Soviet liner
Maxim Gorky *in Marsaxlokk Harbor, Malta,*
December 3, 1989

————————

The modern Atlantic alliance was born at sea. It was on a battleship off the coast of Canada that Franklin D. Roosevelt and Winston Churchill met during Europe's darkest hours—great leaders, a rendezvous at sea, a rendezvous with destiny. The legacy of that meeting became known as the Atlantic Charter, significant not for its details but for its vision. And it spoke of a day when nations would resolve their differences at the negotiating table, not on the field of battle.

Tonight, I've come to Brussels to share with our friends and our allies the results of that vision, results born of strength and solidarity, continuity and commitment. It seems like the world is changing overnight. But the yearning for freedom lives within all of us and always has. And that simple truth is manifested in the thunderous events that are taking place just a few hundred kilometers to the east. And that simple truth brought Mikhail Gorbachev and me together on a windswept harbor off Malta.

The seas were as turbulent as our times, but it was not an ill wind carrying us on our mission. No, it was the wind of change—strong and constant, profound. And today, as the sun broke through the clouds there at Malta, we could see a new world taking shape, a new world of freedom.

Remarks at a welcoming ceremony at Zaventem Airport,
Brussels, December 3, 1989

"The Days of the Dictator Are Over"

During the President's first year in office, Central America dominated the hemispheric agenda. Along with a dramatic bipartisan breakthrough on policy toward Nicaragua—which eventually helped force the Communist leader of the Sandinistas, Daniel Ortega, to hold free elections—Panama was front and center through 1989. In the Panamanian election held in early May, an international panel of observers led by former President Jimmy Carter, the Catholic Church, and others documented widespread vote fraud by dictator Manuel Noriega. The people backed opposition candidate Guillermo Endara by a three-to-one margin, and Noriega's thugs resorted to violence to complete their theft. The Bush administration joined other hemispheric leaders in condemning the action . . .

Today elected constitutional government is the clear choice of the vast majority of the people in the Americas, and the days of the dictator are over. Still, in many parts of our hemisphere, the enemies of democracy lie in wait to overturn elected governments through force or to steal elections through fraud. All nations in the democratic community have a responsibility to make clear, through our actions and our words, that efforts to overturn constitutional regimes or steal elections are unacceptable. If we fail to send a clear signal when democracy is imperiled, the enemies of constitutional government will become more dangerous.

Remarks and a question-and-answer session with reporters
on the situation in Panama, White House Briefing Room,
May 11, 1989

A message to Nicaragua's Communist leader, Daniel Ortega . . .

The President. I wish Mr. Ortega had been there when [Costa
Rican President Oscar] Arias was sworn in, and I'll tell you
why. . . . Maybe you were there this day I'm talking about. I
represented the United States as Vice President. You had thirty
thousand people in a stadium in the capital. Remember that
day?

Q. The national stadium?

The President. The national stadium, exactly. And what you did
was to go in there, everybody lined up behind their flag. And
I'm saying to myself, I don't know what kind of reception I'm
going to get—the U.S. Stars and Stripes and the Vice President
of the United States—I know we've got good relations with
Costa Rica, but a lot of other countries [are] represented. I
swear to God, to the die I day I'll never forget the reception for
my country. It wasn't me—they didn't know who the hell I
was—but marching in behind the Stars and Stripes with our little delegation, and people were cheering, and it was democracy.
It overlooked any kind of regional differences, and it was so
moving and touching.

And to Manuel Noriega . . .

Q. Mr. President, on Mr. Noriega—we each asked our questions. Will you answer one question on Noriega?

The President. Yes, I'd be delighted to. He's not my favorite character, but what is it? [Laughter]

Q. You've been criticized in this country—politically and some of
the media—for the way you reacted to the coup in Panama.

The President. Yes.

Q. You said you acted according to what you felt.

The President. I wasn't criticized by any of the countries around
this table, I noticed—not one.

Q. Right. But some of the media in this country and some in
Congress—

The President. We've got a lot of hawks out there; we've got a lot of macho guys out there that want me to send somebody else's kid into battle. And what I will do is prudently assess the situation at the time, and I've seen nothing in terms of intelligence or fact coming in later that would make me have done something differently. And that doesn't mean under some provocation or some denial of our rights as the United States of America, that I'd be afraid to use force. But for these instant hawks up there to—those doves that now become instant hawks on Capitol Hill, they don't bother me one bit because the American people supported me by over two to one, and I think I sent a strong signal to the countries represented around this table that we are not imprudently going to use the force of the United States.

If somebody lays a glove on an American citizen there in the Canal Zone or where we have certain treaty rights, then we've got another story.

> *Interview with Latin American journalists,*
> *White House Roosevelt Room, October 25, 1989*

Today, Noriega may think his lead-pipe politics have won, but he's won nothing more than a fragile status quo. And democracy really will triumph in Panama—I'm confident of that. It's a question of when, not if.

> *The President's news conference in Hotel Cariari Convention Hall,*
> *San José, Costa Rica, October 28, 1989*

Announcing Operation Just Cause . . .

I am committed to strengthening our relationship with the democratic nations in this hemisphere. I will continue to seek solutions to the problems of this region through dialogue and multilateral diplomacy. I took this action only after reaching the conclusion that every other avenue was closed and the lives of American citizens were in grave danger. I hope that the people of Panama will put this dark chapter of dictatorship behind them and move forward together as citizens of a democratic Panama with this government that they themselves have elected.

*Address to the nation announcing U. S. military action
in Panama, Oval Office, December 20, 1989*

Q. Mr. President, this spring you indicated that you would accept Noriega going to a third country where he could be free of prosecution. What has changed now that that's no longer acceptable?

The President. The death of one marine, the brutalization of a wife of a lieutenant, the death of a lot of our kids—that's what's changed.

*Question-and-answer session with reporters in Houston, Texas,
on the situation in Panama, Houstonian Country Club,
December 30, 1989*

A LEGACY OF SERVICE:
To Country, to Community

No President, no government, can teach us to remember what is best in what we are. But if the man you have chosen to lead this government can help make a difference; if he can celebrate the quieter, deeper successes that are made not of gold and silk but of better hearts and finer souls; if he can do these things, then he must.

*Inaugural Address, U. S. Capitol West Front,
January 20, 1989*

To serve and to serve well is the highest fulfillment we can know.

*Remarks at the Boy Scout National Jamboree at Fort A. P.
Hill, Bowling Green, Virginia, August 7, 1989*

"Beneath the Great Seal"

President Bush has often stated that the President has an obligation to set a high moral tone for the country, as well as his own administration. Ethics was a major focus of the first few weeks . . .

The mission is great. But it really has to be accomplished in the finest tradition of our nation: pride, honesty—spirit of idealism when it comes to public service, knowing that our actions must always be of the highest integrity. It's not really very complicated. It's a question of knowing right from wrong, avoiding conflicts of interest, bending over backwards to see that there's not even a perception of conflict of interest.

Remarks at a swearing-in ceremony for members
of the White House staff, White House East Room,
January 23, 1989

Our principles are clear: that government service is a noble calling and a public trust. I learned that from my mom and dad at an early age, and I expect that that's where many of you learned it— there or in school. There is no higher honor than to serve free men and women, no greater privilege than to labor in government beneath the Great Seal of the United States and the American flag. And that's why this administration is dedicated to ethics in government and the need for honorable men and women to serve in positions of trust. . . .

Government should be an opportunity for public service, not private gain. And I want to make sure that public service is valued and respected, because I want to encourage America's young to pursue careers in government. There is nothing more fulfilling than to serve your country and your fellow citizens and do it well. And that's what our system of self-government depends on.

And I've never known a finer group of people than those that I worked with in government. You're men and women of knowledge, ability, and integrity. And I saw that in the CIA. I saw that when I was in China. I saw it at the United Nations. And for the last eight years, I saw that in every department and agency of the United States government. And I saw that commitment to excellence in the federal workers I came to know and respect in Washington, all across America, and, indeed, around the world. You work hard; you sacrifice. You deserve to be recognized, rewarded, and certainly appreciated. I pledge to try to make federal jobs more challenging, more satisfying, and more fulfilling. I'm dedicated to making the system work and making it work better.

Remarks to members of the senior executive service,
DAR Constitution Hall, January 26, 1989

On ethical conduct for former Presidents . . .

Q. You've mentioned ethics in a number of ways, and you've talked about the value of service this year. The last two days we've picked up headlines in the papers, and they've read President Reagan has a $5-million book deal. He's got a $50,000-a-speech deal. With all respect for the office and the former President, do you think it's appropriate to cash in on the presidency?

The President. I don't know whether I'd call it cashing in. I expect every President has written his memoirs and received money for it. Indeed, I read that a former President—was it Grant? Grant got half a million bucks. That's when half a million really meant something. [Laughter] . . . so I think there is plenty of tradition that goes with Presidents writing memoirs and being paid for it.

Q. But you've also talked about perceptions. Is there a perception problem here?

The President. No, because I think there has been a long history of that, and I don't think it's ever been challenged as inappropriate.

The President's news conference, White House Briefing Room,
January 27, 1989

I believe in government service. I believe that it plays a vital role. But it must complement individual service. And nothing can replace personal commitment, both in our jobs and in our private lives. Many people look to you, the people in government, to do all things and solve all problems. Well, I think as a people we need to renew our sense of commitment, to take greater responsibility not only for ourselves but for one another.

*Remarks at the swearing-in ceremony for Elizabeth H. Dole
as secretary of labor, Department of Labor Great Hall,
January 30, 1989*

George Bush served as the U.S. permanent representative to the United Nations from 1971 to 1972, when President Nixon asked him to head the Republican National Committee. Here he recounts a few memories from his UN days . . .

The memories of my time here in 1971 and 1972 are still with me today—the human moments, the humorous moments that are part of even the highest undertaking.

With your permission, let me share one story from many of the sessions of the Security Council. I was the permanent representative of the United States. I was forty-five minutes late getting to the meeting, and all forty-five minutes were filled by the first speaker to take the floor. And when I walked in and took my seat, the speaker paused and said with great courtesy, "I welcome the permanent representative of the United States, and now, for his benefit, I will start my speech all over again from the beginning." [Laughter] That's a true story. And at that moment, differences of alliance, ideology, didn't matter. The universal groan that went up around that table from every member present, and then the laughter that followed, united us all. . . .

I do remember sitting in this hall. I remember the mutual respect among all of us proudly serving as representatives. Yes, I remember the almost endless speeches—and I don't want this to be one of them—[laughter]—the Security Council sessions, the receptions, those long receiving lines, the formal meetings of this Assembly and the informal discussions in the delegates' lounge over here. And I remember something more, something beyond the frantic pace and sometimes frustrating experiences of daily life here: the heartbeat of the United Nations, the quiet conviction that we could make the world more peaceful, more free. What we sought then—all of us—now lies within our reach.

Address to the Forty-fourth Session of the United Nations
General Assembly, UN General Assembly Hall,
September 25, 1989

"AMERICA'S PRIDE"

Here, addressing the troops for the first time as commander in chief, President Bush briefly recounts his stay on the USS *Finback*—**the submarine that picked him up in 1944 after he was shot down over the Pacific island of Chi Chi Jima . . .**

I've been in a submerged submarine while depth charges were going off all around it. And I know what it's like to hear the vessel strain and shake and pray to God . . .

Remarks aboard USS America, *Norfolk, Virginia,*
January 31, 1989

Using a personal example to underscore how the United States earned its role as a Pacific power. This was President Bush's first address to a foreign legislature as President . . .

I first came to the Asian Pacific region during World War II, more than forty-five years ago. I was a teenager, nineteen years old. I was flying torpedo bombers in the United States navy. It was then, for the first time in my life, that I truly appreciated the value of freedom and the price we pay to keep it. Believe me, I have never forgotten.

Remarks to the National Assembly at the National
Assembly Hall, Seoul, Korea, February 27, 1989

On April 19, forty-seven sailors aboard the USS *Iowa* were killed in an explosion. Several days later, President Bush traveled to Norfolk, Virginia, to address a memorial service. As he recounted in his diary: "I kept rehearsing and reading my speech aloud. I did pray for strength, because I cry too easily, so I read it over and over again. I tried not to personalize it when I gave it. I tried not to focus on a grieving parent or a grieving spouse; I tried to comfort individually in the speech; but then I got to the end, I choked up and had to stop . . ." (*ATB*, p. 423).

To the navy community, remember that you have the admiration of America for sharing the burden of grief as a family, especially the navy wives, who suffer most the hardships of separation. You've always been strong for the sake of love. You must be heroically strong now, but you will find that love endures. It endures in the lingering memory of time together, in the embrace of a friend, in the bright, questioning eyes of a child.

And as for the children of the lost, throughout your lives you must never forget, your father was America's pride. Your mothers and grandmothers, aunts and uncles, are entrusted with the memory of this day. In the years to come, they must pass along to you the legacy of the men behind the guns.

Remarks at the memorial service for crew members
of the USS Iowa *at Norfolk Naval Air Station Hangar LP-2,*
Norfolk, Virginia, April 24, 1989

Following the service, President Bush traveled to Chicago to address an Associated Press luncheon. Before the lunch, William Keating of the Detroit Newspaper Agency and Lou Boccardi of AP asked President Bush the status of Terry Anderson, an AP reporter who was being held hostage in the Middle East, prompting the following comment at the start of the President's luncheon remarks.

I vowed when I came into the presidency not to talk about the burden of the presidency, the loneliness of the job or the great toughness that nobody understands. I learned from my immediate predecessor—eight years and I never once heard a call for sympathy or a call for understanding along those lines. But I will say that when you do take that oath of office, you do feel a disproportionate concern for a fallen sailor or an individual held hostage against his or her will anywhere in the world.

Remarks at the Associated Press luncheon
at the Hyatt Regency Hotel Grand Ballroom,
Chicago, Illinois, April 24, 1989

"A THOUSAND POINTS OF LIGHT"

From now on in America, any definition of a successful life must include service to others.

Remarks to students at University Field House,
Washington University, St. Louis, Missouri,
February 17, 1989

When a President talks about volunteerism, there are a few cynics around who suggest he's trying to escape the responsibility of the federal government, he's trying to say let somebody else do it. I'm saying, and I believe it with a fervor, that this narcotics problem in this country is not going to be solved without the Thousand Points of Light. Not just a thousand organizations, but literally a million efforts to get out there and try to work the problem. It isn't going to be done by the government.

Remarks and a question-and-answer session with students
at the school library, James Madison High School,
Vienna, Virginia, March 28, 1989

You understand that helping the less fortunate is in everyone's best interest; that the most powerful gift we can offer anyone is a sense of purpose, a path to self-esteem; that the fabric of family, like that of society, must forever be renewed and rewoven.

Remarks on signing
the National Volunteer Week Proclamation,
Rose Garden, April 10, 1989

The "Iron Horse," New York Yankee Lou Gehrig, was one of George Bush's idols for the way he played baseball, and a Bush hero for the way he lived his life . . .

Lou Gehrig was a Hall of Fame first baseman in the 1920s and 1930s. He played in 2,130 straight games, a record which still stands. But more than that, he was a good and decent man about whom a teammate said, "Every day, any day, he just went out and did his job." Fifty years ago, Lou Gehrig was stricken by a form of paralysis which today bears his name: Lou Gehrig's disease. And even so, he told the crowd at Yankee Stadium, "I consider myself the luckiest man on the face of the earth."

This story has become—certainly among sportsmen and, I think, even more widely—an American parable. But less known is that after he left the Yankees, for much of the last two years of his life, he served his fellow man. He was dying; weaker by the day; he could barely move his body. But as a parole commissioner for the City of New York, he counseled and inspired kids. And they called him the Iron Horse, the Pride of the Yankees. And he was a hero.

Remarks at the presentation ceremony
for the President's Volunteer Action Awards, East Room,
April 11, 1989

We cannot afford to fail, and we won't. For as Americans, we know what is at stake. We know that volunteerism can help those free-falling through society. We know that as citizens and institutions we can use one-to-one caring to truly love thy neighbor. And we know, finally, that from now on any definition of a successful life must include serving others.

Remarks at a luncheon hosted by the New York Partnership
and the Association for a Better New York at the New York
Hilton Hotel Grand Ballroom, New York City,
June 22, 1989

If it weren't for the Points of Light, for these volunteers, the bill to some level of government would be way, way, way higher than it is today. Because neighbor helps neighbor; friend helps friend; people reaching across and trying to lift up those who are hurt—I don't know how you put a price tag on it, but that is the American way. And it's been that way, and it always will be that way.

Exchange with reporters at Pacific Valley Mall during a tour
of the earthquake damage in Santa Cruz, California,
October 20, 1989

If you've got a hammer, find a nail. If you can read, find someone who can't. If you're well, do it like the volunteers I just saw at St. Jude's [Hospital]. Help someone who isn't well. If you're not in trouble, seek out someone who is. Because everywhere there is a need in America, there is a way to fill it. And everywhere there is a dream in America, there's a way to make it come true.

Remarks at the Commercial Appeal's Thanksgiving Celebration,
Commercial Appeal front lawn, Memphis, Tennessee,
November 22, 1989

IN THE ARENA:
Ups and Downs, Ins and Outs

You may have noticed my special greeting from [Pistons' forward] Bill Laimbeer. He and his wife, Chris, were with [us] in

October, and he told me ... he'd see me at the White House in June. Actually, he was sure he'd be here, but not so sure about me.

Remarks congratulating the Detroit Pistons on winning the National Basketball Association Championship, Old Executive Office Building, Room 450, June 20, 1989

PUBLIC LIFE

The other day I got a little lesson in how impatient the American people are. In the morning mail ... I found letters from seventh-graders at a church school in California. It was dated Inauguration Day, January 20, and it said, and remember this was just on the day that I was taking office, "Dear Mr. President, Would you please do something about pollution? I'm not saying you're doing a bad job, but could you put a little more effort into it?" [Laughter]

Remarks at the swearing-in ceremony for William K. Reilly as administrator of the Environmental Protection Agency, Waterside Mall, February 8, 1989

During the 1988 campaign, then Vice President Bush temporarily mistook September 7 as Pearl Harbor Day (December 7). This would not be the last time he would poke fun at himself for that lapse ...

Last year I told the American Legion about Pearl Harbor being on September 7. [Laughter] Just think, if Franklin Roosevelt had listened to me, think what we could have spared the nation. [Laughter]

Remarks at the annual conference of the Veterans of Foreign Wars, Sheraton Washington Hotel Ballroom, March 6, 1989

Addressing the blurring line between privacy and the right to know on his first trip back to Houston as President . . .

Q. Is the increased attention being given to the private lives of public officials and candidates a good thing or a bad thing for politics and government in this country?

The President. Well, I think there are excesses. I think there are intrusions into people's private lives that go beyond the public trust or go beyond one's ability to serve. And I don't like the excesses.

> *Remarks at a luncheon hosted by the Forum Club*
> *of Houston, Texas, at the George R. Brown Convention Center,*
> *March 16, 1989*

On his White House role models . . .

Q. Your resident scholar, Dr. [Roger] Porter [chief domestic policy adviser], gave us a brief history lesson this morning on the presidency. And he recalled a conversation he had with you about the great Presidents of the past, and why we don't have great Presidents today—talking about Jefferson and Monroe and Madison. Who are your two favorite great Presidents?

The President. First, I'd make the point that everyone looks better over time. [Laughter]

Q. But who are your two?

The President. Herbert Hoover looks better today than he did forty years ago, doesn't he?

Q. No.

The President. People remember—[laughter]—not to you, but to a lot of people . . . they remember the compassionate side of the man. You couldn't even talk about that thirty or forty years ago.

Q. Is he your model?

The President. No, he's not. [Laughter] But I was trying to make the point that time is generous to people. I remember the hue and cry around Harry Truman from guys like me and Republicans. Now we're kind of moderated and think the good things and leave out some of the contentious matters.

So history is basically kind to American Presidents. A model, I think . . . would be Teddy Roosevelt. He comes out of the same elitist background that I do. [Laughter] And he had the same commitment to the environment that I did, although the rules on hunting have changed dramatically since he used to shoot with no limits out there in South Dakota, or North Dakota.

But he was a man of some action; he was a person that understood government, didn't mind getting his hands dirty in government. I remember part of his life being on the Police Board in New York City. Ask Gabe Pressman about that. Probably combat pay was required in those days. So, he was an activist.

I have great respect for Eisenhower. I'm not trying to compare myself to any of these people, but in Eisenhower's case, he was a hero. . . . . He led the Allied forces and helped free the world from imperialism and Nazism. And he brought to the presidency a certain stability. Others may have had more flair, and he presided . . . in fairly tranquil times, but he did it. He was a fair-minded person, strong leader, and had the respect of people. And I think he was given credit for being a compassionate individual. So, those are two I would throw out there. And you can't live in this house and do as I do: have my office upstairs, next door to the Lincoln Bedroom, in which resides the handwritten copies of the freedom doctrine that will live forever—Emancipation Proclamation—right there in our house. So I think all of us—I think almost all Americans put Lincoln on that list someplace.

Q. Any Democrats in your pantheon, sir?

The President. Well, I respect certain things about Harry Truman. He liked to go for walks. [Laughter] But he was tough—said what he thought and had respect from people. Won them over, did it his way, and I respect him for being a fighter. They had him written off in '48. I bet ten bucks against him and on Tom Dewey. And I lost. So did a lot of other people who thought the polls would be correct. So I respect a guy that fights back, and Truman did that.

. . . I had a lot of differences with Lyndon Johnson, but there were certain things about him that were good. . . . We had a little insight that came from a personal knowledge of the man. And he got all caught up in Vietnam, but people forget that—for his legislative agenda—he got through what President Kennedy couldn't get through. We ought to give a little credit for somebody who can do that. He controlled both houses of the legislature, which is slightly different than the forty-first President of the United States is facing. . . .

You can't live here without becoming more of a student of history . . . [and] you begin to pick up the redeeming features of those you maybe hadn't had down as a hero or hadn't even thought much about in the history of this country.

So I don't think that—I would argue with your premise. I could just go on forever here—[laughter]—but I would argue with what I thought was the premise that great leaders were all back there somewhere. I'm not sure of that.

Let me just end on one that—I learned a lot from Ronald Reagan. . . . One thing I learned from him is, I never once in eight years, no matter how difficult the problem, heard him appeal to me or to others around him for understanding about the toughest, loneliest job in the world—how can anyone be asked to bear the burden single-handedly? Never—and when Reagan left office, you never heard the presidency is too big for one man—never heard it.

Back in 1980, people like Lloyd Cutler, for whom I have great respect, were saying, look, this is so complex today that maybe we need a parliamentary system. He wasn't proposing it; he was saying it ought to be looked at. Reagan came in; stood on certain principles, stayed with them, and never asked for sympathy or never asked for understanding of the great, over-whelming burden of the presidency, and left with 61 percent of

the people saying, "Hey, wait a minute! He did a good job."
Good lesson right here in modern history.

White House luncheon for journalists, East Room,
March 31, 1989

One of many exchanges on the topic of presidential vacations . . .

Q. Mr. President, you have this wonderful home, a beautiful Cigarette boat, and yet the average Mainer makes about $14,000 a year. And I was wondering if you could tell us how you manage to stay in touch with the average man's realities.

The President. Well, I do my very best. I've got a lot of friends from all walks of life. And there is a tendency in this job to get isolated, but you—

Q. We see you riding the boat every night on TV and playing tennis and having a great time.

The President. But I don't think people feel anything other than that isn't it nice to have a good vacation. And I try to have as much contact as I can.

Q. Do you think the average Mainer can afford to have a vacation like you have, sir?

The President. I don't think so. I'm very privileged or lucky in that regard, but I also don't think the average Mainer begrudges me a vacation of any kind. In fact, the response from the townspeople here has been the way it's been for the sixty-four other years I've been here—very good. They're just wonderful.

And presidential security . . .

Q. Knowing you're always a target for terrorists, do you feel safe strolling about Kennebunkport?

The President. Yes, but I can't stroll quite as freely as I used to before I was in government work. And I don't worry about it. We've got extraordinarily able Secret Service and I just don't—I honestly don't spend one second of the day thinking about that.

The President's news conference, Walker's Point,
August 23, 1989

Not every President is blessed with a green thumb. Five months ago, I planted an elm to mark North Dakota's new campaign. It turned out they had some kind of moth disease. [Laughter] So, in the interest of public safety here in Sioux Falls, they specifically asked me not to dedicate a building. [Laughter] Well, so far, my luck in this tree business is about like this—as I had in fishing.

Remarks at the South Dakota Centennial Celebration
at Sioux Falls Arena, Sioux Falls, September 18, 1989

During their fifty-six years of marriage, the Bushes have lived in well over thirty houses—from Odessa, Midland, and Houston in Texas, to New York, Beijing, and, as we see here, Washington, D.C. . . .

Ira [Gribin, president of the National Association of Realtors] mentioned to me that my speech is a special occasion for this association, and I said I was honored. And then Ira said, "Well, it's not often that we're addressed by someone who lives in public housing . . ." [Laughter]

When I was elected to Congress—and I get reminded about this by Barbara—when I was elected to Congress in 1966, we needed to make housing arrangements up in Washington. We were in Houston. And at that time, Senator Al Simpson's father, Milward Simpson, was retiring and moving back to Wyoming. So, I bought the Simpson house, sight unseen, over the telephone. And when we got to Washington, there were just two problems: we found out right away that the house wasn't quite big enough for our family, and we found out when we put the place up for sale that it wasn't worth quite as much as we paid for it. [Laughter] And that's my claim to fame in your business. I'm the only person who ever lost money in Washington real estate in the last twenty years. [Laughter] Ira, where the hell were you when I needed you? [Laughter]

But few people have done more for the real estate industry than Barbara and I have. We've moved twenty-eight times—this is true—we have moved twenty-eight times in our forty-four years of marriage. [Laughter] You ought to be smiling. Now, I know what you're thinking—what a dream client my family would make for any Realtor. [Laughter] In fact, Dick Darman over at OMB is calculating the commissions we've paid over the years, measured as a percentage of the gross national product.

Remarks announcing the HOPE (Homeownership and Opportunity
for People Everywhere) Initiative to the National Association
of Realtors at Loew's Anatole Hotel Chantilly Ballroom,
Dallas, Texas, November 10, 1989

Every week, I receive up to sixty thousand letters from every state in the Union and from nearly every country in the world. You can get a lot of free advice in this job.

Remarks at the opening session of the Universal Postal Union Congress,
John F. Kennedy Center for the Performing Arts,
November 13, 1989

CONGRESS AND DEMOCRATS:
A Kinder, Gentler Take

I speak to you today with great respect and in accordance with the plan our Founding Fathers designed two centuries ago: as a President of the United States addressing the freely elected government of a sovereign state. And I speak to you in the spirit of bipartisanship. I've got to; you've got us outnumbered. [Laughter]

Remarks to the South Carolina state legislature,
State Capitol House Chamber, Columbia, February 15, 1989

Our challenge now is to keep it [economic growth] going. We can, and we will. We've all heard the naysayers. I think there are a few out there whose predictions of economic disaster are now in the seventy-eighth straight month. [Laughter]

Remarks to the U.S. Chamber of Commerce,
DAR Constitution Hall, May 1, 1989

I'm a big believer in alternative fuels and conservation. This winter I'm putting windmills in Washington. Henceforth, hot air is going to heat the city.

Remarks at the University of Nebraska,
Bob Devaney Sports Center, June 13, 1989

Marshall [Coleman], you're our candidate. Certainly you have my full support, and you know Virginia better than I do, but let me give you a little free advice: don't film your TV ad riding around in a tank.

Remarks at a Republican Party fund-raising dinner
at the Richmond Center Exhibition Hall, Richmond, Virginia,
June 21, 1989

Q. Mr. President, do you have some advice for [Democratic activist] Jesse Jackson if he wants to run for mayor of the District? Would you like to get involved in that?

The President. I gave Jesse my advice last year—[laughter]—all during the campaign, in a gentle, kind way. And I might note, he gave me plenty, too—and still is.

Remarks and a question-and-answer session with reporters
during a meeting with District of Columbia police chief
Maurice Turner, Oval Office, July 27, 1989

I have to tell you I was mightily impressed with that centennial cattle drive. It captured the hearts of America—three thousand cattle, sixty miles in six days. Now, maybe I can get a few of those drovers to come back with me to Washington. There's a herd back on Capitol Hill that I'd like to move in my direction.

Remarks at the Montana Centennial Celebration
at the State capitol grounds, Helena, September 18, 1989

Back in 1889, when President Harrison sent a letter—telegram, rather, to the first governor of Washington to tell him that Washington had become the forty-second state, he sent the telegram collect. Well, that's one way to balance the budget. [Laughter]

Remarks at the Washington Centennial Celebration
at Riverfront Park, Spokane, September 19, 1989

The Dallas paper reported last week that [Texas Governor] Bill Clements was dining in a restaurant when a holdup and shoot-out occurred right in front of him. The most remarkable part of all, however, is that not once during the whole ordeal did he put down his hamburger. [Laughter] And I'm not sure if that was Texas courage or hunger or the need for a new pair of glasses or a hearing aid. . . .

I don't often quote Franklin D. Roosevelt on partisan matters, but the little story he told to make fun of his Republican opponents fits the liberal Democrats so well today. Remember the story of the unfortunate chameleon which turned brown when placed on a brown rug and turned red when placed on a red rug, but who died a tragic death when they put him on a Scotch plaid?

Remarks at the Republican Governors' Association Annual
Dinner, Capitol Hilton Presidential Ballroom,
October 17, 1989

Two references here to Governor Ann Richards, who, at the 1988 Democratic National Convention, said George Bush was "born with a silver foot in his mouth" . . .

Bill, you and I do go back a long way—long before either of us got into politics. And we shared common goals in business and in politics. We also have a lot in common as public speakers. We've certainly been accused of making our fair share of verbal gaffes. But so what if we've been known to put our foot in our mouth from time to time? I just hope that your foot is as silver as mine. . . .

A Texas Democratic friend of mine had his own ideas about the election. He offered me his prediction that the next governor of the state would be that smart, silver-haired, feisty, outspoken Lone Star lady with a sharp sense of humor. And I said, no way, not possible—Barbara is very happy in the White House.

*Remarks at a Republican fund-raising dinner honoring Governor
Bill Clements at the Grand Kempinski Hotel Crystal Room,
Dallas, Texas, November 10, 1989*

SPORTS

For each of his four years in office, President Bush threw out the first pitch to help the Texas Rangers baseball team—then partly owned by his son George W.—open their Major League season. Here, a participant in a business meeting queries the President about his first official pitch in office . . .

Q. Mr. President, Red Scott from southern California.
The President. Yes, sir?
Q. Was that pitch a curve or wasn't it, yesterday?
The President. That pitch—you mean at the Baltimore game? [Laughter] I got into the locker room and warmed up with Mickey Nettleton [Tettleton], the catcher. Sixty-four—your old arm gradually got a little looser. But it was high and outside. But here's my problem. [Laughter] He stepped in front of the plate before it could break down across the middle. That's my side of it, and I'm going to stick with it.

. . . Walk out there, and you're always wondering about getting booed. . . . Last year, I go to the All-Star Game in Cincinnati—and we're in the middle of a campaign—saying this is suicide, man, what are you going to do out here? You know you're going to get booed. So, right there as I was about to walk out, I saw two Little Leaguers—one eleven-year-old kid, big, tall guy, you know, and a little eight-year-old blond girl. And I said, "Who are these?" And they said, "Well, these are Little Leaguers. They're going out first." So, I got with them, and I said, "You guys nervous?" [Laughter] And I said, "Well, why don't we all walk out together?" [Laughter] There wasn't a boo in the house—[laughter]—it worked!

Remarks at a White House briefing for members of the American Business Conference, Old Executive Office Building, April 4, 1989

I played in 1947 in the first College World Series finals. It started in Kalamazoo, Michigan. I think they played there two or three years before a move to Omaha. And next year, '48, again our Yale team reached the finals, but there was one problem. We had a good coach—great National League baseball player, Ethan Allen; and we walked the eighth hitter, bases loaded, I think, to get to the ninth hitter. The ninth hitter was their pitcher, Jackie Jensen, who went on to be one of the greatest sluggers the Boston Red Sox ever had. And he hit a ball that's still rolling in Kalamazoo, Michigan. . . . So, we lost both times.

Remarks congratulating the Wichita State University Shockers on winning the NCAA Baseball Championship, Rose Garden, June 16, 1989

Fishing, I guess, is my favorite form of relaxation. And it's with a rod and reel that I tend to count my blessings, especially if I'm out there with one of our grandkids or with Barbara, the only woman on earth who can read and fish at the same time—[laughter]—and catch every word and every fish.

Remarks at the Boy Scout National Jamboree at Fort A. P. Hill, Bowling Green, Virginia, August 7, 1989

Putting New York City politics in the proper perspective . . .

Rudy has the energy, the intelligence, and the will to solve New York's problems. He knows that when he becomes mayor, he'll have the second-toughest job in America. The first, of course, is managing the New York Yankees.

Remarks at a fund-raising dinner for mayoral candidate
Rudolph W. Giuliani at the Hilton Hotel Grand Ballroom,
New York City, October 12, 1989

As the distinguished mayor said, Acres Homes was a part of my congressional district twenty-some years ago. In fact—little known fact—this was the home turf for the George Bush all-star championship women's softball team. . . . He [Bobby Moore] and I started this team in 1960. And we had good teams, and these— I want to say girls; they were then, now women—but they almost won the state championship. Traveled all over the state and played out of De Soto Park, which is just down the road a bit, so I do feel at home.

Remarks at the Acres Homes War on Drugs rally
at Andrew Wizner Park, Houston, Texas,
December 7, 1989

At one point or another, Lady Luck spurns all fishermen (and women), as it did George Bush during his 1989 summer vacation. Here, with his friend Brian Mulroney at his side, he attempts to "spin" his lack of success . . .

This is getting out of hand. And so, between now and when I leave on Monday, I guarantee you—I positively guarantee you—that this jinx will be broken. I've seen a lot of good .350 hitters bat about .178 for a while. Then they come out of the slump and move forward. My record fishing in these waters is well-known. It's a superb record, a record of bountiful catches. And somehow, something's gone wrong for the last thirteen days—[laughter]—

something's happened. . . . We're thinking of having a poll to take a media person with us when Barbara and I go out to thwart these evil rumors that I don't know what I'm doing fishing. It's gotten out of hand. When I see it on national television, I know we've got to put an end to this monkey business. So, we will prevail. And besides that, everyone knows fishing is a team sport.

News conference of the President and Prime Minister
Brian Mulroney of Canada at Walker's Point, Kennebunkport,
Maine, August 31, 1989

Before I go any further, I want to put an end to the rumor, ugly rumor that's making the rounds since I was up in Maine about a covert amphibious operation off the coast of the American Northeast. There is no truth to the rumor that the bluefish I finally caught was hooked on the line by a navy frogman—not true, not true at all.

Remarks at the National Hispanic Heritage
Presidential Tribute dinner at the Omni Shoreham
Hotel Regency Ballroom, September 12, 1989

THE PRESS "PACK"

The relationship between the media and any President is inherently, and historically, confrontational. President Washington referred to the "exaggerated and indecent terms as could scarcely be applied to a Nero, a notorious defaulter, or even to common pick-pocket" that the press aimed in his direction after Chief Justice John Jay, acting on orders from the White House, signed a controversial treaty with Great Britain in 1795. President Bush's tenure in office was certainly no exception. And yet, it is clear that he frequently enjoyed bantering with members of the "fourth estate" . . .

Adlai Stevenson said, "An editor is the person who separates the wheat from the chaff and prints the chaff." [Laughter] So I know

I'm probably responsible for providing more than my fair share of chaff, but after all, I am the guy that said during the campaign, "A kitchen in every pot"—[laughter]—and also that "America's freedom"—I was reminded by some of these back here—"America's freedom is the example by which the world expires." [Laughter]

Remarks to the American Society of Newspaper Editors,
J. W. Marriott Hotel Grand Ballroom, April 12, 1989

President Bush had a particular fondness for the people he called the "photo dogs"—the White House press photographers who accompanied the reporters just about everywhere he went for four years. During their annual dinner, he clicks off a few shots of his own . . .

One of the things I do like about Larry [Downing, *Newsweek* photographer], though, is his loyalty. In Beijing, the microphones picked up his patriotic challenge to some Chinese security guards: "Stop pushing me," he said. "Our President may sound like an idiot, but he's our President, and we're going to take pictures of him."

Remarks at the Annual White House News Photographers
Association Dinner, Washington Hilton Hotel International
Ballroom, May 23, 1989

You're wondering why we're all dressed up. We're off to the *Wall Street Journal*'s one hundredth anniversary here in a few minutes, and the *Wall Street Journal* maintains a more dignified air with its no-photos policy. If they were ever to run a swimsuit issue, it would be [former Chrysler chairman] Lee Iacocca in thongs.

Remarks at a Republican Party fund-raising dinner
at the New York Hilton Hotel Grand Ballroom,
New York City, June 22, 1989

In 1979, the *Wall Street Journal* became the largest-circulation daily in the nation, but one rival complained that was only because so many subscribers were at an age where they forgot to cancel. [Laughter]

Speaking of age—and literally apropos of absolutely nothing—Bob Hope told this story of aging at the Joe Gibbs charity dinner in Washington this week that Barbara and I attended, and that our guest here Kay Graham's son sponsored. Two men, two old men, sitting on a park bench—and the first one said, "Do you know how old I am?" The second one said, "Stand up, turn around, drop your trousers down. Now pat yourself on the back. Okay, pull up your trousers, sit back down here on this bench." The man said, "Well, how old am I?" He said, "You're ninety-three years old, four months, and three days." The first guy said, "How did you know that?" He said, "You told me yesterday."

Remarks at the Wall Street Journal Anniversary Dinner
at the World Financial Center Winter Garden,
New York City, June 22, 1989

With tongue firmly in cheek, the President concludes a passionate, yet reasoned, appeal for legislation outlawing flag desecration . . .

I would now be glad to take questions, all of which I'm sure will be on the flag.

The President's news conference, White House Briefing Room,
October 13, 1989. (The President fielded thirty-one questions,
mostly on the situation in Panama and on abortion funding,
before the flag desecration issue was raised by reporters.)

Years ago, this industry—I was going to say "yours," but as one who had a tiny interest in gas wells years ago, "ours"—added an agent to natural gas that gave it a characteristic scent. And that was so that if there ever was a leak in someone's house, they'd have a better chance of detecting the leak. It doesn't work that way in

the White House—[laughter]—so I would ask for your technological assistance.

Remarks to the members of the Natural Gas Supply Association,
Old Executive Office Building, Room 450, October 19, 1989

Lifting a Glass

**Obviously referring to stars from both the political and sports
arenas, the President adds a lighter note to the proceedings at
10 Downing Street . . .**

This is a most distinguished gathering, and if I start singling out
the excitement that Barbara and I felt about meeting the various
individuals here, I'd get into serious trouble. I love politics, and
we've got some good, competitive politics around this table. Neil
[Neil Kinnock, British Labour Party leader], nice to see you, sir,
and the associates on the other side. I love sports, and I could learn
about that stiff left arm and looking at the pin and not getting
nervous on putting from one distinguished guest here, or bending my knees and volleying properly from another. And so, you
have adequately accommodated my insatiable quest for being the
name-dropper of the year by the distinguished guests here.

Toast at a dinner hosted by Prime Minister Margaret Thatcher
in London, June 1, 1989

**Opening the Education Summit with the nation's fifty gover-
nors . . .**

Welcome, welcome. I will try to keep it short. You see, the record
has already been set for toasts here in Charlottesville at the university. Back in 1824, Mr. Jefferson hosted a dinner in the Dome
Room of the Rotunda for the Marquis de Lafayette attended by
former Presidents Monroe and Madison. It was an elegant dinner.
The libations flowed freely—so freely, in fact, that thirteen formal

toasts ensued—[laughter] . . . looking around here, to be followed by thirty-seven more impromptu toasts. That's the one tradition I would like to discourage tonight.

Toasts of the President and Governor Terry Branstad of Iowa
at the Education Summit dinner at Monticello in Charlottesville,
Virginia, September 27, 1989

We first met last November, sir, in Houston, Texas. We met, if I might add this personal note, the day after your Harvard football team fell to the mighty men of Yale. It seemed at the time like an inauspicious start, somehow, but we've learned anew how special the relationship—you're trying to get even—[laughter]—the relationship between Mexico and the United States can be. . . .

Speaking of trust, I trust that you dried out from the golf-cart tour of Camp David on Sunday. [Laughter] There was a true downpour. President and Mrs. Salinas came up there in the mountains. But I was anxious for the President to look around, so he and I set out on a golf cart in this driving rain. Barbara was convinced that I had just dealt a severe blow to Mexican–United States relations.

Toast at the state dinner for President Carlos Salinas de Gortari
of Mexico, State Dining Room, October 3, 1989

EDUCATION PRESIDENT

A student told me a while ago that high school is a great place to learn about personal risk-taking. I asked him, "How do you figure?" And he said, "Have you ever tasted cafeteria food?"

Remarks at the Cheltenham High School commencement ceremony
in Wyncote, Pennsylvania, June 19, 1989

When we talk about merit schools and merit teachers, there could hardly be a better example than this year's winner, the founder of the Westside Preparatory School in Chicago's inner city, Marva Collins. Says Marva, "Any child can learn if they are not taught so thoroughly that they cannot." [Laughter] Think about that one, now.

She got results, working with students who have been written off by the public schools. It's said that 98 percent of her students go on to high school and then college. And her students got results. It was reported one of Marva's six-year-olds could recite Jesse Jackson's 1988 convention speech from memory. [Laughter] Now look, Marva, Jesse is a very gifted speaker, and you're being too tough on those kids. [Laughter] Give them my convention speech, and I bet they can do it at age three. [Laughter]

But I've also heard one young girl who began pounding her lunch box on the desk in the middle of class. Marva told the girl, "No, darling, no one is going to be handing out good jobs to people who pound their lunch boxes on their desks. President Bush does not pound his lunch box on the desk." [Laughter] Obviously, Marva's never been to one of our cabinet meetings.

Remarks at the annual meeting of the American Association
of University Women at the Sheraton Washington Hotel Ballroom,
June 26, 1989

Q. Are all the Presidents rich? [Laughter]

The President. No. In our history, some didn't have much money at all. And that certainly should never be a requirement. I hope that some people are thinking: Just because we come here, you see, maybe I'll be President someday. Do you ever think about that? You should, because it's fun to dream about stuff.

Q. How does it feel to be President?

The President. Sometimes it feels good, and sometimes it feels less good. But most of the time it's wonderful because I like my job, and I like a lot of parts of it. Some of it I don't like. There are some parts I don't like, but I like what I'm supposed to be doing, and so does my wife . . . she's trying to help people on literacy. And I like this part of the job. You meet people. And you can say to a school principal and hope people hear it all over the country, "Hey, you're doing a first-class job." And so there's some wonderful things.

You know what I got to do? Some of the boys are interested. Just before I came here, I got to meet the quarterback for the Denver Broncos football team. And I know Mike Ditka, and I know some of the others. So, I get some fun stuff to do in sports. Then you think—you're President; you think you're helping.

We're going off to meet Mr. Gorbachev, and in a week or so you're going to be reading about all that because it will be in every paper. And why are we doing it? Well, we're trying to make the world a little more peaceful. We want it to be a place where you grow up—that you don't have to worry about having to go off to war. You can think about what this guy's thinking about—maybe getting to be President or maybe getting a good education or going out and helping others.

Q. How come you became President?

The President. How did I get to be President? Well, I was in politics a long time, and I was in business, and I worked hard. I decided in the late seventies that I wanted to be President, and then I went out and worked for it. And I had a lot of help. You can't do it alone. You get help. Your governor helped me; and this congresswoman, Lynn Martin, was extraordinarily helpful to me. And then people that aren't in office—they helped. So, you have to get a lot of people behind your case and your cause. In my case, I ran and lost for the Senate, for example. I got up—friends pick you up, dust you off, put you back in the game, and you try again. Then I ran for President and lost in 1979. And then President Reagan suggested to our convention that I be Vice President, and then we were elected. And then for eight years I was Vice President. And then I ran again.

So, it's that way. But you have to work at the grass roots; you have to care about people, I think. But you have to be willing to try, to risk something. And you've got to learn that if somebody says something ugly about you, don't worry about it. I used to be very worried when I was much—fifteen, twenty years ago. Somebody said something that was critical, I would worry about that. I don't worry about that anymore. So, you have to have a fairly thick skin, but never so thick that you don't care about people.

Remarks and question-and-answer session with students
at Pickard Elementary School, Room 305, Chicago, Illinois,
November 20, 1989

CHAPTER TWO

1990:
DARKNESS IN
THE DESERT SKY

President and Mrs. Bush at a Thanksgiving prayer service
aboard the USS *Nassau*. November 22, 1990.

A year that would end with an unprecedented international coalition of nations standing together against Iraq's invasion of Kuwait would begin with America's President forging a different kind of international coalition—this one with Presidents Virgilio Barco of Colombia, Alan Garcia of Peru, and Jaime Paz Zamora of Bolivia. On February 15, amid great concerns over security, President Bush traveled to Colombia to attend the drug summit and sign the Declaration of Cartagena—which provided a framework to help the four countries better coordinate the war against drugs. A week later, the President met with Germany's Chancellor Helmut Kohl at Camp David, where the two men discussed the prospects for a unified Germany in NATO. On October 2, after forty-five years of postwar division, Germany was reunified.

On the home front, President Bush hosted Mikhail Gorbachev at the Washington Summit in late May and welcomed the G-7 leaders to his hometown of Houston, Texas, in July. He also won passage of two landmark pieces of legislation: the Clean Air Act amendments, and the Americans with Disabilities Act. Last, but not least, on March 22, President Bush—in his own words— "liberated many four-, five-, and six-year-old kids who shared my hate for broccoli" when he defiantly declared he would no longer eat the vegetable.

FAITH, FAMILY, AND FRIENDS:
Lightness Against the Dark

I want my grandchildren to come here. I want them to feel reassured that there always will be comfort here in the presence of God, and I want them to delight in the colors and the

sounds and the tapestries and mosaics to the fine old hymns. And I want them to know a very special way of understanding this place—studying the brilliant stained-glass windows. From where we now stand, the rose window high above seems black and formless to some, perhaps, but when we enter and see it backlit by the sun, it dazzles in astonishing splendor and reminds us that without faith we, too, are but stained-glass windows in the dark.

Remarks at the Washington National Cathedral Dedication,
September 29, 1990

FROM MULESHOE TO WINK TO NOTREES

I remember the first place Barbara and I lived in, when our son George was just a baby—a tiny, ramshackle shotgun house in the oil town of Odessa, Texas. It had a makeshift partition down the middle that cut the house into two apartments, leaving us with a small kitchen and a shared bathroom, and the old water-drip window unit—you remember those cooler units they used to use out there—cranked up like a west-Texas dust storm still couldn't drown out the noise of the all-night parties next door.

Remarks at the annual convention of the National Association
of Home Builders at the Omni Coliseum, Atlanta, Georgia,
January 19, 1990

Barbara and I realized on the way down here that we're talking forty-two years ago next month that we moved to Texas. Of course, that was in a '47 Studebaker, and today it was in Air Force One. More legroom now. [Laughter] But all the same, it's just a wonderful feeling of coming home. And Texas remains larger than life in our hearts. It is a place of family and duty and loyalty and honor. But then, what more could you expect from a state whose name means "friend"?

. . .More than forty years ago, as a salesman peddling drilling bits . . . I crisscrossed all across west Texas in my car, from Muleshoe to Wink to Notrees, from the panhandle down . . . to Fort Stockton. I learned a lot about the people then. Shared barbecues and saw their pain when they were laid off and the paychecks weren't there. Listening to the pulse of people—that's how you hear the heartbeat of Texas, and that's how Texas gets into your blood. Sticks to you like a tumbleweed in a barbed wire fence. And you know, once it's there, it never leaves.

. . . On Inauguration Day, I talked . . . about a new breeze blowing. Let me tell you, standing back here in Texas, I can feel it. It is the warm gulf breeze of a state where people are independent-minded and open, as bold as its frontiers. It's the wind of a land where risk-taking comes from the strength of your beliefs and where your spirit is as big as the Texas sky.

. . . When I was running, with a spectacular lack of success, for the Senate back in 1964, my first speech was about building a two-party system in Texas. Barbara listened, and three other people listened, and that was it. [Laughter] And that's the gospel truth.

Remarks at a Republican Party fund-raising dinner
at Loews Anatole Hotel Chantilly Ballroom,
Dallas, Texas, May 18, 1990

You can make your own life an adventure. Next month will be forty-two years since my own graduation. And like so many of you, I, too, was presented with some choices on my graduation day: further study or maybe a law firm or a bank or the stock market, and probably for me in New York or in the East—honorable, interesting professions, all. But the truly great decisions we make in life are rarely logical or practical. And so, I packed up, Barbara and I packed, and I drove my red Studebaker from the Eastern states of our upbringing to the oil fields of west Texas. And we chose a future that would be uniquely our own. And like most Americans, we were free to live where we pleased, do what we wanted. We came of age at a time when the postwar world possibilities of America seemed limitless.

Remarks at the University of Texas commencement ceremony
at Neuhaus-Royal Athletic Complex, Austin, May 19, 1990

FAMILY

When Barbara and I became the official caretakers of the White House for four years, the first thing we did was invite all of our children and our grandchildren to spend the night here together upstairs as a family. My family is very, very important to me, and I feel lucky to have been blessed with a wonderful wife and children and, of course, now twelve grandchildren. . . .

Our children are precious. And you're the reason all of us came together here today: to tell you how special you are to us and how glad we are that you are in the family. You know, our son Marvin and his wife, Margaret, just adopted their second child, a little grandson, our grandson Walker. And if I do say so myself, this guy is really something. And so is his sister, Marshall, who's also adopted. And they're an important part of our family, and we love them.

Remarks to special-needs adopted children and their parents,
White House East Room, January 26, 1990

The anchor in our world today is freedom, holding us steady in time of change, a symbol of hope to all the world. And freedom is at the heart of the very idea that is America. Giving life to that idea depends of every one of us. Our anchor has always been faith and family.

In the past few days of this past momentous year, our family was blessed once more, celebrating the joy of life when a little boy became our twelfth grandchild. When I held the little guy for the first time, the troubles at home and abroad seemed manageable and totally in perspective.

Now, I know you're probably thinking, well, that's just a grandfather talking. Well, maybe you're right. But I've met a lot of children this past year across this country, as all of you have, everywhere from the Far East to Eastern Europe. And all kids are unique, and yet all kids are alike—the budding young environmentalists I met this month who joined me in exploring the Florida Everglades; the Little Leaguers I played catch with in Poland, ready to go from Warsaw to the World Series; and even the kids who are ill or alone—and God bless those boarder babies, born addicted to drugs and AIDS and coping with problems no child should have to face. But you know, when it comes to hope and the future, every kid is the same—full of dreams, ready to take on the world—all special, because they are the very future of freedom. And to them belongs this new world I've been talking about.

And so, tonight, I'm going to ask something of every one of you. Now, let me start with my generation, with the grandparents out there. You are our living link to the past. Tell your grandchildren the story of the struggles we waged at home and abroad, of sacrifices freely made for freedom's sake. And tell them your own story as well, because every American has a story to tell.

And, parents, your children look to you for direction and guidance. Tell them of faith and family. Tell them we are one nation under God. Teach them that of all the many gifts they can receive, liberty is their most precious legacy, and of all the gifts they can give, the greatest is helping others.

And to the children and young people out there tonight: With you rests our hope, all that America will mean in the years and decades ahead. Fix your vision on a new century—your century—on dreams we cannot see, on the destiny that is yours and yours alone.

Address before a joint session of the Congress on the State of the Union, U.S. Capitol House Chamber, January 31, 1990

I'm delighted to be here at this relatively early morning breakfast. It reminds me of the time I told our oldest grandson that the early bird gets the worm. He says, "I think I'll sleep in and have pancakes."

Remarks at a fund-raising breakfast for Governor Kay Orr
at the Peony Park Ballroom, Omaha, Nebraska, February 8, 1990

George Bush possesses a well-publicized aversion to broccoli. Perhaps his most fervent antibroccoli statement as President was this Shermanesque declaration outside the White House during an exchange with reporters . . .

Q. Mr. President, have you lost the broccoli vote?

Q. What about it, since you brought it up?

Q. Yes, can you give us a broccoli statement?

The President. Now, look, this is the last statement I'm going to have on broccoli. [Laughter] There are truckloads of broccoli at this very minute descending on Washington. My family is divided. [Laughter] I do not like broccoli. [Laughter] And I haven't liked it since I was a little kid and my mother made me eat it. And I'm President of the United States, and I'm not going to eat any more broccoli. [Laughter]

Wait a minute. For the broccoli vote out there, Barbara loves broccoli. [Laughter] She's tried to make me eat it. She eats it all the time herself. So, she can go out and meet the caravan of broccoli that's coming in.

The President's news conference, White House South Grounds,
March 22, 1990

Referring to a speech given by his grandson George P. Bush . . .

It's nice to know there's at least one charismatic, silver-tongued devil in the family.

Remarks at a Republican Party fund-raising dinner
at the Orange County Convention Center, Hall E,
Orlando, Florida, April 20, 1990

Perhaps you saw on the news that Millie was hanging around, just over the other side, down in the ivy there, when something bit her on the nose. I'm not sure if it was a squirrel or a rat, but I had to investigate.

And of course, anyplace you go here—I do, as President— there's a bunch of Secret Service guys following right along. So imagine this: the seven of us—[laughter]—poking around in the hedges, looking for the culprit, when, you guessed it, the sprinklers came on. [Laughter] So I just want you to know there's a real life inside this magnificent complex.

Remarks at the presentation ceremony for the Achievement
Against All Odds Awards, Rose Garden, May 3, 1990

In this country, the combination of grandchildren and computer games has produced some unexpected results. This is a true story, Mr. President. The most popular computer game in America is called Teenage Mutant Ninja Turtles. [Laughter] Don't worry about the translation; it doesn't make sense in English, either. [Laughter]

Toast at the state dinner
for President Zine al-Abidine Ben Ali of Tunisia,
White House State Dining Room, May 15, 1990

One of the first political challenges to land on President Bush's Oval Office desk, early in 1989, was the savings and loan crisis. Moving quickly and working with Congress, he sent legislation to Capitol Hill on February 6, and signed the Financial Institutions Reform, Recovery, and Enforcement Act of 1989 that August to begin addressing the financial fallout from roughly 750 failed S&Ls.

The President's political challenge over for all intents and purposes, the S&L issue was to turn very personal for the Bush family in 1990—as one of the companies to come under close congressional scrutiny was a Colorado institution, Silverado. Many have since speculated that the Silverado case received special attention because the President's son Neil sat at one time on the S&L's outside board of directors.

President Bush shared this view, as he related in a December 1989 letter to his old Yale friend and retired congressman Lud Ashley, writing in part: "I can't believe that his [Neil's] name would appear in the paper if it was Jones not Bush. In any event, I know that the guy is totally honest" (*ATB*, p. 449). Here, eight months later, the President comments on the issue publicly . . .

This is not easy for me as a father. It's easy for me as a President because the system's going to work. I will not intervene. I have not suggested any outcome. But what father wouldn't express a certain confidence in the honor of his son? And that's exactly the way I feel about it, and I feel very strongly about it. And for those who want to challenge it, whether they are in the Congress or elsewhere: let the system work; and then we can all make a conclusion as to his honor and his integrity.

It's tough on people in public life to some degree. I've got three other sons, and they all want to go to the barricade. Every one of them, when they see some cartoon they don't like, particularly those that are factually incorrect and demeaning of the honor of their brother, they want to do what any other kids would do. And I say, "You calm down now. We're in a different role now. You can't react like you would if your brother was picked on in a street fight. That's not the way the system works."

But we have great emotions that I share with Barbara, I share with my sons and my daughter, that I won't share with you except to say: One, as President, I'm determined to stay out of this and let it work and let it work fairly. And secondly, I have confidence in the honor and integrity of my son. And if the system finds he's done something wrong, he will be the first to step up and do what's right.

The President's news conference
following the Houston Economic Summit, George R. Brown
Convention Center Assembly Hall, July 11, 1990

I'd like to just clear up one thing. And this is just if the Canadian press would drop all notebooks and not write this down and consider this off-the-record. This is just for the American press.

The other day our dog Ranger appeared at a press conference, and he was called "Millie." He's a strong male dog here, as you can see, and his feelings were slightly hurt. And some decreed that because Ranger looked so frisky that Millie was—well, calling Ranger "Millie." So I'd like to clear it up as best I can. Knowing my way with the English language, I hope that's got it clear for you guys. [Laughter]

Remarks and a question-and-answer session
with reporters at Walker's Point, Kennebunkport, Maine,
following a meeting with Prime Minister Brian Mulroney
of Canada, August 27, 1990

I probably shouldn't do this, but I might tell you of a frustration— not an overwhelming frustration but a frustration that I have. I think Barbara Bush is secretly in love with Hume Cronyn.

Remarks at the presentation ceremony for the National Medal
of the Arts, White House East Room, September 10, 1990

Let me convey apologies of a very close member of the family who couldn't make it tonight. As it turns out, Millie is back East, promoting her new book. [Laughter] Her celebrity status has gone to her head. [Laughter] I gave her a bowl of Alpo, and she asked to see the wine list.

Remarks at a fund-raising dinner for gubernatorial candidate
Pete Wilson at Westin Bonaventure Hotel San Francisco Ballroom,
Los Angeles, California, September 18, 1990

FAITH

There is no denying that America is a religious nation. And sure, differences exist over sect and theology. I'm reminded of what that French statesman Talleyrand once said of America: "I found there a country with thirty-two religions and only one sauce."

Remarks at the annual convention of the National Religious
Broadcasters, Sheraton Washington Hotel Ballroom,
January 29, 1990

―――――――――

Let me close, then, with a story of two such heroes, both Romanian, and how their example illumined decency, courage, and love. The first was a Lutheran minister, Laszlo Tokes, who dared to speak of freedom. So last November in Timisoara, masked thugs broke into the small apartment of Tokes and his pregnant wife. And they beat him, and they stabbed him. And the government allowed them no food, and even parishioners were not permitted to bring bread. And finally, the police arrived to deport the minister, but the flock protected him, forming a human chain around his apartment. And in time, the chain grew across the land until, as we celebrated Christmas, Romania's quest for freedom summoned lightness against the dark. Today, Laszlo Tokes ministers to ever larger numbers, preaching his faith, but now preaching it without any fear at all.

As does another, Gheorghe Calciu, a Romanian Orthodox minister. His story proves that . . . you can't destroy the human will. Father Calciu has spent twenty-one of his sixty-four years in jail—twenty-one of his sixty-four years, a third of his entire life, in prison. And in fact, he found God there while in prison for opposing the government. Released, he risked freedom by preaching a series of Lenten sermons. And for that he was imprisoned again, tortured beyond belief. Father Calciu had faith. He refused to break and was sentenced to death. And as he stood in the corner of the prison yard praying for his wife and son, awaiting death, it was then that something remarkable occurred. His two executioners called to him, and surely he thought, this was the end. "Father"—that was the first time they had ever called him that—"we have decided not to kill you." And three weeks later he asked permission to celebrate the divine liturgy and, while making preparations, heard these two same men approach. And he turned around and was astonished—his would-be executioners were on their knees on the cold concrete of the cell.

Remarks at the annual convention of the National Religious
Broadcasters, Sheraton Washington Hotel Ballroom,
January 29, 1990

Nature's beauty has a special power, a resonance that at once elevates the mind's eye and yet humbles us as well. Before nature, the works of humanity seem somehow small. We may build cathedrals, temples, mosques, monuments, and mausoleums to great men and women and high ideals, and still we know we can build no monuments to compare with nature. Our greatest creations really can't equal God's smallest.

Remarks at the closing session
of the White House Conference on Science and Economics Research
Related to Global Change, J. W. Marriott Hotel Grand Ballroom,
April 18, 1990

Diary: "There is no way to adequately describe the moving time in the desert. We went first to the Air Force, then up to an Army base in the sand, then over by chopper to the USS *Nassau* in international waters where we had a nice prayer service for Thanksgiving on the deck: and finishing with the first Marines back in the desert. . . . I wasn't sure I could get through the speeches, and I did choke up in the hangar, on the flight deck of *Nassau* at the Church service. The kids look so long and yet they are gung-ho . . ." (*ATB*, p. 489).

I reminded some at an army base a while ago that this reminds me a bit of a Thanksgiving I spent forty-six years ago on a carrier, USS *San Jacinto* CVL30, off the coast of the Philippines during World War II. I found then that the Lord does provide many blessings to men and women who face adversity in the name of a noble purpose. They are the blessings of faith and friendship, strength and determination, courage and camaraderie and dedication to duty.

And I found that the Lord allows the human spirit the inner resolve to find optimism and hope amidst the most challenging and difficult times. He instills confidence when despair tries to defeat us and inspires teamwork when the individual feels overwhelmed by the events of day to day.

Remarks during a Thanksgiving Day service
on the flight deck of the USS Nassau in the Persian Gulf,
November 22, 1990

FRIENDS

Susan [Molinari] found a scrawny little mutt on Election Day in 1988. We were all waiting for the returns to come in, but the dog wasn't doing well, and they didn't think it would make it. But it was a good dog—loyal, cautious, prudent, some would say timid—and it pulled through. I still can't figure out why Susan named the dog George. [Laughter] But she did. And being a female pup—[laughter]—she'll have it even tougher. Life ain't easy for a girl named George. [Laughter] Let me give you a little serious, political, inside advice, one single word: puppies—worth ten points, believe me.

Remarks at a fund-raising luncheon
for congressional candidate Susan Molinari
at the Shalimar Hall Grand Ballroom, Staten Island,
New York, February 28, 1990

On the Bushes' admired friend and fellow Texan, Lady Bird Johnson . . .

She was his [LBJ's] anchor and his strength. And she never failed him. And she was always there. And as she has once again today, Lady Bird brought to the White House dignity and warmth and grace. And she was never onstage, never acting out some part, always the same genuine lady no matter what the setting. Her gift of language is a combination of both elegance and simplicity, and vivid imagery that charms our country to this very day.

Remarks at the twenty-fifth anniversary celebration
of President Lyndon B. Johnson's inauguration,
White House State Floor, April 6, 1990

While in office, President Bush turned often to Canada's Prime Minister Brian Mulroney for counsel. The two forged a close working relationship, and their friendship continues to this day in private life. Here, the President assesses his colleague to the north before they threw out the first pitches in Toronto . . .

I found that this prime minister tells it as it is, with no coloration; and I view that as extraordinarily helpful to the United States, the way a good friend, the head of a very friendly country, should do. And he's very forceful. We have some differences; but most of the time, on these big issues that he was referring to [NATO, trade], I think we have broad agreement.

News conference of the President and Prime Minister Mulroney
at the Sky Dome Founders Club Lounge, Toronto, Canada,
April 10, 1990

As this needling suggests, former Wyoming senator Al Simpson is another close Bush family friend loved for his sense of humor and, most of all, loyal friendship . . .

On the rest of our leadership: Al Simpson, back from a landslide, proving that adage that you can fool some of the people all of the time. [Laughter]

Remarks at a dinner for the Senate Republican leadership,
Union Station East Hall, November 13, 1990

"THE CORE OF VALUES"

The values I'm talking about have a home in the family, in our churches, and in our communities. And these institutions are strong, much stronger than the alarmists out there would have us believe. Each of them contributes to our public life, enriches it in ways beyond measure. Each of them makes this nation strong, gives it a sense of purpose and a role in the world.

Remarks at the American Spectator *annual dinner,*
Willard Hotel Ballroom, January 22, 1990

Whether talking about a nation or an individual, character is measured not by our tragedies but by our response to those tragedies.

Remarks to the National Leadership Coalition on AIDS,
Crystal Gateway Marriott Arlington Ballroom, March 29, 1990

I'm not pessimistic about America. We go through cycles. We went through a cycle in the Vietnam War where our own sons and, to some degree, daughters were told that our cause was immoral— people feeling as strongly as they did. I was old enough or blind enough, or whatever, not to accept that view. I still don't accept that view, because when I look at Southeast Asia and I see a Vietnam where the charge was against us—if we'd only get out; this is an indigenous civil war; you'd have a little more democracy there—that hasn't worked out that way. . . .

But the point is . . . we had a generation of Americans that were taught about a deep conviction by professors and politicians and others that our purpose, our cause, was wrong. And then we condoned as a society certain excesses that we should have condemned. And I'm talking about an elevation of understanding about narcotics, for example, which gets right to the core of values.

Well, you've got to understand. I even think we condoned graffiti as an expression of people's—wasn't this marvelous—

creativity, when all it was, was littering and cluttering up not exactly beautiful subway cars but—[laughter]—nevertheless, we condoned things we should have condemned. I have confidence that the country goes somewhat cyclically, but always moves forward to our fundamental values.

I'm not discouraged about it. I wrestle with things that I think are important—and I don't want to get into a debate with you all about the flag amendment. I happen to feel strongly about it, and I'd like to see the debate . . . without having to call the other guy a demagogue. . . . And I've fought for it because I do think there was a unique symbol there. And there's pretty good understanding on the part of the American people. The debate can go on without denigrating the other person's convictions that disagrees or feels that amending the Bill of Rights or the Constitution would be an egregious error.

But I keep coming back, as I listen to the debates on all these questions . . . that we have a way of finding our way through, in the United States, these—what appear to be—dilemmas or these challenges. And the reasons is, I think, there is fundamental understanding that we are one nation under God, that we have great respect for religious diversity, and that as we see the social problems of the day we return more and more to the importance of family.

. . . I want to be very careful about censorship and about demagoguing these issues, whatever they are. But I don't feel I ought to address myself, in a legislative sense, to helping with this question because I think we can sort it out as people. And I'm confident not only of our decency and honor as a country but of our tremendous generosity as a country. We've got some big problems here at home, and I've got to address myself perhaps more effectively to some of those. But I don't put down as one of them the weakening of the moral underpinning of this country. I hope I'm right.

Remarks and question-and-answer session with the Magazine Publishers of America, Old Executive Office Building, Room 450, July 17, 1990

Perhaps their [troops in the Gulf] sacrifice will make those of us
at home this Thanksgiving Day reflect even more greatly. So
that when we give thanks for our food, we will think of those rav-
aged by hunger; when we give thanks for our health, we will think
of those imprisoned by pain or illness or despair; when we give
thanks for our freedom, we will also think of those who live in
darkness or tyranny; when we give thanks for our future, we will
think of those who don't know hope. And we will realize that we
have two obligations above all others. First, we must not take for
granted the blessings of our lives. And second, for our lives to have
true meaning, we must share with others. For this holiday reminds
us that it's inner riches, not external wealth, by which we are measured. After all, Thanksgiving is not a time of the year, but it really
is an attitude of the heart.

Remarks at the Thanksgiving turkey presentation ceremony,
Rose Garden, November 14, 1990

"THE VISION THING":
Not to Demagogue but Deliver

A line has been drawn in the sand.

The President's news conference, White House Briefing Room,
August 8, 1990

**I think we've got all kinds of potential for peace, given the fact
that we've come together almost unanimously, standing up
against this brutal dictator. And out of that and out of the con-
texts that go with that, I hope we can be catalytic in solving
other problems; and I think that will lead to a new world
order that has a much better chance for peace for our children
and our grandchildren.**

Remarks and a question-and-answer session with reporters
following discussions with President Muhammad Hosni
Mubarak at the Itihadia Palace Main Hall, Cairo, Egypt,
November 23, 1990

"Tough Decisions"

The calendar offers each of us convenient launch points for a fresh start. Sometimes it's a new day, a new year—now, a brand-new decade. And the beginning of the nineties invites America to clearly put its signature on the twentieth century, to write the next chapter in a book of spectacular achievements, world leadership. I welcome the nineties with a genuine sense of optimism. It's an ideal time to renew our vows and our values, time to look beyond the next paycheck and the next personal problem, time instead to look to the next generation.

And so, I am optimistic about our future for one compelling reason: to succeed, we do not have to acquire any new qualities. The courage, ingenuity, and compassion that made us the leader of the free world is still in every one of us. And we simply have to remember that the American adventure isn't over—it's just begun.

Remarks at the American Spectator *annual dinner,*
Willard Hotel Ballroom, January 22, 1990

In July of 1989, in the wake of the Tiananmen Square repression, President Bush sent his trusted National Security Advisor, General Brent Scowcroft, to Beijing on a secret diplomatic mission. Here the President explained the need for secrecy . . .

In diplomacy, I don't think you make progress by throwing down a list of things, telling somebody else how to behave. I do think you adhere to your own principles, and I think sometimes you have to undertake the kind of diplomacy I engaged in here to reiterate principles and to explain the severity of problems to people. But if you do it publicly all the time and you do it so you're painting someone in a corner, I don't think you get results.

The President's news conference, White House Briefing Room,
January 25, 1990

Response when asked to comment on his being "at near-historical public approval ratings now for well into your first term: eighty percent or more . . ."

These things come and go. And you know where I learned it? Back in Illinois in 1980. . . . I remember Vic Gold [who helped then-Vice President Bush write his 1987 autobiography, *Looking Forward*] lecturing me on hanging my hat on polls.

That's not the way I try to call the shots on the policy. You just raised a question about China. If I had my finger in the wind, I might have done that one differently. I might have done differently about going to Cartagena if I put my finger in the wind in terms of polls, but that's not the way I run this administration.

The President's new conference,
White House Briefing Room,
March 13, 1990

On one of his favorite Presidents, Dwight David Eisenhower, and "the vision thing" . . .

He was decisive, acting on instincts that were invariably wise. You know, some critics can't figure out how Eisenhower was so successful as a President without the vision thing. Well, his vision—[laughter]—his vision was etched on a plaque, sitting on his desk, that many of you around here remember because you were there: "Gently in manner, strong in deed." And he used that vision not to demagogue but deliver.

Remarks at a luncheon commemorating
the Dwight D. Eisenhower centennial, White House State
Dining Room, March 27, 1990

It is said that Lincoln's hand shook as he dipped his quill into the inkwell before he signed the Emancipation Proclamation. Perhaps he felt the weight of history. Perhaps he was weary. In any event, he waited a moment to steady his hand so that no one would think he wavered on such an important decision. Through the vision of one man, millions were freed.

Remarks at the twentieth anniversary dinner of the Joint Center
for Political and Economic Studies, Washington Hilton Hotel
International Ballroom, April 4, 1990

Once again asked to comment on the polls, this time when asked how criticism of Prime Minister Margaret Thatcher would affect her reputation . . .

I don't think you deal with heads of government based on whether they're up or down in the polls, or even speculate. . . . I'm enough of a politician to know that people can be down one moment and then soaring like an eagle the next.

Interview with foreign journalists, Oval Office,
April 17, 1990

Bigotry and hate regrettably still exist in this country, and hate breeds violence, threatening the security of our entire society. We must rid our communities of the poison we call prejudice, bias, and discrimination.

Remarks on signing the Hate Crimes Act,
Old Executive Office Building, Room 450, April 23, 1990

I have offered you my hand and my word that together we can and will make America open and equal to all.

Remarks at a meeting with the Commission on Civil Rights,
Rose Garden, May 17, 1990

One of the landmark pieces of legislation to become law during the Bush presidency was the Americans with Disabilities Act of 1990, which President Bush would later call "really the world's first comprehensive declaration of equality" for disabled people.

As he wrote his friend Mike Deland, head of the Council on Environmental Quality and a leader in the disabilities movement, the day after the signing ceremony: "As I looked out at the audience yesterday, I was saying to myself 'don't choke up'— hang in there . . ."

Together we must remove the physical barriers we have created and the social barriers we have accepted. For ours will never be a truly prosperous nation until all within it prosper.

Remarks on signing the Americans with Disabilities Act of 1990,
White House South Lawn, July 26, 1990

As Americans, we're slow to raise our hand in anger and eager to explore every peaceful means of settling our disputes; but when we have exhausted every alternative, when conflict is thrust upon us, there is no nation on earth with greater resolve or stronger steadiness of purpose.

Address to the people of Iraq on the Persian Gulf crisis,
taped in the Oval Office on September 12 and broadcast unedited
on Iraqi television, September 16, 1990

Completing a "double play" of sorts, after addressing a newly reunified Germany on German national TV, President Bush once again took to the airwaves—this time to urge his fellow Americans, for the first time, to contact their congressional representatives to pass the controversial budget agreement he had reached with the Democrats. The agreement gained some notoriety because, among the spending restraints and tax cuts, it also included a tax increase in the 28 percent income tax bracket to 31.5 percent—and, as such, violated then-candidate Bush's "no new taxes" pledge. Here the President refers to both the imperfection of the agreement and the urgency of the moment . . .

Clearly, each and every one of us can find fault with something in this agreement. In fact, that is a burden that any truly fair solution must carry. Any workable solution must be judged as a whole, not piece by piece. Those who dislike one part or another may pick our agreement apart. But if they do, believe me, the political reality is, no one can put a better one back together again. Everyone will bear a small burden. But if we succeed, every American will have a large burden lifted. If we fail to enact this agreement, our economy will falter, markets may tumble, and recession will follow.

Address to the nation on the federal budget agreement,
Oval Office, October 2, 1990

Response when asked if his presidency was "on the line" . . .

We've got two big things coming together now. One is the deficit, and one is this crisis halfway around the world. But I'm telling you honestly, I don't look at it in terms of whether it's good for a Bush presidency or popular politically. And that's why last night I tried to give cover to members of Congress, Democrat and Republican, and say, "You don't have to support crossing every *t* and dotting every *i,* but say the President encouraged you to do it. Blame me." Because I know what's best for our country, but I don't suspect it's politically popular.

Remarks and a question-and-answer session
with regional newspaper editors, Old Executive Office Building,
Room 450, October 3, 1990

The President and the leaders of both houses have to be responsible for the overall good of the country, have to make something happen. I can't get it done just my way. I don't control both houses of Congress. I'd love to think that luxury will come my way someday, but it hasn't. Therefore, we've had to compromise. So, I will keep trying in that spirit—that cooperative, positive spirit.

The President's news conference on the federal budget crisis,
White House West Driveway, October 6, 1990

Not surprisingly, going into the 1990 midterm election, both the budget and the standoff with Iraq weighed equally on his mind . . .

I will hold everyone's feet to the fire and make them up there, to the best of my ability, do the right thing. I really do believe in what I'm doing, and I believe that the national interest is more important than my own political interest and certainly more important than the special interest.

Remarks to White House interns, Old Executive Office Building,
Room 450, October 18, 1990

We've made the tough decisions, and now it's time to move on.

Remarks on the federal budget agreement and an exchange
with reporters at the Center for Cultural Exchange Between East
and West, Honolulu, Hawaii, October 27, 1990

Addressing the hardest part of his job as President—sending somebody else's son or daughter into combat. Here the President reiterates the message he delivered in person to the troops the week before—that there will be "no more Vietnams." By this, he meant he was determined not to "tie the hands of the military" and, instead, let them "fight to win" . . .

Q. Mr. President, if you ultimately feel that you have to ask Americans to support the use of force, what that, of course, means is that you have to ask some parents to give up the lives of their children.

The President. I know it.

Q. What I was wondering was, we all know how important your children are to you. Do you feel this issue is important enough to you that you could conceive of giving up one of their lives for it?

The President. You know, Maureen [Santini, *New York Daily News*], you put your finger on a very difficult question. People say to me, "How many lives? How many lives can you expend?" Each one is precious. I don't want to reminisce, but I've been there. I know what it's like to have fallen comrades and see young kids die in battle. It's only the President that should be asked: "Is it worth it? How many lives is it worth? Is it worth it to commit one life, put one life in harm's way to achieve these objectives?" And that's why I want to get a peaceful resolution to this issue.

You ought to read my mail. It is so heart-moving. Supportive, and yet: "Please bring my kid home. Please bring my husband home." It's a tough question. But a President has to make the right decision. These are worldwide principles of moral importance. I will do my level best to bring those kids home without one single shot fired in anger. And if a shot is fired in anger, I want to guarantee each person that their kid, whose life is in harm's way, will have the maximum support, will have the best chance to come home alive, and will be backed up to the hilt.

Because of that question which weighs on my mind, I added that language this morning about how this will not be another Vietnam. They can criticize me for moving force. And if we've got one kid that's apt to be in harm's way, I want him backed up to the hilt by American firepower, and others as well. That's why I'm working as hard as I am not only to hold this coalition together but to strengthen it. The best way to safeguard the lives of Americans is for Saddam Hussein to do what he should have done long ago. And if force has to be used, the best way to safeguard lives is to see that you've got the best and you're willing to use it. That's my posture.

The President's (sixty-sixth) news conference,
White House Briefing Room, November 30, 1990

Capitalizing on the wave of political and economic reform sweeping through Latin America—including Chile's return to democracy and Nicaragua's free election earlier in the year—the President announced his Enterprise for the Americas Initiative

on June 27 to help foster economic growth and stable currencies throughout the hemisphere. During a five-day trip to Brazil, Uruguay, Argentina, Chile, and Venezuela, President Bush made good on his pledge to regional leaders to stay engaged . . .

Territories may end at borders, but mankind's capacity for progress knows no bounds. Continents may end at water's edge, but human potential knows only those limits set by human imagination. The Americas' role in the world is not defined by geography; it is defined by its peoples and its ideals. I truly believe that we are approaching a new dawn in the New World.

Our thinking must be bold; our will, resolute. Our challenge now is to hew out of the wilderness of competing interests a new kind of opportunity in the Americas. To fulfill the New World's destiny, all of the Americas and the Caribbean must embark on a venture for the coming century: to create the first full democratic hemisphere in the history of mankind, the first hemisphere devoted to the democratic ideal—to unleash the power of free people, free elections, and free markets.

Remarks to a joint session of the Congress,
Brazilian Congress Building House Chamber, Brasilia, Brazil,
December 3, 1990

Less than a decade from now, we will enter the twenty-first century. Already, we see the outline of that century. It will be a world in which those nations which modernize and compete will prosper, a world in which investment and trade will create opportunity and growth. So, my message today is, let's join together to work towards this new world of progress. And it's a new world of hope, I might add, for all the peoples of the Americas.

Remarks at the American Chamber of Commerce breakfast,
Holiday Inn Crowne Plaza Hotel Salón de Directorio, Santiago,
Chile, December 7, 1990

Toward a "Commonwealth of Freedom"

Television, which began as the American forum, has become the world forum. And so, when a lone brave man stood up to a column of tanks in Tiananmen Square, the world stood with him. When the people of Prague sang the first Christmas carols in over forty years, the world sang with them. And when the first German took the first hammer to that wall of shame in Berlin, the world shared in an historic act of courage.

Remarks at the annual convention of the National Association
of Broadcasters, Georgia World Congress Center
Thomas P. Murphy Ballroom, Atlanta, Georgia,
April 2, 1990

———————

On May 31, Mikhail Gorbachev arrived in Washington for the second of five bilateral summit meetings with George Bush. Perhaps the most stunning development during the four days of talks in Washington and Camp David came on the first afternoon, when, sitting in the Cabinet Room of the White House, the Soviet chairman indicated he would let the people of united Germany decide if they wished to be in NATO. That first night, President Bush toasted his counterpart . . .

We meet at a time of great and historic change in the Soviet Union, in Europe, and around the world. Such profound change is unsettling, but also exhilarating. And we don't shrink from the challenges before us, but we welcome them, determined to build the foundations of enduring peace and security.

Toast at the state dinner for President Mikhail Gorbachev
of the Soviet Union, State Dining Room,
May 31, 1990

———————

Sharing a Malta memory while again toasting his counterpart, this time as the guest at the Soviet embassy . . .

Yesterday we welcomed the Gorbachevs back to Washington still filled with memories of the things we shared at Malta: friendship, cooperation, seasick pills.

Toast at a dinner hosted by President Mikhail Gorbachev
of the Soviet Union, Soviet embassy Golden Dining Room,
June 1, 1990

A new world of freedom lies before us, hopeful, confident—a world where peace endures, where commerce has a conscience, and where all that seems possible is possible.

Remarks at the welcoming ceremony for the Houston
Economic Summit, Rice University Academic Quadrangle,
July 9, 1990

When people are free to choose, they choose freedom.

Remarks on presenting the final communiqué
of the Houston Economic Summit, George R. Brown
Convention Center Assembly Hall, July 11, 1990

While the events of this past year have been a glorious beginning, there is still much to do—because peace is more than just the absence of war.

Remarks to the thirtieth biennial
Greek Orthodox Church Clergy-Laity Congress,
Sheraton Washington Hotel Sheraton Ballroom,
July 12, 1990

At long last we are writing the final chapter of the twentieth century's third great conflict. The Cold War is now drawing to a close, and after four decades of division and discord, our challenge today is to fulfill the great dream of all democracies: a true commonwealth of freed nations. To marshal the growing forces of the world, to work together, to bring within reach for all men and nations the liberty that belongs by right to all.

Remarks at the Aspen Institute Symposium,
Aspen Institute Music Tent, Aspen, Colorado, August 2, 1990

Sharing his vision for the Americas with the world at the UN . . .

I see a world of open borders, open trade, and most importantly, open minds; a world that celebrates the common heritage that belongs to all the world's people, taking pride not just in a hometown or homeland but in humanity itself. I see a world touched by a spirit like that of the Olympics, based not on competition that's driven by fear but sought out of joy and exhilaration and a true quest for excellence. And I see a world where democracy continues to win new friends and convert old foes and where the Americas—North, Central, and South—can provide a model for the future of all humankind: the world's first completely democratic hemisphere. And I see a world building on the emerging new model of European unity, not just Europe but the whole world whole and free.

Address before the forty-fifth session of the United Nations
General Assembly, United Nations General Assembly Hall,
New York City, October 1, 1990

On October 2, President Bush separately addressed the peoples of two countries: Germany and the United States. Germany was celebrating the day few had dared dream might happen just a year before—the reunification of East and West Germany into one nation. On this historic day, the President closed his videotaped remarks saying . . .

Today the Wall lies in ruins, and our eyes open on a new world of hope. Now Germany is once more united. Now the Wall no longer divides a nation and a world in two. The last remnants of the Wall remain there at the heart of a free Berlin, a ragged monument in brick and barbed wire, proof that no wall is ever strong enough to strangle the human spirit, that no wall can ever crush a nation's soul.

Address to the German people on the reunification
of Germany, broadcast on German TV,
October 2, 1990

We must recognize that no people, no continent, can stand alone, secure unto itself. Our fates, our futures, are intertwined . . .

Every new nation that embraces these common values, every new nation that joins the ranks of this commonwealth of freedom, advances us one step closer to a new world order, a world in which the use of force gives way to shared respect for the rule of law. This new world will be incomplete without a vision that extends beyond the boundaries of Europe alone. Now that unity is within reach in Europe is no time for our vision of change to stop at the edge of this continent.

Remarks to the Federal Assembly, Federal Assembly Hall,
Prague, Czechoslovakia, November 17, 1990

"THIS WILL NOT STAND"

On the evening of August 1, National Security Advisor Brent Scowcroft and NSC Middle East expert Richard Haas confronted President Bush in the White House Medical Office with the news that Iraq was about to invade Kuwait—a probability confirmed an hour later. That set in motion a series of events with ramifications felt even to this day, particularly in Iraq.

The next morning, before his first meeting with the National Security Council on the invasion, President Bush met the press. Of that encounter, he recalled: "Among the forest of boom and

hand-held microphones, I was careful in my remarks. I condemned the invasion and outlined the steps we had taken. . . . I
did not want my first public comments to threaten the use of
American military might, so I said I was not contemplating
intervention, and, even if I knew we were going to use force, I
would not announce it in a press conference. The truth is, at that
moment I had no idea what our options were. I did know for
sure that aggression had to be stopped, and Kuwait's sovereignty
restored. We had a big job ahead of us in shaping opinion at
home and abroad and could little afford bellicose mistakes at the
start. What I hoped to convey was an open mind about how we
might handle the situation until I learned the facts . . ." (*AWT,*
p. 315).

We view the situation with the utmost gravity. We remain committed to take whatever steps are necessary to defend our long-
standing, vital interests in the Gulf, and I'm meeting this morning
with my senior advisers here to consider all possible options
available to us.

> *Remarks and an exchange with reporters on the Iraqi invasion*
> *of Kuwait, White House Cabinet Room, August 2, 1990*

———————

Later that day, after consulting by phone with Hosni Mubarak
of Egypt, King Hussein of Jordan, Secretary of State James
Baker, and others while he was en route to Aspen, Colorado,
the President consulted with Prime Minister Margaret
Thatcher of the United Kingdom at the residence of the U.S.
ambassador to the UK, Henry Catto. "At about two o'clock,
Margaret and I stepped out to a patio for a press conference. We
condemned Iraq's aggression and called for a peaceful solution, with the withdrawal of Iraqi troops and the restoration of
the Kuwaiti leadership. She put her finger on the most important point—whether the nations of the world had the collective
and effective will to implement the resolutions of the [United
Nations] Security Council and compel withdrawal and restora-

tion. It would be up to American leadership to make that happen . . ." (*AWT*, p. 320).

We're not ruling any options in, but we're not ruling any options out.

Remarks and a question-and-answer session with reporters
in Aspen, Colorado, following a meeting with Prime Minister
Margaret Thatcher of the United Kingdom, August 2, 1990

Diary: "I flew down to Washington from Camp David on the afternoon of Sunday, August 5. Haas met me as I emerged from the helicopter on the South Lawn and brought me up to date on the latest developments. I walked up to the crowd of waiting reporters for a few informal remarks. Although over the weekend I had been thinking about the need to voice my determination to the American people, I had not decided when I should do it. At the moment, I just planned to fill everyone in on the diplomatic steps we were taking and the international reaction. I explained that none of our allies was willing to accept anything less than total Iraqi withdrawal from Kuwait, nor would they tolerate a puppet government. . . . Everyone, of course, wanted to know what measures we would take ourselves to protect Americans in Kuwait, especially in view of Iraqi threats to close down foreign embassies. To this, I answered . . ." (*AWT*, p. 332).

This will not stand. This will not stand, this aggression against Kuwait.

Remarks and exchange with reporters on the Iraqi invasion
of Kuwait, White House South Lawn, August 5, 1990

We succeeded in the struggle for freedom in Europe because we and our allies remained stalwart. Keeping the peace in the Middle East will require no less. We're beginning a new era. This new era can be full of promise, an age of freedom, a time of peace for all peoples. But if history teaches us anything, it is that we must resist aggression or it will destroy our freedoms. Appeasement does not work. . . .

America does not seek conflict, nor do we seek to chart the destiny of other nations. But America will stand by her friends. . . .

Standing up for our principles is an American tradition. As it has so many times before, it may take time and tremendous effort, but most of all, it will take unity of purpose. As I've witnessed throughout my life in both war and peace, America has never wavered when her purpose is driven by principle. And in this August day, at home and abroad, I know she will do no less.

Address to the nation announcing the deployment
of United States armed forces to Saudi Arabia,
Oval Office, August 8, 1990

We've worked for decades to develop an international order, a common code and rule of law that promotes cooperation in place of conflict. This order is imperfect; we know that. But without it, peace and freedom are impossible. The rule of law gives way to the law of the jungle. And so, when the question is asked, Where does America stand? I answer, America stands where it always has—against aggression.

Remarks to Defense Department employees,
Pentagon Building River Entrance, August 15, 1990

On September 7, President Bush set off for Helsinki to meet with Gorbachev about the Iraqi crisis. "We had a lot of turbulence on the flight, so I didn't sleep much and was dead tired on Saturday when we arrived. But Finland was wonderful, and President Mauno Koivisto, an old friend, gave us a warm welcome . . ."

Much is at stake, and there is much the world stands to gain if we succeed. If the nations of the world, acting together, continue, as they have been, to isolate Iraq and deny Saddam the fruits of aggression, we will set in place the cornerstone of an international order more peaceful, stable, and secure than any that we have known.

Remarks at the arrival ceremony at Helsinki-Vantas Airport,
Helsinki, Finland, September 8, 1990

After a roller-coaster day of negotiations with the Soviets, a steadfast Iraqi patron during the Cold War, the President got the strong joint statement with Gorbachev he was seeking . . .

Our preference is to resolve the crisis peacefully, and we will be united against Iraq's aggression as long as the crisis exists. However, we are determined to see this aggression end, and if the current steps fail to end it, we are prepared to consider additional ones consistent with the UN Charter. We must demonstrate beyond any doubt that aggression cannot and will not pay.

Soviet Union–United States Joint Statement
on the Persian Gulf crisis, September 9, 1990

"On September 11, I addressed a joint session of Congress to report on the Gulf situation and my talks with Gorbachev. I hoped to strengthen support for our approach to the crisis, and underscore the long-term importance of what we had accomplished at Helsinki. . . . The speech that evening was warmly received, and I felt a charge of adrenaline as I addressed the crowded chamber. . . . What pleased me the most that evening was that there was strong support for the actions I had already taken (moving troops) and what I might yet have to do if there was provocation. As long as there was Congressional backing, I felt I had a good chance to prevail. Yet I saw confrontation brewing over the question of force . . ." (*AWT*, pp. 369–371).

We stand today at a unique and extraordinary moment. The crisis in the Persian Gulf, as grave as it is, also offers a rare opportunity to move toward an historic period of cooperation. Out of these troubled times, our fifth objective—a new world order—can emerge; a new era—freer from the threat of terror, stronger in the pursuit of justice, and more secure in the quest for peace. An era in which the nations of the world, East and West, North and South, can prosper and live in harmony. A hundred generations have searched for this elusive path to peace, while a thousand wars raged across the span of human endeavor. Today, that new world is struggling to be born, a world quite different from the one we've known. A world where the rule of law supplants the rule of the jungle. A world in which nations recognize the shared responsibility for freedom and justice. A world where the strong respect the rights of the weak.

Address before a joint session of the Congress
on the Persian Gulf crisis and the federal budget deficit,
U.S. Capitol House Chamber, September 11, 1990

Diary: "We've been to Czechoslovakia in a very moving and historic visit—the first visit of an American President to Czechoslovakia. . . . I spoke in Wenceslas Square, one year after the Communists went out. Estimate was 750,000 people. It was wall to wall. I regretted we had to be in a Plexiglas cocoon—dictated by the security people. But even that did not detract from the moment . . ." (*ATB,* p. 488).

There is no question about what binds our nations, and so many others, in common cause. There is no question that ours is a just cause and that good will prevail. The darkness in the desert sky cannot stand against the way of light.

Remarks in Prague, Czechoslovakia, at a ceremony
commemorating the end of Communist rule, Wenceslas Square,
November 17, 1990

Iraq's aggression is not just a challenge to the security of Kuwait and the other Gulf neighbors but to the better world we all hope to build in the wake of the Cold War. We're not talking simply about the price of gas; we are talking about the price of liberty.

Remarks to Allied armed forces near Dhahran, Saudi Arabia,
November 22, 1990

I have asked the secretary of state to be available to go to Baghdad anytime, up to and including January 3, which is over five months after the invasion of Kuwait and only twelve days before the United Nations deadline for withdrawal. That deadline is real.

To show flexibility, I have offered any one of fifteen dates for Secretary Baker to go to Baghdad, and the Iraqis have offered only one date. In offering to go the extra mile for peace, however, I did not offer to be party to Saddam Hussein's manipulation.

Saddam Hussein is not too busy to see . . . Kurt Waldheim, Willy Brandt, Muhammad Ali, Ted Heath, John Connally, Ramsey Clark, and many, many others on very short notice. It is simply not credible that he cannot, over a two-week period, make a couple of hours available for the secretary of state on an issue of this importance—unless, of course, he is seeking to circumvent the United Nations deadline.

Remarks on the nomination of the secretary of labor
and the Persian Gulf crisis and a question-and-answer session
with reporters, White House South Lawn, December 14, 1990

LEGACY OF SERVICE:
From Within

Block by block, neighborhood by neighborhood, life by life, we can reclaim those living in the darkness.

Remarks and exchange with reporters prior to a luncheon
with the founding directors of the Points of Light
Initiative Foundation, White House Diplomatic Room,
March 30, 1990

What we do for ourselves dies with us; what we do for others remains.

Remarks to members of the National Conference
of State Legislatures, Old Executive Office Building,
Room 450, February 9, 1990

LIFE BY LIFE

I know how much Barbara's work in literacy means to her and to others. And she often talks about what volunteers are doing around the country. So, I know you do give a lot. But you are not giving dignity, for that cannot be conferred, or education, because that must be acquired. You're not bestowing ambition, because ambition's got to come from within. What the men and women of VISTA do achieve is even more miraculous: you impart to so many disadvantaged Americans the means to build pride, to earn a degree or a skill, to believe in themselves.

For an individual, dignity comes when he realizes that he's the true author of his destiny; for a troubled community, it comes by finding leadership that comes from within.

Remarks at the White House ceremony commemorating
the twenty-fifth anniversary of VISTA,
White House Roosevelt Room, January 31, 1990

A close friend of mine sent me a poem recently which eloquently embodies this spirit of giving: "I sought my soul, but my soul I could not see. I sought my God, but my God eluded me. I sought my brother and found all three."

Thousands of Americans are finding their soul, finding their God, by reaching out to their brothers and sisters in need. You've heard me talk about a Thousand Points of Light across the country. Americans are working through their places of worship, through community programs, or on their own to help the hungry or the homeless, to teach the unskilled, to bring the words of men and the word of God to those who cannot even read.

Remarks at the Annual National Prayer Breakfast,
Washington Hilton Hotel International Ballroom,
February 1, 1990

There is nothing that hurts more than a child afraid of the darkness whose cries go unheard, a lonely child whose tiny spirit is wrapped up in a brave fight too big for its years.

Remarks at the ribbon-cutting ceremony for the Children's Inn
at the National Institutes of Health in Bethesda, Maryland,
June 21, 1990

Commenting on community efforts responding to Hurricane Hugo in Charlotte, North Carolina, and the Flight 232 crash in Sioux City, Iowa . . .

No hand was idle, and certainly, no heart was untouched.

Remarks at the presentation ceremony
for the All-American Cities Awards, August 6, 1990

PUBLIC SERVICE

We know well where the real heavy lifting happened out there in the campaign—out in the field. And I'm talking about what you all know so well: the phone work, the sign making, the all-nighters, the creative chaos, and the just plain making do with what you got. . . .

In the '88 election, we sought power for its potential to help people. We wanted progress for a clean environment and the fight against drugs that savage our streets, and for the sake of the family, free institutions, free speech, and free markets, to make Amer-

ica second to none in education, to ensure economic opportunity
for all Americans. We knew what remained to be done.

Remarks at the Bush-Quayle campaign reunion,
Washington Hilton Hotel International Ballroom,
January 18, 1990

**Commemorating the twenty-fifth anniversary of Lyndon
Johnson's 1965 inauguration, the President salutes the tireless
public service rendered by his fellow Texan and Oval Office
predecessor . . .**

LBJ often spoke about the strength that comes from the power for
good that lies out there in the fertile lands and great cities of America, about America's deep confidence in itself—its conviction
that we don't have any problem that we are not big enough to solve
ourselves, and always remembering that all our successes can
always be improved. He tried with all his heart and to be the best
President this country ever had for the people who are pressed
against the wall, whose cries are not often heard. But he heard.
Lyndon Johnson heard.

Remarks at the twenty-fifth anniversary celebration
of President Lyndon B. Johnson's inauguration,
White House State Floor, April 6, 1990

"Home of the Brave"

Our servicemen and -women are proving that America could
not be the land of the free if it were not the home of the brave.

Remarks at a rally for senatorial candidate Lynn Martin,
Rosemont Horizon Arena, Chicago, Illinois, September 26, 1990

The world is still a dangerous place, and those in uniform will
always bear the heaviest burden. And we want every single Amer-

ican home. And this we promise: no American will be kept in the Gulf a single day longer than necessary. But we won't pull punches. We're not here on some exercise. This is a real-world situation, and we're not walking away until our mission is done, until the invader is out of Kuwait.

Remarks to the Military Airlift Command
at Dhahran International Airport, Dhahran, Saudi Arabia,
November 22, 1990

Seeing you all here brings back a personal memory of another Thanksgiving—another group of young Americans far from home—and for me it was November 23, 1944. And I was twenty years old and six days away from my last mission as a carrier pilot. And our ship, the *San Jacinto,* laid off the coast of the Philippines. And while we celebrated without family that year, like you, we all came together as friends and as part of something bigger than ourselves to thank God for our blessings. And we joined together then, as you are now, as part of a proud force of freedom. . . .

No President, believe me, no President is quick to order American troops abroad. But there are times when all nations that value their own freedom and hope for a new world of freedom must confront aggression.

Remarks to the U.S. army troops near Dhahran, Saudi Arabia,
November 22, 1990

Variations of the phrase "each life is important" appear in several areas during the 1990 holiday season, including a hand-typed letter to each of the Bushes' five children sent from Camp David a week after this message . . .

Tonight the star of Bethlehem and the candles of the menorah will cast their light in American outposts around the world with a timeless message of hope and renewal that radiates to people of all faiths. Each of you is precious. Each life is important because it touches so many other lives. And while you may be out of America's sight, rest assured no matter where you serve, you will never be out of America's hearts.

Christmas message to American troops,
broadcast on Armed Forces Radio and Television Network,
December 24, 1990

IN THE ARENA:
Intellectual Complexity

Right here in this auditorium, almost eighty years ago, Teddy Roosevelt came to meet with the citizens of Milwaukee. His speech that day saved his life—literally. He was shot by a deranged assassin while on his way here. And TR had his draft speech folded up in his jacket pocket, where it helped blunt the bullet. Tough guy. He delivered the speech anyhow. But the moral is: it's not whether a speech is long or short; what matters most is how thick it is.

Remarks at a fund-raising luncheon
for Governor Tommy Thompson at Mecca Auditorium,
Milwaukee, Wisconsin, June 7, 1990

"Milking a Bull"

Getting a good farm bill through Congress is like milking a bull.

Remarks to the American Farm Bureau Federation
at Orange County Convention/Civic Center, Hall D,
Orlando, Florida, January 8, 1990

Happy memories at the 1988 Bush-Quayle campaign reunion . . .

It was a long, hard campaign. We all have our memories, but I can remember riding in planes and kissing babies and hugging pigs and marching in parades and driving stagecoaches and tractor trailers and playing shuffleboard in Florida and standing under

confetti cannons in California and waiting for yet one more balloon drop. But tonight, I really came over to thank you for one
thing you did not ask me to do: you never asked me to make a
video riding in a tank. [Laughter]

Some of the members of the press corps who had the good fortune—or ill fortune, depending on how they looked at it—of
being assigned to our campaign would know that this is a true one,
but I'll never forget it. Barbara and I were traveling in the car when
they told us to look out the window to wave because these photo
dogs were coming alongside for a photo opportunity. And so, we're
both sitting there, smiling and waving and looking enthusiastic—
you know how you do in campaigns. [Laughter] And the truck full
of photo dogs pulls up next to us, and they all look over and say
in unison, "Pardon me, sir. Do you have any Grey Poupon?"
[Laughter] Don't say these guys don't have a sense of humor.

The Secret Service never really got into the act too well. They
had one comedian, though. I'd been singing to myself in the car—
this is also a true story—and as Barbara and I were getting out, she
heard a quiet voice from behind the wheel in front say, "If I were
you, sir, I wouldn't give up your day job." [Laughter]

Barbara tells a story about staying in her hotel and not having
her bathrobe with her. In the morning, the room service knocked
on the door with coffee, and she looked all over for a robe—no
luck. So, when the room service guy opened the door, the future
First Lady was standing there, looking quite elegant, wrapped in
a bedsheet. [Laughter]

. . . The toughest part, for me, was the debates. Some time has
passed, so I want to take a moment to recognize my opponent.
He was strong, tough, tenacious, a real fighter. I gained newfound
respect for Dan Rather.

Remarks at the Bush-Quayle campaign reunion,
Washington Hilton Hotel International Ballroom,
January 18, 1990

It was in this very hall a year and a half ago that the party oppo-
site from mine held their 1988 convention. And of course, I have

fond memories of that convention. It gave me a very good excuse to go fishing with Jim Baker. [Laughter] And the question was appropriately raised, "Where was George?" Albeit a year and a half later, I'm proud to say, "Here I am," proud to be with the Home Builders. Isn't it great to live in a country with no limits? Who would have thought that I would ever put my silver foot where Ann Richards talked?

> *Remarks at the annual convention of the National Association*
> *of Home Builders at the Omni Coliseum, Atlanta, Georgia,*
> *January 19, 1990*

———————

I understand that this is actually the *American Spectator*'s 1989 annual dinner. [Laughter] Now, that's true conservatism, you see. Wait until the year's over—completely over—until you decide whether it's worth celebrating about.

> *Remarks at the* American Spectator *annual dinner,*
> *Willard Hotel Ballroom, January 22, 1990*

———————

Some say reapportionment has been a political gold mine for both parties. They may be right. The Democrats get the gold and we get the shaft.

> *Remarks referring to the 1981 gerrymandering plan enacted*
> *by California Democrats, at a fund-raising dinner*
> *for gubernatorial candidate Pete Wilson at the St. Francis Hotel*
> *Grand Ballroom, San Francisco, California, February 28, 1990*

———————

Response when asked if Representative Dick Gephardt of Missouri, House Democratic leader, "gets under [his] skin" . . .

I don't want to knock the man. Maybe he'll come on a good idea one of these days.

> *The President's news conference, White House Briefing Room,*
> *March 13, 1990*

———————

Q. Have you ever flown a kite before?
The President. Yes. I have a large inventory of kites.
Q. You do?
The President. I'm one of the better kite fliers. I'm often told to go fly my kite.

> *Exchange with reporters aboard Air Force One,*
> *April 13, 1990*

I'm not one to dwell on surveys recently, but I will point out that people understand that the Congress bears a greater responsibility for this. But I'm not trying to assign blame. That's why I'm not doing it right now.

> *Referring to budget negotiations, the President's news conference,*
> *White House Briefing Room, May 24, 1990*

Larry, I understand that when you were a boy, a farm boy in Midvale, you house-trained a pig. [Laughter] Imagine that, your senator-to-be house-trained a pig. [Laughter] That ought to help him in Congress.

> *Remarks at a fund-raising dinner for senatorial candidate*
> *Larry Craig at the Boise Convention Center Eyries Ballroom,*
> *Boise, Idaho, July 19, 1990*

So far, I've talked about Bill's views—some of his views and achievements. And if that isn't enough for you, think about this one: last month he won the celebrity cow-milking contest at the Michigan State Fair. [Laughter] But even without that experience, Bill Schuette knows that it's the cows who should be milked, not the taxpayers.

> *Remarks at a fund-raising dinner for senatorial candidate*
> *Bill Schuette at the Westin Hotel Renaissance Ballroom,*
> *Detroit, Michigan, September 27, 1990*

Congress has got to stop being manic-depressive: manic on spending, depressive for the economy.

Remarks at a fund-raising dinner for senatorial candidate
Bill Schuette at the Westin Hotel Renaissance Ballroom,
Detroit, Michigan, September 27, 1990

Fellow Gladiators: Past and Present

Martin Luther King Jr. . . .

He was a crusader and an evangelist, bore the weight of a pioneer. He was a force against evil. His life was a metaphor for courage. His goal was an America where equality and opportunity could coexist and where goodness could prevail. . . . He went to cities and towns, large and small, places like Selma and Birmingham and Montgomery—wherever he was needed. And wherever he found hatred, he condemned it. Wherever there was bigotry, he assailed it. And wherever there was segregation, he defied it. He endured death threats and these obscene phone calls in the dead of night, but he refused to be intimidated. And through his courage, Dr. King changed forever America for the better.

Remarks on signing the Martin Luther King Jr.
Federal Holiday Proclamation, Old Executive Office Building,
Room 450, January 9, 1990

Jimmy and Rosalynn Carter . . .

I couldn't come to Atlanta without taking note of one such Point of Light: a part-time carpenter and his wife, who have provided shelter for so many in this very city. And of course, I'm talking about the former President, Jimmy and Rosalynn Carter. They deserve our thanks, as do all the people behind Habitat for Humanity.

Remarks at the annual convention of the National Association of Home
Builders at the Omni Coliseum, Atlanta, Georgia, January 19, 1990

Mikhail Gorbachev . . .

The dealings I've had with him here, and then on the sidelines when George [Shultz] and President Reagan were dealing with him, is that he's a man who you can talk to; he's quite open in his negotiations. He damn sure will tell you if he doesn't agree with you. . . .

I find we can talk quite openly. And I'm looking forward to a summit meeting. I don't know why all meetings have to be called summits. [Laughter] We tried to call the Malta meetings something else, and it lasted about two days.

Remarks and question-and-answer session at a luncheon hosted
by the Commonwealth Club at the Hilton Hotel Grand Ballroom,
San Francisco, California, February 7, 1990

Vaclav Havel . . .

[His] life has been one of miraculous transformations from the world of drama to the world of dissent, from the life of an artist to the life of an activist, and of course in the space of just one short year, the most miraculous journey of all, from prison to the presidency.

Remarks following discussions with President Vaclav Havel
of Czechoslovakia, White House South Portico, February 20, 1990

I took him [Havel] up to the Lincoln Bedroom, which is not normally the thing when you have these official visits. But I wanted him to see the room in which Abraham Lincoln had signed the Emancipation Proclamation. And I think I detected tears in his eyes, this playwright who not so many months ago was in jail and here he is the president of a fine, new, burgeoning democratic country. It was a very moving experience.

Remarks at the presentation ceremony for the Charles Stark Draper
Prize for Engineering, Department of State Ballroom,
February 20, 1990

Richard Nixon . . .

He had an intellectual's complexity. Knowing how you feel about some intellectuals, Mr. President, I don't mean to offend you. [Laughter] But he was an author—eight books, each composed on those famous yellow pads—who, like his favorite author, Tolstoy, admired the dignity of manual labor. And yet he worked in the most pragmatic of arenas and yet insisted that politics is poetry, not prose.

Remarks at the dedication of the Richard M. Nixon
Presidential Library in Yorba Linda, California,
July 19, 1990

Justice William Brennan . . .

His powerful intellect, his winning personality, and importantly, his commitment to civil discourse on emotional issues that, at times, tempt uncivil voices have made him one of the greatest figures of our age.

Remarks announcing the nomination of David H. Souter
to be an associate justice of the Supreme Court of the United States
and a question-and-answer session with reporters,
White House Briefing Room, July 23, 1990

The Iron Lady . . .

She's been a staunch friend and ally. She's a woman of principle; she's stood for what she believes. You always knew where she was and what she believed. I think everybody in America would agree that Margaret Thatcher has been an outstanding ally for the United States.

Exchange with reporters on confirmed reports that Prime Minister
Thatcher was preparing to resign, near Dhahran,
Saudi Arabia, November 22, 1990

"Uncatchable"

I was hoping to get out here for the Reds' opening day. But they tell me I'm three months too early. Same problem I ran into on Pearl Harbor Day. . . .

The jury is no longer out. Markets work. Government controls do not work. And since the debate has all but ended on this issue, perhaps our most die-hard ideologues can now turn their attention to the real question that divides America: Is it Texas or Cincinnati that produces the world's best chili?

Remarks to the Chamber of Commerce,
Hyatt Regency Hotel Ballroom, Cincinnati,
Ohio, January 12, 1990

Faithfully, and impartially, discharging his fiduciary duties despite an urgent plea from the hometown team . . .

Even though we're in opposing political parties, Kathy [Whitmire, mayor of Houston] and I have always gotten along. For instance, she's never held it against me that a member of my family owns the other baseball team in Texas. [Laughter] And for my part, I've tried to return her kindness. So, I picked up the phone when she called a couple weeks ago. She asked me to declare a disaster area, and I told her I did not think the Houston Oilers were that bad.

Remarks to the U.S. Conference of Mayors,
Capitol Hilton Hotel Presidential Ballroom,
January 26, 1990

The Berlin [1936] games were to be the showcase of Hitler's theories on the superiority of the master race until this twenty-three-year-old kid named Jesse Owens dashed to victory in the 100-, 200-, and the 400-meter relay. It was an unrivaled athletic triumph. But more than that, it really was a triumph for all humanity.

Remarks at the posthumous presentation
of the Congressional Gold Medal to Jesse Owens, White House
Roosevelt Room, March 28, 1990

It's been a big day for me. I received some of the Olympic leaders in the Oval Office, and just now I've been given some wonderful Olympic sweats backstage. I'll wear them with pride and hope I don't get in trouble for impersonating an athlete. . . .

In ancient Greece . . . competing in the [Olympic] games was the highest honor a citizen could receive. And back then, athletes that won didn't pay taxes for the rest of their lives. Let me get back to you on that.

Remarks at the United States Olympic Committee dinner,
Omni Shoreham Hotel Regency Ballroom,
March 28, 1990

A mother once told her son, "I have a pretty good idea that you skipped your piano lesson and played baseball." The son said he hadn't, and the mother said, "Are you sure?" And the son said, "Yes, I have the fish to prove it."

Remarks at a White House briefing for conservative leaders,
Old Executive Office Building, Room 450, April 26, 1990

It [the Hubble Space Telescope] will see to the furthest reaches of the universe, to the very edges of time. It will, quite literally, even enable astronomers to see back in time, perhaps far enough back to when the Dallas Cowboys had a winning season.

Remarks at the Texas A&I University commencement ceremony
at Javelina Stadium, Kingsville, May 11, 1990

I remember coming to Glacier National Park last year with a grandson and being told that Montana has 896 catchable fish per square mile. [Laughter] My question is, why don't they count the uncatchable fish?

Remarks at a fund-raising breakfast for senatorial candidate
Allen Kolstad at the Billings Trade Plaza Center,
Billings, Montana, July 20, 1990

"Free-Associating"

Around the world, there is, as we've heard here tonight, rapid and welcome change, as people from Panama to Prague strive for democracy. Self-determination is contagious. They even want it in Malibu, I understand.

Remarks at a Republican Party fund-raising dinner at the Century
Plaza Hotel Los Angeles Ballroom, Los Angeles, California,
February 6, 1990

Let me begin with a story that will show you my understanding of engineering. It concerns three men that were scheduled to be executed on the same day of the French Revolution. One was a lawyer, another a politician, the third an engineer. First came the lawyer. He put his head in the guillotine, and the blade went two-thirds of the way down the track and then stopped. The man was set free. Next, the politician. When the guillotine stopped short of his head, he, too, was spared. Finally came the third man, the engineer, and he focused on the matter at hand. "I think that guillotine has a problem," he told the executioner. "But don't worry; I think I have the solution."

Remarks at the presentation ceremony
for the Charles Stark Draper Prize for Engineering,
Department of State Ballroom, February 20, 1990

When I heard the citations of my fellow honorees, this distinguished five, I was reminded of the story of the kid that threw a rope around his mongrel dog and started heading over to Madison Square Garden. And they said, "Well, where are you going?" He said, "Well, I'm going to enter him in the Madison Square Garden pet show." And they said, "Well, do you think he has a shot at winning?" He said, "No, but he's going to be in some damn fine company."

Remarks at the centennial celebration of the Johns Hopkins
University Medical Institutions, Shriver Auditorium,
Baltimore, Maryland, February 22, 1990

Being President does have its advantages. And this is true: I have a TV set there in the White House with five screens, one big one in the middle, four small ones around it. Now I don't have to miss the nightly news while I watch *Wheel of Fortune.*

In my State of the Union, I announced six national education targets to be met by the year 2000. And this morning I want to add a seventh goal: by the year 2000, all Americans must be able to set the clocks on their VCRs.

Remarks to the Academy of Television Arts and Sciences
at the Century Plaza Hotel Los Angeles Ballroom,
Los Angeles, California, March 2, 1990

I really feel comfortable talking to this group because most people think I've been free-associating for years.

Remarks to the American Society of Association Executives,
Washington Convention Center, Hall A, March 6, 1990

One reason that I'm so pleased to be here is that if my speech is a disaster, relief is at hand.

Remarks to the Bethesda–Chevy Chase Rescue Squad
in Bethesda, Maryland, April 25, 1990

The success that's he's [Michael Eisner, CEO of Disney] achieved at Disney is the envy of CEOs worldwide. His secret's simple: just surround yourself with the best—Dopey, Dumbo, Goofy.

Remarks at the University of South Carolina
commencement ceremony, Carolina Coliseum,
Columbia, May 12, 1990

Back in 1492, Christopher Columbus was searching not for a new world but a new way—a passage to the riches of the Far East. In fact, Columbus was so confident he carried a letter from Queen Isabella to be delivered to the emperor of China. This marked history's first known case of mail getting lost on its way.

Remarks at the swearing-in ceremony
for David H. Souter as an associate justice
of the Supreme Court of the United States,
White House East Room, October 8, 1990

A Day in the Life

What I do in terms of pleasure is to read mostly novels, some of them not so—I wouldn't say that they were particularly weighty. *Bonfire of the Vanities* is one which was pretty darn good and was up near the top of the list. I'm reading *Network News* right now. I'm halfway through that. I read a couple of books on Teddy Roosevelt. I'm reading Caro's *Lyndon Johnson.* I say reading—I've got about two or three books going right now. . . . But it's relaxed reading. It is relaxed kind of reading, and it's novels. I find I can do that just before—instead of taking one of these Halcion sleeping tablets, a good novel will help. [Laughter]

Remarks and question-and-answer session
with the Magazine Publishers of America, Old Executive
Office Building, Room 450, July 17, 1990

I remember the last time I was in this state. It was for Montana's one hundreth birthday, when Allen was chairman of the centennial commission. For my part, I planted a tree. Now, you may know that my record's not too good in that respect. [Laughter] I planted a tree in North Dakota, and regrettably, it got attacked by gypsy moth. [Laughter] And I planted a tree in Spokane, Washington, and I hadn't left town before some vandals ripped off the whole tree. [Laughter] And so, you can understand why they've asked me not to dedicate any buildings here. [Laughter] But the tree—when I climbed off the plane, I got a firsthand report from the governor, who confessed to a certain nervousness about the tree. But the tree I planted in Helena—believe it or not, it's alive.

Remarks at a fund-raising breakfast for senatorial candidate
Allen Kolstad at the Billings Trade Plaza Center,
Billings, Montana, July 20, 1990

For four years, in addition to his serious responsibilities as the President's spokesman, it was clear that Marlin Fitzwater also frequently served as President Bush's "straight man." To wit . . .

Q. Marlin Fitzwater at one point said that you were pretty adamant or stubborn about it [vacation], saying to him at one point that you needed the rest. [Laughter] Is that what it boiled down to? [Laughter]

Mr. Fitzwater. I beg your pardon. [Laughter]

The President. I need to rest, and I haven't gotten as much as I would like. But I wouldn't call it adamant or stubborn because I refuse to—

Mr. Fitzwater. Neither would I. [Laughter]

The President. He better not have, either. [Laughter] Marlin's going through kind of a downer, though, because the Iraqi spokesman has the matching tie and hankie, you know, so he's been a little—[laughter]

The President's news conference on the Persian Gulf crisis,
White House Briefing Room, August 30, 1990

The timing of these awards is fortuitous. A year ago this week, Barbara and I awarded medals to some of the artistic giants of our time: Alfred Eisenstaedt and Dizzy Gillespie and John Updike, among others. And with all that assembled talent, guess what led the evening news: the Rose Garden presentation of the national turkey. [Laughter] So, you're in luck. [Laughter] This year the turkey doesn't get here until Thursday.

Remarks at the presentation ceremony for the National Medals
of Science and Technology, White House East Room,
November 13, 1990

You know, Bart Simpson dropped me a line the other day when I told him you were coming—true story—and he wrote me saying: "When I mess up my bedroom, my mom comes in and yells, but eventually she cleans it up and everything's cool. But when we mess up the environment, we're the ones who will be yelling, and it definitely won't be cool." Well, this is one of those rare moments when Bart makes sense. [Laughter]

. . . If it's true, as some say, that we're all borrowing the earth from future generations, it's also true that the earth will be preserved by millions of small decisions made every day by every one of us. And they're the kind of small decisions that make a world of difference, whether it's recycling aluminum cans, conserving water, turning off a lightbulb, even just keeping the refrigerator door closed.

Like that scene in the *Teenage Mutant*—bear with me—*Ninja Turtles*. [Laughter] They're standing in front of the refrigerator, deciding what to have for dinner. And one of them is standing with the door open. So, another one says, "Think with the door closed, then get what you want." "Okay," the first one says, "I'm thinking tonight we'll have broccoli." [Laughter] And fortunately, he pulls out a pizza. So there's a happy ending to this story.

Remarks at the presentation ceremony
for the President's Environmental Youth Awards, Old Executive
Office Building, Room 450, November 14, 1990

I want to assure those of you who fear that a terrible fate awaits Tom Turkey that we've decided to spare him. He will not be subjected to questions from the Washington press corps after this ceremony.

Remarks at the Thanksgiving turkey presentation ceremony,
Rose Garden, November 14, 1990

CHAPTER THREE

1991:
THE LIBERATION
HAS BEGUN

The Commander-in-Chief greeting military families
at Fort Stewart, Georgia. February 1, 1991.

One of the most indelible images of the twentieth century occurred Christmas Day, 1991, when the sickle and hammer of the red Soviet flag was drawn down from atop the Kremlin's domed Council of Ministers building and up flew the three broad and bright stripes of democratic Russia into the Moscow night. Earlier in the day, Mikhail Gorbachev resigned as the eighth and last leader of the USSR, and President Bush formally recognized the independence of all twelve former Soviet republics. The New York Times *reported that the Soviet Union flag was lowered at 7:32 that night and that the "muted moment of awe was shared by the few pedestrians crossing Red Square." In a peaceful instant, the Revolution of 1918 yielded to the Revolution of 1989.*

The drama unfolding in Moscow capped a highly momentous year for President Bush's administration—as the coalition forces scored their historic victory against Iraq; the Russian people elected Boris Yeltsin president in June; a coup against Gorbachev failed in August; and the Baltic states gained their long-sought independence in September. In October, together with Gorbachev and the Soviets, President Bush convened the Madrid Peace Conference, with Arabs and Israelis negotiating at the same table; and in December, the last American hostage, Terry Anderson, came home from captivity in Lebanon.

On the domestic scene, President Bush fought Congress for comprehensive crime and education reform legislation, prepared for the 1992 campaign, and—to underscore the importance of learning at all ages—resolved to learn how to use a personal computer.

FAITH, FAMILY, AND FRIENDS:
Reserves of Courage and Love

The longer I'm in my job, the more important I come to understand what friendship means.
Remarks at the unveiling of the official bust of the President,
U.S. Capitol Rotunda, June 27, 1991

I worry more about what you put your kids through, what you put your family through, just by being in the arena. It's a little ugly out there, charge and countercharge. And what troubles me is it might get a little worse as the political season goes on.
Interview with Doug Adair of WCMH-TV
at Veterans Memorial Auditorium, Columbus, Ohio,
November 25, 1991

"Moral North Star"

I have been honored to serve as President of this great nation for two years now and believe more than ever that one cannot be America's President without trust in God. I cannot imagine a world, a life, without the presence of the one through whom all things are possible.
Remarks at the annual convention
of the National Religious Broadcasters, Sheraton Washington
Hotel Ballroom, January 28, 1991

I know our country is praying for peace. And across this nation the churches, the synagogues, the mosques, are packed—record attendance at services. In fact, the night the war began, Dr. Graham was at the White House. And he spoke to us then of the importance of turning to God as a people of faith, turning to Him in hope. And then the next morning, Dr. Graham went over to

Fort Myer, where we had a lovely service leading our nation in a beautiful prayer service there, with special emphasis on the troops overseas.

Remarks at the National Prayer Breakfast, Washington Hilton
Hotel International Ballroom, January 31, 1991

So many of us, compelled by a deep need for God's wisdom in all we do, turn to prayer. We pray for God's protection in all we undertake, for God's love to fill all hearts, and for God's peace to be the moral North Star that guide us.

Radio address to the nation on the National Day of Prayer,
February 2, 1991

During the Gulf crisis, Barbara and I, and much of this nation—I think, in this instance, most of the nation—found guidance and comfort in prayer. And throughout the struggle, your prayers sustained us. And so, I want to thank you all and ask that you keep—as Morris [Dr. Morris Chapman, president of the Southern Baptist Convention] generously said—those in the decision-making process, keep us in your prayers.

For me, prayer has always been important, but quite personal. You know us Episcopalians. [Laughter] And like a lot of people, I've worried a little bit about shedding tears in public or the emotion of it. But as Barbara and I prayed at Camp David before the war began, we were thinking about those young men and women overseas. And I had the tears start down the cheeks, and our minister smiled back. And I no longer worried how it looked to others.

Remarks at the annual convention
of the Southern Baptist Convention, Georgia World
Congress Center, Atlanta, Georgia, June 6, 1991

It's hard to face a world in which your children suffer. You ride an emotional roller coaster, and you must draw upon all reserves of courage and love and certainly faith just to make it through each day.

Remarks at the groundbreaking ceremony for the Hospital
for Sick Children, June 13, 1991

FAMILY

Just before Desert Storm started, Mrs. Bush broke her leg while sledding at Camp David—careening out of control into a tree. Several weeks later, her husband compared the incident with Saddam Hussein's environmental decimation in Kuwait . . .

I want to thank everyone for their concern and prayers about Barbara's recent accident. In these days of environmental terrorism—[laughter]—I can happily report that the tree is doing very well and so is Barbara Bush.

Remarks at the National Prayer Breakfast,
Washington Hilton Hotel International Ballroom,
January 31, 1991

Another family-related anecdote, this one from David Frost's historic Camp David interview in the wake of Desert Storm (March 9). Reading from the President's diary . . .

All this time, there were some other things going on. We were worried about security for our children. I was working on a speech to give to the nation when we go in, and then I get a call: "There's an Arab-looking person near Marvin's office, looking suspicious . . ." They pick him up, and in the back of his car is a wig, and a mask—one of these masks you pull down over your face. Right there outside of Marvin's office. When Secret Service find him, they interrogate him; and it turns out that the guy had marital troubles. So what he's doing is trying to spy on his wife—he was there, and he was in the wrong place at the wrong time.

Barbara and I spent a good part of our senior year thinking about, literally, becoming farmers. We talked about life on the land and rising early and working hard and raising a crop and a family. And we looked into the finances of running a farm. In the end, we decided against the whole idea. We realized that when it came to pigs and chickens and cattle or corn, we didn't know the first thing about farming.

So, of course, there was only one alternative: I went west and became an oilman. [Laughter] The very day after a ceremony like this one, I traded the familiar surroundings of this old campus for the dust and grit and searing heat of the Lone Star State.

Remarks at the Yale University commencement ceremony,
University Quadrangle, New Haven, Connecticut,
May 27, 1991

It's [Walker's Point] where my family comes home, and it's our anchor to windward. It has great meaning in terms of family. And we are blessed; [the] Bush family is blessed. The children come home, and they look forward to it.

The President's news conference at the Cape Arundel Golf Course,
Kennebunkport, Maine, May 28, 1991

Response when asked what might deter him from seeking re-election in 1992 . . .

If the family appealed that I not do it, I'd have to say that would weigh with me. Our kids differ, incidentally. Some of them are enthusiastic: "Hey, Mom, I'm on TV." [Laughter] And others want to shun—they want to protect their privacy. I think we've worked out a balance as a family, but in all seriousness, that could have an effect.

Interview with Linda Douglas of KNBC, Jim Lampley of KCBS,
and Paul Moyer of KABC at the Four Seasons Hotel Burton Room,
Los Angeles, California, June 15, 1991

I'm also glad to be with you on Father's Day. I don't know about your kids, but I know about mine, and they guided me through life by using those three magic words: "Ask your mother."

Remarks to the Asian-Pacific community, Mile Square Park,
Fountain Valley, California, June 16, 1991

On July 1, President Bush announced his intention to nominate Judge Clarence Thomas of the U.S. Court of Appeals for the District of Columbia to succeed Justice Thurgood Marshall on the U.S. Supreme Court. Commenting in his diary, the President noted: "It was a hot and sunny day, and I took Clarence back into our bedroom and talked to him briefly. I told him that I did not want to talk about issues; told him he must call 'em as he sees 'em—as an umpire would; and asked him if he would be ready for the bruising fight that lay ahead" (*ATB*, p. 527). For the time being, however, this first encounter with the media was relatively trouble-free and included the following comments about the President's mother, Dorothy . . .

Q. Can you talk a bit about your mother and what she's taught you and why you chose her birthday to announce your nominee? [Laughter]

The President. Well, maybe it's fortuitous. Life goes on. Mother's ninety years old; been an enormous influence in my life and the lives of everybody that's in our enormous family. And I noted . . . what Clarence Thomas . . . had to say about the importance of family in his life. So, if there's symbolism there, one, it was unintended, but two, I think it might be appropriate. Different backgrounds, but the same sense of strength of family. And I think there's a message not just for Clarence Thomas's family or our family but for families all across the country.

And as we celebrate Mother's nintieth birthday, she's not all that well, but she is our moral leader, was since I was old enough to walk on this marvelous point of land here in Kennebunkport, which was just—from my days as an infant. And everyone in this family, young and old, direct or indirect relations, looks up to her. But I have a feeling that's true of a lot of families in this country.

*The President's news conference at Walker's Point,
Kennebunkport, Maine, July 1, 1991*

I'm proud of our country's libraries. And you know, a member of my family wrote a book that's available in most of them. Ironically, Millie is not allowed to get a library card. [Laughter] And there's a great injustice and discrimination out there. [Laughter]

*Remarks at the White House Conference on Library
and Information Services, Washington Convention Center, Hall A,
July 10, 1991*

This is familiar country for Barbara and me. You remember: I'm the one who gets needled from having so many homes in my past, in our past. It was in this city, in Lewiston, that we learned of Franklin Delano Roosevelt's [death] back in 1945. And that's when I was living here briefly. That's when I was flying torpedo bombers out of what was then the Lewiston-Auburn Naval Air Station.

*Remarks to students and faculty in the school gymnasium
of the Lewiston Comprehensive High School, Lewiston, Maine,
September 3, 1991*

I will tell you my reaction when I received the phone call on August 19 saying, "It's a crisis." I responded, "Look, I've already heard enough about Barbara's golf game."

*Remarks to the National Association of Towns and Townships,
Hyatt Regency Hotel Ballroom, September 6, 1991*

People think the problem in our world is crack or suicide or babies having babies, and those are symptoms. The disease is a moral emptiness, though. And we cannot continue producing generations born numbly into despair, finding solace in a needle or vial. If, as President, I had the power to give just one thing to this great country, it would be the return of a moral inner compass nurtured by the family and valued by society.

Remarks at the Substance Abuse Treatment Unit, Department of Veterans Affairs Medical Center, Philadelphia, Pennsylvania, September 12, 1991

Years ago I learned that economics focuses mostly on people, not on numbers. And I do remember those early days in Odessa, 1948, and then Midland right after that. Then, your word was your bond. You shook hands with a guy on an oil deal . . . and it kept; it took. That's all you needed. You didn't need twenty-five thousand lawyers drawing up escrow agreements. You had the values out there.

The neighborhood meant something. The strength of family was strong and meant something. And as Ray [Hunt] touched on it, and this music said, faith was terribly, terribly important. You chose your schools, taught people without being afraid of it, to say the Pledge of Allegiance or to express their patriotism.

Remarks at a Bush-Quayle fund-raising dinner, Hyatt Regency Hotel Reunion Ballroom, Dallas, Texas, November 1, 1991

During the Clarence Thomas hearings in the fall, Wyoming's Senator Al Simpson seemingly took on everyone on Capitol Hill and in the media who attacked the nominee's character. He took plenty of hits in return. Here, President Bush—who was increasingly under fire himself—reflects on his job as 1991 draws to a close . . .

[Wyoming Senator] Al Simpson was coming down on the plane, and he said, "Hey, you're getting clobbered out there by the media these days." And I said, "Yes, that goes with the territory. It takes one to know one." You talk about Simpson telling me about getting clobbered by the press, why—[laughter].

But we reminisced about it. And we both concluded just as friends, no politics, that it is well worth it. I cannot think of a more exciting period in this country to be President of the United States. I'm working hard. I'm doing my level best. I'm absolutely confident that this country's going to turn around and this economy will be back on track. And I am absolutely confident that you, the American people, want me to continue to lead, to have America be the leader around the world.

So, there's some slings and arrows out there. But don't feel sorry for the Bushes. We love it. We feel privileged every single day that we live in the White House.

Remarks to the Bee County community, Bee County Rodeo Arena, Beeville, Texas, December 27, 1991

"Fibrillating Heart"

On May 4, following his graduation speech to the University of Michigan in Ann Arbor, President Bush traveled to Camp David. That afternoon, after a forty-minute nap, he went for a jog. After he tired immediately and repeatedly, the medical unit discovered he was suffering from an irregular heartbeat—called an atrial fibrillation—and ordered him immediately to Bethesda Naval Hospital. He was later diagnosed with Graves' disease, as his wife had in 1989. The situation under control with medication, the President treated the matter with characteristic irreverence . . .

Thank you from the bottom of my former fibrillating heart. . . .

I'm glad to be out of the hospital. It's a little unsettling to turn on the news and see Peter Jennings [ABC News anchor] pointing to a diagram of a heart with your name on it. [Laughter] It's not even Valentine's Day.

Welcoming remarks at the presentation ceremony for the Small Business Person of the Year Award and exchange with reporters, Rose Garden, May 7, 1991

Speaking of my health, which I am reluctant to do, but you might know I just received a note—a true story—from a farmers' organization. And it said: "This wouldn't have happened if you had eaten your broccoli." [Laughter] I don't want to get in a fight with them; just give me thyroid problems any day. [Laughter]

Remarks at the Federal Bureau of Investigation Academy commencement ceremony, Quantico, Virginia, May 30, 1991

FRIENDS

Special Emissary . . .

Arnold—Arnold Schwarzenegger—spent a day with us up at Camp David, and competing with Barbara in tobogganing, she broke her leg. [Laughter] Then, Arnold spent a day with us at the White House promoting fitness, and I ended up in the hospital with atrial fibrillation, or something like that. [Laughter] You'll never eat lunch in my town again, Arnold. [Laughter] But I'm delighted to see you. Come to think of it, you could be my special emissary to Congress. [Laughter] Talk about "The Terminator."

Remarks at the Simon Wiesenthal Center dinner at the Century Plaza Hotel Los Angeles Ballroom, Los Angeles, California, June 16, 1991

The Gipper . . .

Ronald Reagan was born on February 6, but his heart is the Fourth of July. And with his disarming sense of humor, President Reagan was something refreshingly different in Washington: a politician who was funny on purpose. [Laughter] And he also was, though, a visionary, a crusader, and a prophet in his time.

He was a political prophet, leading the tide toward conservatism. He was also a Main Street prophet. He understood that America is great because of what we are, not what we have. Politics can be cruel, can be mean and ugly and uncivil. And unfailingly, Ronald Reagan was strong and gentle. And he ennobled public service. He embodied the American character. He came from the heart of America geographically and culturally. . . .

As President, Ronald Reagan was unmoved by the vagaries of intellectual fashion. He treasured values that last, values that endure. And I speak of patriotism and civility and generosity and kindness, values etched in the American character. Once asked who he admired most in history, he simply responded, "The man from Galilee."

. . . Here's part of what the historians will say of Ronald Reagan. He was the Great Communicator and also the Great Liberator. From Normandy to Moscow, from Berlin to the Oval Office, no leader since Churchill used words so effectively to help freedom unchain our world.

Remarks at the dedication of the Ronald Reagan
Presidential Library, Simi Valley, California,
November 4, 1991

THE VISION THING:
Where Destiny Requires Us to Lead

This experience, this very emotional experience for America, will last us as a people for a long time. We have a sense of pride out across this country now, and it's not a personal thing. I mean, hell, 93 percent today—and these damn polls. It'll be off tomorrow. It'll be something else. These things are transient. But what isn't transient is this renewed sense of self-confidence, and pride, confidence in the young people—all of which came out of this experience in the Gulf.

Secret taping with journalist David Frost,
Camp David, March 9, 1991

No one should assume that the opportunity before us to make peace will remain if we fail to seize the moment. Ironically, this is an opportunity born of war, the destruction of past

wars, the fear of future wars. The time has come to put an end to war. The time has come to choose peace.

Remarks at the opening session of the Middle East
Peace Conference at the Royal Palace Salón de las Columnas,
Madrid, Spain, October 30, 1991

"AGGRESSION IS DEFEATED"

We have seen too often in this century how quickly any threat to one becomes a threat to all. At this critical moment in history, at a time when the Cold War is fading into the past, we cannot fail. At stake is not simply some distant country called Kuwait. At stake is the kind of world we will inhabit.

Radio address to the nation, January 5, 1991

———————

On January 12, both chambers of Congress, after deliberating the moral question of war and the legal question surrounding the War Powers Act, voted to authorize the use of force as enumerated in United Nations resolutions. The vote in the House was 250–183, while the Senate split more evenly at 52–47. In his diary, the President noted that "the big burden, lifted from my shoulders, is this constitutional burden and the threat of impeachment. All of that cleared now by this very sound vote of the Congress" (*ATB*, p. 503). The President returned to the White House from Camp David to speak with reporters and reflected on the debate on Capitol Hill . . .

Q. Mr. President, you spoke of the debate. It was a very somber day up there.

The President. Yes.

Q. People talked about the cost of war. I wondered if you watched it and what effect it had on you.

The President. That's a good question. On the parts of it I saw I couldn't agree more. It was somber, properly somber. It was, I thought, with very little rancor. I thought it was conducted for the most part—not entirely—in a very objective manner in terms of the subject, and yet subjective in terms of the individual speaking. The compassion and the concern, the angst of these members, whether they agreed with me or not, came through loud and clear.

And so, I guess I shared the emotion. I want peace. I want to see a peaceful resolution. And I could identify with those—whether they were on the side that was supporting of the administration or the other—with those who were really making fervent appeals for peace. But I think it was historic. I think it was conducted showing the best of the United States Congress at work. And I keep feeling that it was historic because [of] what it did and how it endorsed the President's action to fulfill this resolution—when you go back and look at war and peace, I think historians will say this is a very significant step. I am pleased that the Congress responded. I'm pleased that they acted and therefore are a part of this.

But I didn't sense—you know, when you win a vote on something you worked hard for, sometimes there's a sense of exhilaration and joy, pleasure. I didn't sense that at all here. I was grateful to the members that took the lead in supporting the positions that I'm identified with. I could empathize with those who didn't vote for us. So, I guess my emotion was somber itself. . . . I didn't watch the whole debate. But what I saw I appreciated because there was very little personal rancor, assigning motives to the other person, or something of that nature. So, it was quite different than some of the debates that properly characterize the give-and-take of competitive politics.

The President's news conference, White House Briefing Room,
January 12, 1991

The liberation of Kuwait has begun.
Statement on Allied military action in the Persian Gulf,
January 16, 1991

President Bush later recalled the evening of January 13, when he "looked over my speech material for my address to the nation . . . trying to capture the right phrases. I read through quotes by Robert Lowell, Thomas Paine, and others, but none captured quite how I was feeling" (*AWT*, p. 447). And just before the speech itself: "I was surprised to find I didn't feel nervous. I knew what I wanted to say, said it, and hoped it resonated. I learned later that I had addressed the largest U.S. audience on record—79 percent of the sets were tuned in . . ." (*AWT*, p. 451).

This is an historic moment. We have in this past year made great progress in ending the long era of conflict and cold war. We have before us the opportunity to forge for ourselves and for future generations a new world order—a world where the rule of law, not the law of the jungle, governs the conduct of nations. When we are successful—and we will be—we have a real chance at this new world order, an order in which a credible United Nations can use its peacekeeping role to fulfill the promise and vision of the UN's founders.

Address to the nation announcing
Allied military action in the Persian Gulf, Oval Office,
January 16, 1991

Appeasement—peace at any price—was never an answer. Turning a blind eye to Saddam's aggression would not have avoided war; it would only have delayed the world's day of reckoning, postponing what ultimately would have been a far more dangerous, a far more costly conflict.

Remarks to the Reserve Officers Association,
Washington Hilton Hotel Ballroom, January 23, 1991

Response when asked why he wouldn't give his State of the Union address from the safety of White House . . .

I am not going to be held a captive in the White House by Saddam Hussein of Iraq. And you can make a note of that one.
Remarks on the nomination of Edward R. Madigan
to be secretary of agriculture and a question-and-answer session
with reporters, White House Briefing Room, January 25, 1991

On January 29, Iraqi ground forces attacked the Saudi border town of Khafji—attempting to draw the coalition into a ground war prematurely. Twelve marines were killed. That night, President Bush went to Capitol Hill to give his State of the Union message . . .

I come to this house of the people to speak to you and all Americans, certain that we stand at a defining hour. Halfway around the world, we are engaged in a great struggle in the skies and on the seas and sands. We know why we're there: we are Americans, part of something larger than ourselves. For two centuries, we've done the hard work of freedom. And tonight, we lead the world in facing down a threat to decency and humanity. . . .

This nation has never found glory in war. Our people have never wanted to abandon the blessings of home and work for distant lands and deadly conflict. If we fight in anger, it is only because we have to fight at all. All of us yearn for a world where we will never have to fight again.

Each of us will measure within ourselves the value of this great struggle. Any cost in lives—any cost—is beyond our power to measure. But the cost of closing our eyes to aggression is beyond mankind's power to imagine. This we do know: our cause is just; our cause is moral; our cause is right.

Let future generations understand the burden and the blessings of freedom. Let them say we stood where duty required us to stand. Let them know that, together, we affirmed America and the world as a community of conscience.

The winds of change are with us now. The forces of freedom are together, united. We move toward the next century more

confident than ever that we have the will at home and abroad to
do what must be done—the hard work of freedom.

*Address before a joint session of the Congress
on the State of the Union, U.S. Capitol House Chamber,
January 29, 1991*

**Four weeks later, after a ground war lasting one hundred hours,
the President first addressed the American people declaring
victory . . .**

Kuwait is liberated. Iraq's army is defeated. Our military objectives
are met. Kuwait is once more in the hands of the Kuwaitis, in control of their own destiny. We share their joy, a joy tempered only
by our compassion for their ordeal.

Tonight the Kuwaiti flag once again flies above the capital of
a free and sovereign nation. And the American flag flies above
our embassy.

Seven months ago, America and the world drew a line in the
sand. We declared that aggression against Kuwait would not
stand. And tonight, America and the world have kept their word.

This is not a time of euphoria, certainly not time to gloat. But
it is a time of pride: pride in our troops; pride in friends who
stood with us in the crisis; pride in our nation and the people
whose strength and resolve made victory quick, decisive, and just.
And soon we will open wide our arms to welcome back home to
America our magnificent fighting forces.

No one country can claim this victory as its own. It was not
only a victory for Kuwait but a victory for all the coalition partners. This is a victory for the United Nations, for the rule of law,
and for what is right. . . .

We must now begin to look beyond victory and war. We
must meet the challenge of securing the peace.

*Address to the nation on the suspension of Allied offensive
combat operations in the Persian Gulf, Oval Office, February 27, 1991*

For the commander in chief, the feeling of victory sank in slowly . . .

The minute we said there will be no more shooting—thousands, hundreds of thousands of families and friends said, "My kids are going to be safe." And I think I was focusing a little more on what's left to be done. But it is contagious . . . the Vice President's been out around the country, and Barbara's been out around the country, and others around here—I sense that there is something noble and majestic about patriotism in this country now. It's there.

The President's news conference on the Persian Gulf conflict,
White House Briefing Room, March 1, 1991

Commending the troops . . .

Americans today are confident of our country, confident of our future, and most of all, confident about you. We promised you'd be given the means to fight. We promised not to look over your shoulder. We promised this would not be another Vietnam. And we kept that promise. The specter of Vietnam has been buried forever in the desert sands of the Arabian Peninsula. . . .

The first test of the new world order has been passed.

Radio address to United States armed forces stationed
in the Persian Gulf region, White House Private Study,
March 2, 1991

And reporting to the Congress . . .

As commander in chief, I can report to you our armed forces fought with honor and valor. And as President, I can report to the nation, aggression is defeated. The war is over. . . .

Tonight in Iraq, Saddam walks amidst ruin. His war machine is crushed. . . .

The consequences of the conflict in the Gulf reach far beyond the confines of the Middle East. Twice before in this century, an entire world was convulsed by war. Twice this century, out of the horrors of war hope emerged for enduring peace. Twice before, those hopes proved to be a distant dream, beyond the grasp of man. Until now, the world we've known has been a world divided—a world of barbed wires and concrete block, conflict, and Cold War.

Now, we can see a new world coming into view. A world in which there is the very real prospect of a new world order. . . . A world where the United Nations, freed from Cold War stalemate, is poised to fulfill the historic vision of its founders. A world in which freedom and respect for human rights find a home among all nations. The Gulf War put this new world order to its first test. And my fellow Americans, we passed that test. . . .

We went halfway around the world to do what is moral and just and right. We fought hard, and with others, we won the war. We lifted the yolk of aggression and tyranny for a small country that many Americans had never heard of, and we ask nothing in return.

Address before a joint session of Congress on the cessation
of the Persian Gulf conflict, U.S. Capitol House Chamber,
March 6, 1991

On March 9, just three days after a triumphant speech before Congress, President Bush granted a secret, and in this instance emotional, interview to British journalist David Frost at Camp David (aired in 1996). Here, the President reflects on the responsibilities of high office . . .

I said when I came into this job, I would never plead for sympathy from people about this being the loneliest and toughest, and this wasn't a lonely period. But there was a certain burden, and it related to the responsibility for the lives of others. That was the toughest, because you just don't need that. . . . But that goes with the territory, and you just have to accept that. . . . That was the tough part.

And addressing Frost's question of "What now?" in the wake of victory . . .

You conduct yourself without arrogance. You lead. You are considerate to the concerns of other countries, large and small. But you stand for something once again. And that gives us a new credibility, and it give us a new force with which to help solve heretofore intractable problems—the obvious one is the problems of the West Bank, Palestine, but we got a lot of others that are still going to be out there.

"Pax Universalis"

The new world order does not mean surrendering our national sovereignty or forfeiting our interests. It really describes a responsibility imposed by our successes. It refers to new ways of working with other nations to deter aggression and to achieve stability, to achieve prosperity and, above all, to achieve peace. . . .

The new world order really is a tool for addressing a new world of possibilities. This order gains its mission and shape not just from shared interests but from shared ideals. And the ideals that have spawned new freedoms throughout the world have received their boldest and clearest expression in our great country, the United States. Never before has the world looked more to the American example. Never before have so many millions drawn hope from the American idea. And the reason is simple: unlike any other nation in the world, as Americans we enjoy profound and mysterious bonds of affection and idealism. We feel our deep connections to community, to family, to our faiths.

Remarks at the Fuel Cell Hangar, Maxwell Air Force Base
War College, Montgomery, Alabama, April 13, 1991

———————

We face a new world, a world in which military confrontation is being pushed aside by constructive economic competition, a world in which nations struggle to build and perfect democracy.

Although we have no road map to guide us through this world, we have a sure compass in principles that both nations hold dear: the peaceful settlement of disputes, free enterprise, an open world economic system, and underlying it all, democracy.

Remarks to the Greek Parliament in Athens,
July 18, 1991

We mourn your lost countrymen but know that they died for the noblest cause of all, the unstoppable tide of freedom that today is changing history swiftly, dramatically. Future generations will look to our age and say, "Here, here in the 1990s began a new world order."

Remarks at the welcoming ceremony
for President Abdou Diouf of Senegal, White House South Lawn,
September 10, 1991

President Bush used his annual UN address to comment how the worldwide "thaw" after the decades-long winter of the Cold War did more than liberate oppressed peoples: it also gave rise to ethnic and religious tensions long repressed by the straitjacket of a divided world . . .

Communism held history captive for years. It suspended ancient disputes, and it suppressed ethnic rivalries, nationalist aspirations, and old prejudices. As it has dissolved, suspended hatreds have sprung to life. People who for years have been denied their pasts have begun searching for their own identities, often through peaceful and constructive means, occasionally through factionalism and bloodshed. This revival of history ushers in a new era teeming with opportunities and perils. . . .

You may wonder about America's role in the new world I have described. Let me assure you, the United States has no intention of striving for a Pax Americana. However, we will remain engaged. We will not retreat and pull back into isolation-

ism. We will offer friendship and leadership. And in short, we seek
a *pax universalis* built upon shared responsibilities and aspirations.
Address to the forty-sixth session of the UN General Assembly
at the UN General Assembly Hall, New York City,
September 23, 1991

The United States will always be a force for peace in the world.
But the peace we seek is a real peace, the triumph of freedom, and
prosperity, not merely the absence of war. We can never know
which war will be the last. But we take as our hope the prophecy
of Isaiah that "nation shall not lift sword against nation, neither
shall they learn war anymore." And yes, we hope, we pray that as
the years progress, the face of war will recede into our distant
memory. But the memory of our veterans and their sacrifice will
never fade.
Remarks at the Tomb of the Unknown Soldier,
Arlington Cemetery, November 11, 1991

The Cold War Ends

On July 29, President Bush arrived in Moscow for his final summit with Mikhail Gorbachev. The Soviet leader was struggling
to hold together an imploding empire. In January a violent
repression of the resurgent Baltic states erupted on the eve of
Desert Storm. In March, only nine of the fifteen republics that
made up the Soviet Union approved a treaty creating a revised
relationship with Moscow in the center. Then on June 12,
Boris Yeltsin, Gorbachev's rival, became the first directly elected
president of Russia. Despite the atmosphere of uncertainty
engulfing his visit, President Bush refers to a "new beginning"
during a speech . . .

For four long decades, our two nations stood locked in conflict as
the Cold War cast its shadow across an armed and uneasy peace.

This summit marks a new beginning, the prospect that we can put an end to a long era as adversaries, write a new chapter in the history of our two nations, forge a new partnership and sturdy peace. We have reason to hope. Indeed, we have good reason to hope. One by one, the cruel realities of the Cold War flicker and fade and a new world of opportunities calls us forward.

Remarks at the Moscow State Institute for International Relations,
Conference Hall, July 30, 1991

As President Bush described it in his diary, signing the Strategic Arms Reduction Treaty was "more than ceremonial—it offers hope to young people all around the world. Idealism is not dead and this significant reduction in these damn intercontinental ballistic missiles is a good thing. I really did feel emotionally involved at the signing ceremony and I felt a sense of real gratitude to the people who worked tirelessly on the treaty. I ad-libbed in Ronald Reagan's name, but there was Rick Burt [U.S. ambassador to Germany] and so many others . . ." (*ATB*, p. 529–30).

By reducing arms, we reverse a half century of steadily growing strategic arsenals. But more than that, we take a significant step forward in dispelling a half century of mistrust. By building trust, we pave a path to peace.

Remarks at the signing ceremony
for the Strategic Arms Reduction Treaty at the Kremlin's
Vladimir's Hall, Moscow, July 31, 1991

Just after midnight on August 18, Brent Scowcroft called President Bush down the road at Walker's Point in Kennebunkport to inform him that the Soviet news agency Tass was reporting that Mikhail Gorbachev had resigned his office due to health reasons. It was a coup. The next morning, a press conference was set for the lawn outside the President's office on the point, but a heavy rain forced everyone indoors—into the cramped Secret

Service command post. The President referred to the Moscow developments as "extraconstitutional" and "disturbing." Responding to a question from Brit Hume, then of ABC News, he sounded this cautionary note . . .

It's not a time for flamboyance or show business or posturing on the part of any country, certainly the United States. We have disproportionate responsibilities in handling these matters with confidence and in a cool and, I think, informed way.

Remarks on the attempted coup in the Soviet Union
and an exchange with reporters at Walker's Point,
Kennebunkport, Maine, August 19, 1991

There [are] some people in this country from one side or another of the spectrum . . . that say you ought to be able to wave a wand and solve a problem of this nature in the city of Moscow instantly. That's not what you can do. But what you can do if you're President is put the full force of the American people, emotionally, morally, behind the democratic forces. And that's what I'm trying to do. And apparently according to Mr. Yeltsin at least, and I think others, that's what we should be trying to do.

The President's news conference on the attempted coup
in the Soviet Union, at Shawmut Inn, Kennebunkport, Maine,
August 21, 1991

On August 24, Gorbachev phoned President Bush to inform him that he was resigning as general secretary of the Communist Party and that he had ordered the government to seize Party property. Several days later, the Soviet legislature made certain Communist Party activities illegal. It was the beginning of the end . . .

Q. Do you think the events of the last week either mark the death or impending death of the Communist Party in the Soviet Union? And after the U.S., after Americans have spent so much time, money, and effort in their struggle against that system, shouldn't Americans take some kind of satisfaction in what's going on there this week?

The President. The answer is yes and yes. Yes, it is clearly the death knell for the Communist movement around the world. There's only a handful of people that stick out like a sore thumb. I think of one down there in Cuba right now that must be sweating because you can't stop . . . this quest for freedom.

What was the second part? The answer is yes, but give me the question.

Q. Should Americans be taking satisfaction—

The President. Of course we should. And so should Canadians and everybody that has stood for freedom for so long. I think back, and Brian and I were talking about this, the days when we talked about the Cold War and what it meant, and the fear of aggression, and what we saw and hated in Hungary. Those days are gone now. And so, the American people should take great pleasure that regardless of politics, Democrat, Republican, whatever it was, they have always stood against totalitarianism and the toughness of those regimes and for exactly what's happening: independence, self-determination, democracy, freedom, moving now—not there yet—moving toward market economies.

The President's news conference with Prime Minister
Brian Mulroney of Canada at Walker's Point, Kennebunkport,
Maine, August 26, 1991

I made a comment the other day that when they appoint a new public works manager in downtown Kiev, that's their business. I got, incidentally, turned in for being testy. I thought that was highly amusing. But obviously, some didn't. [Laughter] I thought it was very funny. But it also has a serious note to it. When it comes to personnel, I don't know, John [Major, prime minister of the United Kingdom], if you've been asked, but every time some guy is in and someone's out, and a new person is appointed that nobody's ever heard of in the West, I'm supposed to be reacting.

Look, they're sorting out an enormous, complex set of new relationships. And so, if President Gorbachev has something to say
about President Yeltsin, knowing President Yeltsin, he's apt to hear
back from him. But that's the way the system is evolving. As you're
struggling for democratic processes, these things happen. And I
really think it is counterproductive for the United States to have
a view on every statement by every leader about what's happening
inside the Soviet Union and in the republics.

What we want to do is adhere to certain values. And as the
process moves to total acceptance of these values, whether it's free
elections or whether it's democracy generally or the whole broad
concept of freedom, we rejoice. But there's going to be some ups
and downs in all of this, and they can sort it out without a lot of
second-guessing from the President of the United States or telling
them where they ought to be the day after tomorrow.

These are monumental changes that have taken place, and the
whole world is excited about it. And there's going to be a hiccup
here, there's going to be criticism there, there's going to be a move
that we didn't expect over here, for example. But it's moving in the
right direction. It has been fantastic. I'm wondering what we're
going to do for an encore next August, John. [Laughter] Because
last year, as you know, it was the Gulf—

*The President's news conference with Prime Minister John Major
of the United Kingdom at Walker's Point, Kennebunkport, Maine,
August 29, 1991*

Diary, September 2: "It's perhaps the clearest day I have ever
seen here. My mind goes back to September 2, 1944—47 years
ago, this very day, I was shot down over the Bonin Islands. So
much has happened—so very much in my life and in the world.
Today I had a press conference. I recognized the Baltics. I
called the presidents of Estonia and Latvia, having talked to
Landsbergis of Lithuania a couple of days ago. I told them
what we were going to do. I told them why we had waited a few
days more. What I tried to do was use the power and prestige of
the United States, not to posture, not to be the first on board,

but to encourage Gorbachev to move faster on freeing the Baltics . . ." (*AWT,* p. 539).

While we await the final outcome, I welcome President Gorbachev's support for the concept that the republics will be free to determine their own future. This new "ten-plus-one" agreement speaks eloquently to that. This is a watershed in Soviet political thinking, equal to the dramatic movements toward democracy and market economies that we are witnessing in the republics themselves. The United States strongly supports these efforts.

The Baltic peoples of Estonia, Latvia, and Lithuania and their democratically elected governments have declared their independence and are moving now to control their own national territories and their own destinies.

The President's news conference at Walker's Point,
Kennebunkport, Maine, September 2, 1991

President Bush later referred to this next address to the nation, delivered September 27 from the Oval Office, as the "broadest and most comprehensive change in U.S. nuclear strategy since the early 1950s, when we launched the containment strategy that saw us through the Cold War. . . . I phoned Gorbachev ahead of the speech, having sent him a letter with the details of the announcement. . . . Gorbachev reacted positively . . ." (*AWT,* p. 546). The speech outlined at least nine major initiatives—including the cancellation of the mobile Peacekeeper intercontinental ballistic missile (ICBM) program—while identifying various areas where the two superpowers could cooperate. With the Soviets prepared to match U.S. force reductions, not to mention their recently announced withdrawals of support for the combatants in Afghanistan and for Cuba, the President aptly noted at the start of his remarks . . .

The world has changed at a fantastic pace, with each day writing a fresh page of history before yesterday's ink has even dried. And mostly recently, we've seen the peoples of the Soviet Union turn to democracy and freedom and discard a system of government based on oppression and fear.

Like the East Europeans before them, they face . . . the daunting challenge of building fresh political structures based on human rights, democratic principles, and market economies. Their task is far from easy and far from over. They will need our help, and they will get it.

But these dramatic changes challenge our nation as well. Our country has always stood for freedom and democracy. And when the newly elected leaders of Eastern Europe grappled with forming their new governments, they looked to the United States. They looked to American democratic principles in building their own free societies. Even the leaders of the USSR republics are reading the *Federalist Papers,* written by America's founders, to find new ideas and inspiration.

Today, America must lead again, as it always has, as only it can. And we will. We must also provide the inspiration for lasting peace. And we will do that, too. We can now take steps in response to these dramatic developments, steps that can help the Soviet peoples in their quest for peace and prosperity. More importantly, we can now take steps to make the world a less dangerous place than ever before in the nuclear age. . . .

The prospect of a Soviet invasion into Western Europe, launched with little or no warning, is no longer a realistic threat. The Warsaw Pact has crumbled. In the Soviet Union, the advocates of democracy triumphed over a coup that would have restored the old system of repression. The reformers are now starting to fashion their own futures, moving even faster towards democracy's horizon.

New leaders in the Kremlin and the republics are now questioning the need for their huge nuclear arsenal. The Soviet nuclear stockpile now seems less an instrument of national security and more of a burden. As a result, we now have an unparalleled opportunity to change the nuclear posture of both the United States and the Soviet Union.

If we and the Soviets take the right steps, some on our own, some on their own, some together, we can dramatically shrink the arsenal of the world's nuclear weapons. We can rely more on defensive measures in our strategic relationship. We can enhance stability and actually reduce the risk of nuclear war. Now is the time to seize this opportunity. . . .

Tonight, as I see the drama of democracy unfolding around the globe, perhaps we are closer to that new world order than ever before. The future is ours to influence, to shape, to mold. While we must not gamble that future, neither can we forfeit the historic opportunity now before us.

It has been said: "Destiny is not a matter of chance; it is a matter of choice. It is not a thing to be waited for; it's a thing to be achieved." The United States has always stood where duty required us to stand. Now let them say that we led where destiny required us to lead, to a more peaceful, hopeful future. We cannot give a more precious gift to the children of the world.

Address to the nation on U.S. nuclear weapons,
Oval Office, September 27, 1991

We've got to write the final chapter of the Cold War conflict. We must help the nations of the East secure the freedoms that they have won. In Central and Eastern Europe, the euphoria of 1989 has worn away. Each country struggles now to build a functioning free market on the ruins of the socialist systems, to rekindle a saving sense of trust essential to democratic society. These nations need our help. They need access to Western markets, financial and technical assistance to ease their transition. For forty long years, the captive nations of the East looked West for a sign of hope. And it's time now to say to these democracies: we will help you. More than that, after such a cold and protracted isolation, it is time for us to extend to them a warm welcome into this commonwealth of freedom.

And yet, while the urgent work of democracy-building and market reform moves forward, some see in freedom's triumph a bitter harvest. In this view, the collapse of Communism has thrown open a Pandora's box of ancient ethnic hatreds, resentment, and even revenge. Some fear democracy's new freedoms will be used not to build new trust but to settle old scores.

All of Europe has awakened to the danger of an old enemy, a nationalism animated by hatred and unmoved by nobler ends. No one need fear healthy national pride, the distinctive and defining traditions, the living history that gives people and nations a sense of identity and principle and purpose. But we must guard against nationalism of a more sinister sort: one that feeds on old, stale prejudices, teaches people intolerance and suspicion, and even racism and anti-Semitism; one that pits nation against nation, citizen against citizen. There can be no place for these old animosities in the new Europe.

The answer lies not in suppressing the dark impulses that destroy nations but in surmounting them, cultivating a spirit of democratic tolerance and peaceful change, a concept of majority rule that respects minority rights. Democracy is not the cause of strife in Eastern Europe and the Soviet Union but rather the solution. Western Europe stands as proof that in the space of little more than one generation, the spirit of democracy can transcend centuries of rivalry, war, nationalistic strife. . . .

Desperate times breed demagogues.

Remarks at a luncheon hosted by Prime Minister Ruud Lubbers
of the Netherlands at the Binnehof Parliamentary Building
Ridderzaal, The Hague, November 9, 1991

President Bush would later reflect on the fall and early winter of 1991 as a time when the republic leaders in the USSR, led by Boris Yeltsin, "began systematically dismantling the old Soviet Union" (*ATB,* p. 542). On December 8, one week after 90 percent of the Ukrainian people voted for independence from the Soviet Union, Boris Yeltsin phoned President Bush to inform him that he, together with Ukraine's President Leonid Kravchuk and Belarus's President Stanislau Shushkevich, had just signed an "accord" containing sixteen articles that created, in Yeltsin's words, a "commonwealth or group of independent states." The Soviet Union had just been dissolved.

On Christmas Day, Mikhail Gorbachev resigned as president of the Soviet Union. The President summed it up: "Our one-time greatest enemy no longer existed. The Cold War was officially over . . ." (*ATB*, p. 542). Later that day, he spoke with the nation . . .

Mikhail Gorbachev's revolutionary policies transformed the Soviet Union. His policies permitted the peoples of Russia and the other republics to cast aside decades of oppression and established the foundations of freedom. His legacy guarantees him an honored place in history and provides a solid basis for the United States to work in equally constructive ways with his successors.

Address to the nation on the commonwealth of independent states,
Oval Office, December 25, 1991

Peace in the Middle East

Every war—every war—is fought for a reason. But a just war is fought for the right reasons, for moral, not selfish reasons. . . .

When this war [Desert Storm] is over, the United States, its credibility and its reliability restored, will have a key leadership role in helping to bring peace to the rest of the Middle East.

Remarks at the annual convention
of the National Religious Broadcasters, Sheraton Washington
Hotel Ballroom, January 28, 1991

On September 12, the President publicly appealed to the Congress to defer a vote on U.S. housing loan guarantees for 120 days. With the Arab-Israeli peace conference tentatively scheduled for October, the administration did not want a contentious debate over Israeli housing policies aggravating a tenuous situation. The Israeli government had established controversial settlements in East Jerusalem, the West Bank, and elsewhere outside the pre-1967 boundaries. This was a source of fierce debate, and worse, between the sparring factions in the region.

Eventually, with bipartisan support for the peace process on Capitol Hill and even in the *New York Times* editorial page, President Bush would gain the deferral he sought, but not before the pro-Israeli lobby waged a bruising fight. This press conference took place just after a meeting with Jewish leaders, who promised to press their case . . .

Q. Mr. President, you talked about powerful political forces at work. It sounds like you're feeling the heat from the Israeli lobby. Do you think there's unfair foreign intervention in the U.S. political process here?

The President. No, I think everybody ought to fight for what they believe in. That's exactly what I'm beginning to do right here. We've laid back, we've been lying in the weeds, saying let's not get all these debate subjects going. The best thing for peace, to move the process forward, is just have this deferral.

But I'm going to fight for what I believe. And it may be popular politically, but probably it's not. But that's not the question here. That's not the question, is whether it's good 1992 politics. What's important here is that we give this process a chance. I don't care if I get one vote. I'm going to stand for what I believe here. And I believe the American people will be with me if we put it on this question of principle. And nobody has been a better friend to Israel than the United States, and no one will continue to be a better friend than the United States. . . .

We've got our policy. We should say clearly what the policy is. And I want this peace process to happen. . . .

We've got to keep our sights on the broad picture of peace in the Middle East. And I would say that includes world peace. They're so closely interlocked when you look at the complex relationships in the Middle East and how they spill over into Europe, into Asia, into the Soviet Union still. So, we're talking about a major chance now for one more tremendous step towards peace. We've seen the evolution in the Soviet Union. And we've seen the defeat of aggression over there in Iraq. We've seen democracy on the move in our hemisphere.

And here is the last place [Middle East] that really needs this peace process to move forward.
The President's news conference, White House Briefing Room,
September 12, 1991

To this day, President Bush frequently remarks on the surreal experience of the Madrid Conference—walking in with Gorbachev at his side, seeing Israelis and Arabs sitting at the same table, ready to discuss a lasting peace . . .

We have seen too many generations of children whose haunted eyes show only fear, too many funerals for their brothers and sisters, the mothers and fathers who died too soon, too much hatred, too little love. And if we cannot summon the courage to lay down the past for ourselves, let us resolve to do it for the children.
Remarks at the opening session
of the Middle East Peace Conference at the Royal Palace Salón
de las Columnas, Madrid, Spain, October 30, 1991

"A Unifying Executive"

I'm here to tell any American for whom hope lies dormant: We will not forget you. We will not forget those who have not yet shared in the American Dream. We must offer them hope. But we must guarantee them opportunity.
Remarks at a meeting of the American Society
of Association Executives, J. W. Marriott Hotel Grand Ballroom,
February 27, 1991

If there's a child hurting, America cares about that.
Question-and-answer session with reporters
in Hobe Sound, Florida, April 3, 1991

Presidents define themselves through their exercise of presidential power. They must use their special authority to serve the whole nation in matters of foreign and domestic policy. They must set a tone for governance, at once leading the people, yet following their desires. They must preserve, protect, and defend the Constitution. And they must encourage deliberative behavior on the part of the Congress.

But the real power of the presidency lies in a President's ability to frame, through action, through example, through encouragement, what we as a nation must do, what is required of communities and institutions, large and small, in schools and factories and the hundreds of daily acts of individuals.

The great joy and challenge of the office I occupy—and believe me, I am honored every single day I walk into that Oval Office by the privilege of being President—the great joy is that the President serves not just as the unitary executive but hopefully as a unifying executive.

As President, I feel honor-bound to strengthen the marvelous system of government bequeathed to us so that we may remain the freest, the most decent, the most prosperous, caring nation in the history of the world.

Remarks at the dedication ceremony of the Social Sciences Complex at Princeton University, Princeton, New Jersey, May 10, 1991

If we want to lead the postwar world, we must not build walls of prejudice and doubt. We must involve ourselves in the world around us. We must build ties of mutual interests and affection everywhere.

Remarks at the Hampton University commencement ceremony at Armstrong Field, Hampton, Virginia, May 12, 1991

Some argue that a nation as moral and just as ours should not taint itself by dealing with nations less moral, less just. But this counsel offers up self-righteousness draped in a false morality. You do not reform a world by ignoring it. . . .

Your destiny and the current of history will most likely inter-
sect more than once. You will have ample opportunity to make
your mark. And take care to make it count.

Remarks at the Yale University commencement ceremony,
University Quadrangle, New Haven, Connecticut,
May 27, 1991

Again using the imagery of the "extended hand" . . .

I learned long ago that if you want something done, give someone a reason for doing it. Don't put them on the defensive; don't
browbeat them. Appeal to the better angels of their nature. . . .

America's magnificent military has helped secure the peace
abroad. Our challenge now is to heal the wounds and the scars at
home and help the extended hand spur harmony and brotherhood, not faction and suspicion.

Remarks at the United States Military Academy
commencement ceremony, Michie Stadium,
West Point, New York, June 1, 1991

**Two extended exchanges with reporters: the first, on the 1980
hostage release . . .**

Q. Eight of the former hostages have called for an investigation of
   the accusations that the Reagan [1980] campaign people
   delayed the release of the hostages until after he was inaugu-
   rated, signed also by a local hostage by the name of Jerry
   Plotkin, local former hostage. I know your feelings on this. Let
   me ask you, you don't like what you call rumormongering and
   the speculation. Wouldn't a bipartisan congressional investigation with subpoena power put all that to rest?
The President. It could, and Congress is looking at it.
Q. Would you like to see it?
The President. I haven't seen any evidence to support it. None. But
   if Congress concludes it, I'd welcome it. But I've seen enough

rumormongering and hate-mongering, accusing me of things inferentially that I don't like, that I can categorically deny, as I did to Morehead Kennedy [former hostage]. I think he's accepted it.

They had me in Paris on October 20. So, what did we do? We put out a play-by-play and hour-by-hour part of the schedule. And so, some of them had the decency to retract that charge. Others were still saying, "Hey, there's evidence out there." Let Congress do it. I think anything by the executive branch would be suspiciously viewed as something less than objective.

Q. But you'd welcome a congressional investigation?

The President. If they see evidence to go forward. But to spend millions of taxpayers' dollars based on rumors, I'm sorry, I don't think that's good.

But let me tell you this on that one. To assign to me the motive that for political gain I would assign an American to captivity one minute longer than necessary, I think is a vicious personal assault on my integrity and my character as President. I don't think I'd deserve to be in this office if for one minute I suggested a person be held hostage so I could get political gain. And I know the same is true of President Reagan.

So, this is what troubles me about these allegations . . . if there's no evidence, I think they ought to say so, to lay it to rest. If I were a hostage—I told Kennedy, "Hey, if I were in your position and read a bunch of allegations about me or anyone else, I'd be heartbroken. I'd want to get to the bottom of it. But that's not the case. So, let me tell you, Morehead, what I know. And I know I had nothing to do with it, and I have no knowledge of anybody who had anything to do with it . . ."

Q. Can you categorically state that there was never any such plan?

The President. To the best of my knowledge, I can. I know of nothing, direct or indirect, that would suggest this. And I can categorically deny that I wasn't in Paris when these rumors and these allegations put me there.

How do you clear your name? Maybe the investigation is

it, but it has to be based on fact. It can't just go out there and have a billion-dollar witch-hunt. So I'd love to get it cleared, and I've done it as emphatically as possible. Because this gets to the heart of character. This gets to your soul. This gets to what's decent and right in the world.

And to suggest that a sitting President or a then Vice President would in any way, direct, indirect, know of and condone this, it touches me much more than some that—like disagreeing on abortion or disagreeing on closing bases. This one gets to the soul. And I'm glad you gave me a chance to wax emotional about it because it really turns me off, these little clever suggestions that I might have been involved. And all I can do is deny any knowledge of it, direct, indirect, for me or anyone else. That's all I can do. And I have a feeling that the American people are fair and they'll understand this.

The second, on the challenges of the presidency . . .

Q. You are perhaps one of the most qualified Presidents in our history in terms of your experience, before you became President, in government. In light of that . . . tell me what is it . . . about this job that's just so . . . much more difficult than you thought it would be?

The President. In many ways it's less hard. But the one thing that's harder, or if I could substitute the word *frustrating,* is the inability to get my domestic program through. We're in a fight on civil rights, for example. I pride myself on having a record of conscience and compassion on civil rights. We have before the Congress a civil rights bill that, in my view, would go a long way to eliminating discrimination in the workplace. And it would not result in quotas, direct or indirect. It wouldn't compel employers to put in quotas in order to avoid lawsuits. I feel strongly about this legislation. I can't get my legislation seriously considered, hearings before committees on it.

So, there's a frustration level, and I guess I'd have to accept your word: it is harder, given the fact that the other party controls both houses of Congress, to get things done that I want done—or put it more broad-mindedly, get the things done that I think I was elected to do. Therein lies a frustration. But I have to accept the fact that the executive branch is ours, the congressional branch is controlled by the [Democratic] leaders. So, when we get into the campaign you're pushing on, I'll go after them. They've already started going after me. And I've started a little bit kinder and gentler so far. But the American people will get this in focus.

But therein is the harder part because I spell out an agenda, I take my case to the people on an agenda, and we're frustrated. The war was something else. We needed the support of the Congress. And I think you go back and look at the history of Desert Storm and Desert Shield, I had to bring the American people along as commander in chief or as President and then, at the appropriate moment, go to the Congress, although I didn't think I had the constitutional responsibility to do this, and say, "Sanction the use of force. Do what every nation in the world has done almost through the United Nations sanctions."

There it was different because the President in foreign policy and in running a war, if you will, has much more power in the ability to [make a] decision. I didn't have to call the subcommittee on defense to ask if the air war should start. . . .

So, that part—not that the war was easy, not that the committing of forces was easy—but from a running-my-job standpoint it was easier. I could assign the duties to [Desert Storm commander] Norm Schwarzkopf, through Colin Powell, through [Secretary of Defense Dick] Cheney, and not have to worry about a subcommittee wanting to take a look. . . .

Q. In a sense, you're saying that, as for your job, the war with Iraq was easier than the war with Congress.

The President. Yes. In terms of making decisions, not in terms of emotion. Not in terms of what's in my heart when I have to say to a mother or a cousin or a brother, "I'm going to put your son in harm's way; I'm going to send your daughter to be the first woman that might be in combat"—thinking of a dead woman who performed heroically, the helicopter pilot . . . but it's easier in getting something to happen.

Interview with Linda Douglas of KNBC,
Jim Lampley of KCBS, and Paul Moyer of KABC
at the Four Seasons Hotel Burton Room, Los Angeles, California,
June 15, 1991

We've had several of these demonstrations, and on each one I listen about it and get, I guess you might say, get the message. Sometimes I agree with it, and sometimes I don't. I was elected President to do what I think is best, and I learn from listening, but I don't learn from some of the excesses that take place, whether it's in front of an abortion clinic or whether it's throwing blood or interrupting somebody's right to be heard.

The President's news conference at Walker's Point,
Kennebunkport, Maine, September 2, 1991

When a President selects a justice to the Supreme Court, he must pick someone who appreciates our Constitution's timeless majesty, who understands the importance of the rule of law in our society. But the nominee must also cherish the values that make our land great, that make our chins quiver in pride and gratitude when troops return home bearing the flag or when Americans through hard work, determination, and dedication expand the frontiers of possibility.

Address to the nation on the Supreme Court nomination
of Clarence Thomas, September 6, 1991

Director of Central Intelligence under President Ford from early 1976 to early 1977, President Bush has a strong affinity

for the intelligence community and views their work as indispensable . . .

By no means can we or should we or will we let our guard down. Let no one mistake our confidence and goodwill for weakness. We're not about to dismantle the intelligence capabilities that we've worked so hard to rebuild, but we must adapt them to new realities. Success in the struggle against Communism does not mean the CIA's work is done. . . .

Tomorrow's intelligence community will need to consolidate and extend freedom's gains against totalitarianism. Intelligence will enhance our protection against terrorism, against the drug menace. Intelligence will help our policymakers understand emerging economic opportunities and challenges. It will help us thwart anyone who tries to steal our technology or otherwise refuses to play by the competitive rules. It will help us seek peace and avert conflicts in regions of dangerous tension.

Remarks at the Veterans of the Office
of Strategic Services dinner, Washington Hilton Hotel,
October 23, 1991

His official announcement still months off, George Bush takes the first step down the 1992 campaign trail . . .

We live in an integrated world. And in that world, you can't neatly divide foreign policy from domestic policy.

Remarks at the Bush-Quayle fund-raising dinner
at the Sheraton Astrodome Hotel, Houston, Texas,
October 31, 1991

If we seek—and I believe that every one of us does—to build a new era of harmony and shared purpose, we must make it possible for all Americans to scale the ladder of opportunity. If we seek to ease racial tensions in America, civil rights legislation is, by itself, not enough. The elimination of discrimination in the workplace is a vital element of the American Dream, but it is simply not enough.

Remarks on signing the Civil Rights Act of 1991,
Rose Garden, November 21, 1991

I think a President owes the American people his judgment.

Interview with Doug Adair of WCMH-TV
in the Veterans Memorial Auditorium chorus room,
Columbus, Ohio, November 25, 1991

Politicians should remember that hot rhetoric won't fill an empty stomach.

Text of the Thanksgiving address to the nation,
November 27, 1991

America can meet the challenges of the new world taking shape around us. Some nations fear the future. They see chaos in change. But America is a nation drawn forward by what is new.

Remarks upon departure for Asian/Pacific nations,
Andrews Air Force Base in Camp Springs, Maryland,
December 30, 1991

LEGACY OF SERVICE:
The Promise of a Renewed America

Today's heroes are our neighbors and family and friends, anyone who gives of themselves by teaching someone to read or by visiting a lonely senior citizen or by helping a lonely child.

Remarks at the Points of Light Award presentation ceremony
for the Henderson Hall/Barcroft Elementary School
Adopt-A-School Program in Arlington, Virginia,
March 11, 1991

"True Patriots"

As someone who has devoted a fair amount of my own life to parts of government and public service, I know that good government simply cannot exist without serious, committed, and hardworking individuals willing to devote their career to public service.

*Remarks at a presentation ceremony for the Senior Executive
Service Presidential Rank Awards, Old Executive Office Building,
Room 450, January 9, 1991*

Like many of you, I have devoted much of my public life to public service. And I, too, cherish public service really as a special honor and personal obligation. And I always have. Long ago, my dad served for years as the moderator of . . . the Connecticut town meeting in our town of Greenwich. It convened once a month, and people came there and talked about whatever concerned them as they always do at town meetings. It could be rowdy or boring. The meetings always, though, gave people a special sense that their opinions made a difference and that they shared something special with their neighbors and friends. Those meetings taught me just what we mean when we talk of government of the people, by the people, and for the people.

*Remarks to public administrations groups on public service,
National Museum of American History,
October 24, 1991*

While our government rests on unchanging principles, it cannot rest on past achievements. Government, like everything else, must evolve. Our long and sturdy tradition of tolerance enables us to test new ideas through public debate. When Congress considers issues, no one minds a tough and honest discussion. We expect it. By the same token, we want and expect our free press to look beneath events, take account of people's motives, and ask tough questions rather than numbly repeating partisan propaganda or baseless rumor. We demand integrity in public behavior and discourse, and when we don't get it, we react.

Remarks to public administrations groups on public service,
National Museum of American History, October 24, 1991

Every time I come out here [CIA headquarters], I still have a sense of homecoming. Today I think of that January day in '76 when President Ford stood here as I took the oath of office as DCI [director of central intelligence], admittedly for a very short period of time. But I treasure having had that one year here, getting to know the people and the institution.

This was without question, if not *the,* certainly one of the most rewarding years of my entire long life. Let me just say to the professionals here, the CIA properly still has a mystique about it. I still get asked, "What was so special for you about your privilege of being the DCI there?" I still say it's the people here, the dedicated, selfless men and women who serve their country, not seeking recognition or honors. They are true patriots. And we're grateful to each and every one of you.

Remarks at the swearing-in ceremony for Robert Gates as director
of central intelligence, Central Intelligence Agency headquarters,
Langley, Virginia, November 12, 1991

"Good Society"

We have within our reach the promise of a renewed America. We can find meaning and reward by serving some higher purpose than ourselves, a shining purpose, the illumination of a Thousand Points of Light. And it is expressed by all who know the irresistible force of a child's hand, of a friend who stands by you and stays there, a volunteer's generous gesture, an idea that is simply right.

Address before a joint session of the Congress on the State
of the Union, U.S. Capitol House Chamber, January 29, 1991

There remain vital tests ahead, both here and abroad, but nothing the American people can't handle. So, we're going to roll up our sleeves, raise up the flag, and stand up for the decent men, women, and children of this great country—block by block, day by day, school by school—for your kids, for mine, for America's kids.

Remarks at the Attorney General's Crime Summit,
Sheraton Washington Hotel Ballroom,
March 5, 1991

Every American involved in service is reaffirming this nation as a community of conscience, a decent land—proud, but not boastful—with a national will reaffirmed and redirected, an America that has rediscovered the can-do attitude.

Remarks on signing the Points
of Light National Celebration of Community Service
Proclamation at the Glenarden Community Center Gymnasium,
Glenarden, Maryland, April 12, 1991

Our nation faces a wide variety of challenges, but the solution to each problem that confronts us begins with an individual who steps forward and who says, "I can help." Government can only do so much and should only attempt so much, but no limits can hold back people determined to make a difference.

Remarks at the Points
of Light Community Service Celebration,
White House South Lawn,
April 26, 1991

Drawing a distinction between LBJ's "big government" approach . . .

We don't need another Great Society with huge and ambitious programs administered by the incumbent few. We need a Good

Society built upon the deeds of the many, a society that promotes service, selflessness, action.

Remarks at the University of Michigan commencement ceremony,
Michigan Stadium, Ann Arbor, May 4, 1991

In the next American century, all of us will have a responsibility to lead. Each part of our communities—the union halls, the police clubs, the chambers of commerce, the parents, teachers—everyone can use their power to solve problems. Because, if you think about it, there isn't a problem in America that isn't being solved somewhere.

Remarks at the California Institute of Technology Commencement
ceremony, Cal Tech athletic field, Pasadena, California,
June 14, 1991

If every community in this land committed itself to sacrifice and action in this work, then each could become a "community of light."

In a community of light, people would discover the fulfillment that comes with helping others. In a community of light, each school, business, place of worship, and group would lead its members toward the light of service as equal partners in solving social problems at their root. In a community of light, people would use their ingenuity, experience, and passion to find solutions that work for their neighborhoods, their communities. They would adapt other people's successful efforts to meet their needs, or if necessary, they would craft their own.

Radio address to the nation on the Daily Points of Light Program,
September 28, 1991

We know that all the world's woes cannot be solved through voluntary service. Our society cannot survive without an efficient, compassionate government that can preserve people's liberties, that can establish a rule of law vital for civilized life, and that can do its part to help those in need in many, many ways. We also know the importance of a vibrant economy and the jobs and opportunities it creates.

But legislation and commerce alone cannot provide the soul that society needs. Real people also must be prepared to respond to the real problems around them. And they must extend the hand of friendship to neighbors, offer their time and concern to those who have fallen upon bad times.

Remarks at the Points of Light Celebration
at the Epcot Center American Gardens Theater, Orlando, Florida,
September 30, 1991

SERVICE IN UNIFORM

On February 1, what he would later call "a moving and emotional day for me," the President traveled to three military bases to meet with the families of service personnel in the Gulf. "I began with Cherry Point Marine Corps Air Station, North Carolina. As we landed, I steeled myself for what I knew would be a wrenching experience . . ." (*AWT*, p. 464).

Unfortunately, there are no medals of valor for military families. If there were, there would be as much decoration on your chests as pride within them.

Remarks to community members
at Cherry Point Marine Corps Air Station, North Carolina,
February 1, 1991

Next it was on to Seymour Johnson Air Force Base, also in North Carolina. "There the emotion, and my reaction to it was just as strong. Once again I tried to get through my text without breaking down. It is hard to do when they play "The Star Spangled Banner" or when they salute you and hold up signs, or when you see a child mouthing the words 'Bring my dad home safe'" (*AWT*, p. 465). The day finished at Fort Stewart, Georgia . . .

I know it's been tough on a lot of you—maybe all of you here at Seymour Johnson. And I know also what it is that you have offered this great nation of ours. I understand what it is that I have asked of you, what General MacPeak has asked of you. Members of this fighting unit have voluntarily set aside their freedom to wage this battle. But while today some may be prisoners of war, and others may have made the ultimate sacrifice, a lifetime of democracy and faith in God keeps their spirit free. No foreign dictator can imprison the love of liberty that beats in the heart of every American.

Remarks to community members at the base picnic grounds,
Seymour Johnson Air Force Base, Goldsboro, North Carolina,
February 1, 1991

They went to the Gulf not because it was the expedient way but because it was the American way. Through their sacrifice as they caused a brutal aggressor to fall, they renewed our faith in ourselves. . . .

Today we hope that this time was the last time, that we stand prepared to respond should there ever be a next time. Our goal is real peace—the triumph of freedom, not merely the absence of war. Our means is the courage and character of the American people.

Remarks at a memorial service for those who died in the Persian
Gulf conflict, Arlington Cemetery amphitheater,
Arlington, Virginia, June 8, 1991

From the fiery birth of our Nation to freedom's latest triumph in the Persian Gulf, America's veterans have always answered the call and given their all whenever freedom was threatened or democracy imperiled.

Address to the nation commemorating Veterans Day, Old Executive
Office Building, Room 459, recorded on November 9 for airing
on November 11, 1991

Remembering Pearl Harbor . . .

I'll never forget the day it happened. I was walking across the school campus. And it just changed my life and the life of everybody then. The country pulled together like never before in our history, with the possible exception of World War I, but I'd say even like never before in our history.

There was an evil there: totalitarianism. And we prevailed. And that spirit that existed in World War II was epitomized by Desert Storm. Different war, different scope, different situation, different body count, but that same spirit of the country coming together is what I remember about World War II.

Interview with Don Marsh of KTVI-TV
at the St. Louis Airport Radisson Hotel, St. Louis, Missouri,
November 13, 1991

I remember exactly where I was when I heard the news about Pearl Harbor. I was seventeen years old, walking across the green at school. And my thoughts in those days didn't turn to world events but mainly to simpler things, more mundane things, like making the basketball team or entering college. And that walk across the campus marked the end of innocence for me.

When Americans heard the news, they froze in shock. But just as quickly we came together. Like all American kids back then, I was swept up in it. I decided that very day to go into the navy to become a navy pilot. And so on my eighteenth birthday, June 12, 1942, I was sworn into the navy as a seaman second class.

And I was shocked, I was shocked at my first sight of Pearl Harbor several months later, April of '44. We came into port on the CVL-30, on the carrier *San Jacinto*. Nearby, the *Utah* was still on her side; parts of the *Arizona* still stood silent in the water. Everywhere the skeletons of ships reached out as if to demand remembrance and warn us of our own mortality. . . .

I wondered how I'd feel being with you, the veterans of Pearl Harbor, the survivors, on this very special day. And I wondered if I would feel that intense hatred that all of us felt for the enemy fifty years ago. As I thought back to that day of infamy and the loss of friends, I wondered: What will my reaction be? What will their reaction be, the other old veterans, especially those who survived that terrible day right here?

Well, let me tell you how I feel. I have no rancor in my heart towards Germany or Japan, none at all. And I hope, in spite of the loss, that you have none in yours. This is no time for recrimination.

World War II is over. It is history. We won. We crushed totalitarianism. And when that was done, we helped our enemies give birth to democracies. We reached out, both in Europe and in Asia. We made our enemies our friends, and we healed their wounds. And in the process, we lifted ourselves up.

The lessons of war itself will live on, and well they should: preparedness; strength, decency, and honor; courage; sacrifice; the willingness to fight, even die, for one's country—America, the land of the free and the brave.

No, just speaking for one guy, I have no rancor in my heart. I can still see the faces of the fallen comrades, and I'll bet you can see the faces of your fallen comrades, too, or family members. But don't you think they're saying, "Fifty years have passed; our country is the undisputed leader of the free world, and we are at peace"? Don't you think each one is saying, "I did not die in vain"?

Remarks to World War II veterans and families
.at Kilo 8 Pier, Honolulu, Hawaii, December 7, 1991

Look into your hearts and minds: you will see boys who this day became men and men who became heroes.

Look at the water here, clear and quiet, bidding us to sum up and remember. One day, in what now seems another lifetime, it wrapped its arms around the finest sons any nation could ever have, and it carried them to a better world.

Remarks at the ceremony commemorating
the fiftieth anniversary of Pearl Harbor, USS Arizona Memorial,
December 7, 1991

IN THE ARENA:
High Hope

Thank you for the warm welcome. *Si res prehensio cano est non oves sic vacio.* **That means, if you're holding up the sign, you can't throw eggs.**
Opening Remarks at the Yale University
commencement ceremony, University Quadrangle,
New Haven, Connecticut, May 27, 1991

———

You take a few shots in this business.
Interview via satellite from the Old Executive Office Building. Room 459, with Warner Saunders of WMAQ-TV in Chicago, Illinois, November 20, 1991

"Je Serai Parfait"

Looking around at this dais and at the audience, I wonder who's home minding the GNP.
Remarks and a question-and-answer session at a meeting of the Economic Club at the New York Hilton Hotel Grand Ballroom, New York City, February 6, 1991

———

I feel a little funny being here. After all, I'm the CEO now of an outfit that's lost money thirty-three of the last thirty-five years.
Remarks at a meeting of the American Business Conference, Department of Commerce Great Hall, April 9, 1991

———

The admiral [Vice Admiral William O. Studeman, director of the National Security Agency] said this visit is a bit of a departure from the routine here at NSA. This isn't exactly the kind of place where you can pull off a surprise party.

Remarks at a presentation ceremony
for the National Security Agency Worldwide Awards in Fort Meade,
Maryland, May 1, 1991

It's really something to look out over this outstanding military audience. Now I know how Bob Hope feels. [Laughter] Also, let me say it was good of you to invite a navy man to speak at West Point. I left the goat outside, but I'm glad to be here. [Laughter]

Remarks at the United States Military Academy
commencement ceremony, Michie Stadium,
West Point, New York, June 1, 1991

First, I want to say that there's absolutely no rule here that says that the person giving the speech has to be as smart as the students receiving the scholarships.

Opening remarks at the presentation ceremony
for the Presidential Scholars Awards, White House South Lawn,
June 19, 1991

It wasn't until the War of 1812 and the decisive defeat—with all respect, Ambassador Acland [of the United Kingdom]—[laughter]—of the British forces—if I'd known you were going to be here, I would have changed this—[laughter]—at the Battle of New Orleans.

Remarks at the presentation ceremony for the Presidential Medals
of Freedom and Presidential Citizen's Medals,
White House East Room, July 3, 1991

The President. Merci beaucoup. Un grand plaisir. Je pratique mon
francais. [Thank you very much. A great pleasure. I am practicing my French.] How do you say "next time"?

The Prime Minister. La prochaine fois. [Laughter]
The President. La prochaine fois, je serai parfait en français. [Next
time, I will be perfect in French.] [Laughter]
> *The President's news conference*
> *with Prime Minister Brian Mulroney of Canada at the SkyDome,*
> *Toronto, July 9, 1991*

**During the Moscow Summit, President Bush takes the oppor-
tunity to share a friendly warning with Russia's new entrepre-
neurs that capitalism has its ups and downs . . .**

A young man became the manager of a company. And his predecessor handed him three envelopes and said that if he was ever in
trouble, to open the envelopes. So, one day when business was not
going well, the man decided it was time to open envelope number one. The message inside read: Blame your predecessor. So he
did, and things improved for a while. But then they got worse
again. So he decided to open up envelope number two. It read:
Blame the accounting department. So he did that. But sales con-
tinued to go downhill. And finally, with much hesitation, he
opened envelope number three. And it said: Prepare three
envelopes.
> *Remarks to Soviet and United States businessmen in Moscow,*
> *Radisson Hotel Composer's Hall, July 31, 1991*

I want to thank the Hispanic Chamber of Commerce for its
endorsement of our America 2000 education strategy. I am grateful for your initiatives to teach economics and entrepreneurship
to our kids, beginning in kindergarten. And now, if only some
could do the same for economists, I think we'd be in pretty good
shape around here.
> *Remarks at the annual convention of the United States*
> *Hispanic Chamber of Commerce, Hyatt Regency Hotel,*
> *Chicago, Illinois, September 20, 1991*

SPOTLIGHT ON THE MEDIA

Some say that if Edison had invented the lightbulb today, we'd have scores of studies citing the dangers of electricity. [Laughter] And the newspapers would headline the story "Candle Industry Threatened."

Remarks to the American Association for the Advancement of Science,
Old Executive Office Building, Room 450, February 15, 1991

———————

President Bush still enjoys showing the *Saturday Night Live* **clip he references here . . .**

Q. The French foreign minister says that a date has been set for the start of the ground war and that we're on the eve of the pre-eve. Do you disagree with that?

The President. I don't comment on anything to do with the military . . . although the decision on ground forces will be made by me for UN ground forces. But I would simply not comment on that. It reminds me of *Saturday Night Live.* Remember the questions they ask on *Saturday Night:* "Hey, tell us how we can help the Iraqi soldiers the most" or "What is the password?" or "Please give me some information that will do in our troops." I mean, I'm not in that business—come on.

Exchange with reporters at Walker's Point beach,
Kennebunkport, Maine, February 17, 1991

———————

I know many of the reporters out there were roughing it lately. Sam Donaldson, though, said it wasn't so bad staying at the Sheraton Riyadh. In fact, he said the towels were so fluffy he could barely get his suitcase closed.

Remarks at the Gridiron Dinner, Capitol Hilton Hotel
Presidential Ballroom, March 23, 1991

———————

Explaining the President's ever-present observers to students . . .

They [White House press corps] come on most of the trips, not all. Sometimes we answer the questions, and then they write the stories. . . . Now, whether *Time* magazine over here—you ever heard of *Time*? Well, see, now, he's going to write a glowing piece about this education program. [Laughter] We've got high hope.

Question-and-answer session with students
at the Discourse Room, Saturn School of Tomorrow,
St. Paul, Minnesota, May 22, 1991

Referring to the Iraqi invasion of Kuwait in 1990 and the attempted Soviet coup in 1991. Both took place in August, and both required President Bush to manage the crises from Maine . . .

Don't say we never give you any news up here.

Remarks on the attempted coup in the Soviet Union
and an exchange with reporters at Walker's Point,
Kennebunkport, Maine, August 19, 1991

Not quite ready to start the 1992 campaign . . .

The President. When they [Democratic candidates] go after me, I'll go right back after them, if I decide to run. And I told you I will let you know when the candidacy becomes formal. I don't want to get out ahead of all these legal arrangements.

Q. —could do it now.

The President. No, but it's too small a crowd. If I do that, I want a great big crowd. And I don't want the golf course in the background, maybe. [Laughter]

Exchange with reporters at Holly Hills Country Club,
Ijamsville, Maryland, October 13, 1991

Indoctrinating a foreign journalist to the ways of the West
Wing . . .

Q. Mr. President, I have two questions, if I may, sir.
The President. You get one, but they call it a follow-on. You can
use that technique. [Laughter]
> *The President's news conference*
> *at the U.S. ambassador's residence, Rome, Italy,*
> *November 8, 1991*

FREEDOM'S FRIENDS

Margaret Thatcher . . .

We will never forget her courage in helping forge a great coalition
against the aggression which brutalized the Gulf. Nor will I forget
one special conversation that I had with the prime minister. In the
early days of the Gulf crisis—I'm not sure you remember this one,
Margaret—in the early days of the Gulf crisis I called her to say
that though we fully intended to interdict Iraqi shipping, we were
going to let a single vessel heading for Oman enter port down at
Yemen—going around Oman down to Yemen—without being
stopped. And she listened to my explanation, agreed with the decision, but then added these words of caution—words that guided
me through the Gulf crisis, words I'll never forget as long as I'm
alive. "Remember, George," she said, "this is not time to go wob-
bly." [Laughter]

Those who work with me in the White House know we use
that expression often and have used it during some troubling days.
And never, ever will it be said that Margaret Thatcher went wob-
bly. [Laughter]

Finally, think of what Margaret Thatcher meant to the world.
Her resolution and dedication set an example for all of us. She
showed that you can't lock behind walls forever when moral
conviction uplifts their souls. And she knew tyranny is powerless
against the primacy of the heart.

Margaret Thatcher helped bring the Cold War to an end, helped the human will outlast the bayonets and barbed wire. She sailed freedom's ship wherever it was imperiled. Prophet and crusader, idealist and realist, this heroic woman made history move her way.

Prime Minister, there will always be an England, but there can never be another Margaret Thatcher.

Remarks upon presenting the Presidential Medal
of Freedom to Margaret Thatcher, White House East Room,
March 7, 1991

Queen Elizabeth II . . .

You've been freedom's friend for as long as we remember—back to World War II when, at eighteen, you joined the war against fascism. It was then that America first began to know you as one of us, came to love you as standing fast with freedom, summoning across the oceans our values and our dreams.

Remarks at the welcoming ceremony for Queen Elizabeth II
of the United Kingdom, White House South Lawn, May 14, 1991

Irving [Kristol] has devoted so much of his effort the past three decades to making the world safe for democratic capitalism. That message now opens new worlds from Moscow to Warsaw. And I just wish we could say the same thing for Washington, D.C. [Laughter]

Remarks to the American Enterprise Institute,
Willard Hotel, December 4, 1991

POLITICS

Agriculture Secretary Clayton Yeutter's move to chair the Republican National Committee opened the way for this presidential pun . . .

Let it be said of Clayton that he's moved on to another fertile field.

Remarks at the swearing-in ceremony for Edward R. Madigan
as secretary of agriculture, Agricultural Building,
March 12, 1991

Jim [Secretary of State Baker] put it well. We have been friends. And I have total confidence in him. Remember 1980? He's the guy who told me in New Hampshire, "Don't worry; let the guy from California pay for the mike."

Remarks at the Gridiron Dinner, Capitol Hilton Hotel
Presidential Ballroom, March 23, 1991

I think back to the times that we worked together as perm reps [permanent representatives] up there twenty years ago, and I still wonder how it is that I ended up with the easier job.

Remarks following discussions with Secretary-General Javier Perez
de Cuellar de la Guerra of the United Nations,
White House East Room, May 9, 1991

Imagine: a son of Yale getting a Princeton degree. "Son of Yale"—you can snicker, but you ought to hear what they call me in Washington.

Remarks at the dedication ceremony of the Social Sciences Complex,
Princeton University, Princeton, New Jersey, May 10, 1991

I must confess I wish I were with you in Orlando. Instead, I'm stuck up here at Disney World North.

Remarks in a teleconference from the Old Executive
Office Building, Room 459, with the annual meeting of the Public
Broadcasting Service in Orlando, Florida, June 11, 1991

Referring to his request that Congress pass a crime bill and a transportation bill in one hundred days . . .

Lyndon Johnson, in his State of the Union address in January of 1964, challenged Congress to act on at least eight broad domestic issues, all within five months. And I thought one hundred days was fairly reasonable. I wasn't asking Congress to deliver a hot pizza in thirty minutes. [Laughter] That would be revolutionary for a Congress.

Remarks on the administration's domestic policy,
White House South Lawn, June 12, 1991

They had some protesters out at CalTech [California Institute of Technology] where I spoke yesterday. As I said to the crowd there, it was kind of beneath the dignity of my office because there were so few. [Laughter]

Interview with Linda Douglas of KNBC,
Jim Lampley of KCBS, and Paul Moyer of KABC
in the Four Seasons Hotel Burton Room, Los Angeles, California,
June 15, 1991

Grading a fellow pilot, who also happened to be the Brazilian president . . .

I hear that, yesterday, en route from Brasilia to Washington, the president himself piloted the plane and even helped land it. I'm glad he didn't pull a barrel roll over the South Lawn. [Laughter] But all our Brazilian guests are here tonight, so I guess the passengers weren't too much in danger. Captain Collor got them here a half hour early, and nobody lost their luggage—[laughter]—so things are going very well to start off our visit.

Toast at the state dinner for President Fernando Collor de Mello
of Brazil, State Dining Room, June 18, 1991

Response to a reporter when asked before a meeting with the Republican congressional leadership if the meeting was political in nature . . .

Label this as a nonpolitical conversation this morning, but you'll know. [Laughter] It's like [Supreme Court Justice] Potter Stewart on pornography: you'll know it when you see it. [Laughter]
Exchange with reporters, Cabinet Room, June 19, 1991

My schedule read that it was time to motorcade to the Capitol for this unveiling of my bust, and I started worrying about the headlines on that one. [Laughter] No, not what you're thinking. "Bush Goes for Bust" maybe, or "Bush Gets Busted." [Laughter]
Remarks at the unveiling of the official bust of the President,
U.S. Capitol Rotunda, June 27, 1991

Today is the anniversary of Zachary Taylor's death. The poor guy has really suffered his share of indignities recently—[laughter]—digging him up. But I want to set the historical record straight about Zachary. I was told that his last words were "Pass the broccoli." [Laughter] Not so. His last words were really "I have endeavored to do my duty."
Remarks at a meeting of the American Defense
Preparedness Association, J. W. Marriott Hotel Grand Ballroom,
July 9, 1991

Let me say to our very able secretary of education [Lamar Alexander] from whom you heard a minute ago: I promise I will keep up with my computer lessons, but I'll need a little more time to write my report on "what I did on my summer vacation." [Laughter] And if you think mine's a tough assignment, how about President Gorbachev, what he did on his summer vacation. [Laughter]
. . . Your world, the whole world, trembles with new possibil-

ities. One day, we scratch out our thoughts with paper and pen; the next, it seems, we use computers and laser printers. One day the Soviet Union, bellicose and threatening, stares at us from across the sea. But in a single dramatic week, we saw seventy years of history swept away. With the dizzying changes that surround us, history books and atlases seem to have a shorter shelf life than milk. [Laughter]

Remarks to students and faculty in the school gymnasium,
Lewiston Comprehensive High School, Lewiston, Maine,
September 3, 1991

Looks like something that started out in Washington as a trench and went over budget.

Remarks at an environmental agreement signing ceremony
at the Grand Canyon National Park, Arizona, September 18, 1991

I've come here today fresh from—that means "immediately from," not necessarily "fresh feeling"—[laughter]—from two days of meetings over at the UN in New York City.

Remarks at a Republican Party fund-raising dinner
at the East Brunswick Ramada Renaissance Hotel,
East Brunswick, New Jersey,
September 24, 1991

Sonny and Ger . . .

Let me also salute a guy who wants to trade a star on Hollywood Boulevard for a seat in the Senate, mayor of Palm Springs, my friend Sonny Bono. I've got one question for him: What makes Sonny think that someone from the California entertainment industry can succeed in national politics? [Laughter] And Sonny, a little advice for you, if you want to practice debating, skip over Connie Morella, who's sitting next to you, and go a couple of seats down with Geraldine Ferraro and be ready. It's tough. I've been there; I know. [Laughter]

> *Remarks at the National Italian-American Foundation*
> *fund-raising dinner, Washington Hilton Hotel,*
> *October 5, 1991*

Let me just welcome you to the White House complex. That's what this is called for various reasons.

> *Opening remarks on signing the Columbus Day Proclamation,*
> *Old Executive Office Building, Indian Treaty Room,*
> *October 10, 1991*

A little more than two months ago, the Vice President outlined our agenda for civil justice reform before the American Bar Association. That speech unleashed a national debate, a flurry of mail here at the White House, I might add, and some of the best lawyer jokes that I've heard in years.

> *Remarks on signing the executive order on civil justice reform,*
> *White House Roosevelt Room, October 23, 1991*

Responding to a question by ABC's Ann Compton regarding a departing White House employee, the President suggests what his retirement plans might not include . . .

I don't know that it would be the function of the President to suggest what employment somebody should take. If you ask me, would I like to go out there, leave my job, and go to work for this sheikh when I get through being President, no, I wouldn't like to do that. [Laughter]

> *The President's 106th news conference,*
> *White House Briefing Room, October 25, 1991*

Turning a presidential double play . . .

While you all are here, I have a special announcement to make. We talk a lot about recycling. Well, today we're going to save a few trees by giving two speeches at the same time—[laughter]— piloting a new program in recycling audiences, too. [Laughter]

Remarks following the presentation of the President's Environment
and Conservation Challenge Awards and before signing
the executive order on federal recycling, Rose Garden,
October 31, 1991

Missing in action are two members of Congress who were supposed to be here, but let's hope they're not doing bad things up there on the Hill.

Opening remarks at the swearing-in ceremony for William Taylor
as chairman of the Federal Deposit Insurance Corporation,
Old Executive Office Building, Room 450, October 31, 1991

I am going to continue to support environmentally responsive access to ANWR, the Alaskan refuge, for energy production. We need it. And if you're worried about the caribou, take a look at the arguments that were used about the [Alaskan] pipeline. They'd say the caribou would be extinct. You've got to shake them away with a stick. They're all making love lying up next to the pipeline. And you've got thousands of caribou up there. And yet the same voices, the same voices are arguing against ANWR today. I mean, come on. [Laughter]

Remarks at the Bush-Quayle fund-raising dinner
in Houston, Texas, Sheraton Astrodome Hotel, October 31, 1991

Dedicating the Ronald Reagan Presidential Library, the soon-to-be candidate refers to President Carter's presence along with four Republican Presidents (Nixon, Ford, Reagan, and Bush) . . .

I feel very badly that you haven't met a Democratic President yet, but please don't do anything about that. [Laughter]

Remarks at the dedication
of the Ronald Reagan Presidential Library, Simi Valley, California,
November 4, 1991

After a welcome like this, there's no place I'd rather be. And there is also no place better than sitting up here with Miss America, Carolyn Sapp. [Laughter] I'd like to be the one sitting there, but it seems my friends and assistant Fred McClure switched the place cards. [Laughter] So I have a question for him. Fred, how did you used to like working at the White House? [Laughter]

Remarks to the Future Farmers of America
at the Kansas City Municipal Auditorium, Kansas City, Missouri,
November 13, 1991

I've really enjoyed my visits here to both exchanges today, the board and then here. I've seen the future. It uses hand signals, at least for now. [Laughter] But then, I've also glimpsed at the fact that that's changing. Speaking of hand signals, I saw a few riding in here. [Laughter] They have a nice way of making one feel at home. [Laughter] No, actually it's been very, very friendly.

Remarks following a tour of the trading floor
to the Chicago Mercantile Exchange, Chicago, Illinois,
December 10, 1991

LEARNING THE COMPUTER

Part of the America 2000 education plan called for the country to become a "nation of students." Here, the President explains he was convinced to offer leadership by example . . .

To prove no one's ever too old to learn, Lamar [Alexander, secretary of education], with his indefatigable determination and leadership, has convinced me to become a student again myself. Starting next week, I'll begin studying. And I want to know how to operate a computer. [Laughter] Very candidly—I don't expect this new tutorial to teach me how to set the clock on the VCR or anything complicated.

Address to the nation on the National Education Strategy,
White House East Room, April 18, 1991

First day back at school . . .

I am computer illiterate. Everybody in this room, obviously, knows how to run a computer. But I would like to report to you that I intend to undertake and fulfill that commitment, and today I learned to turn one on—[laughter]—push the button down here and one up here with the green thing on it—[laughter]—and out came a command to somebody that I had written on the—I pushed a button; I was worried what might happen there. [Laughter]

Remarks at the presentation of a Points of Light Award
to the U.S. Naval Academy/Benjamin Banneker
Honors Mathematics and Science Society Partnership,
at the U.S. Naval Academy Bancroft Hall,
Annapolis, Maryland, April 23, 1991

Our America 2000 strategy for education lays out a series of bold challenges: to create better and more accountable schools that parents can choose, to reinvent the American school by developing a new generation of American schools, to turn our land into a nation of students and, in the process, me into a computer genius.

Remarks to the National Federation of Independent Businesses,
Capitol Hill Hyatt Regency Ballroom, June 3, 1991

I was asked for a report. It's been almost six months since my first computer lesson, and I'm making progress. I make the same mistakes, but I do it five times faster. It's marvelous. [Laughter]

> *Remarks at the presentation ceremony for the National Medals*
> *of Science and Technology, Rose Garden,*
> *September 16, 1991*

Sports

On taking his presidential strike count to 3–0 and comparing notes with General Colin Powell, chairman of the Joint Chiefs of Staff . . .

I had a bad day opening the Rangers game. Got to throw out the first ball for the Rangers game, Milwaukee/Rangers, and I— curve ball, broke a little early, went into the ground. That's my side of the story, and I'm staying with it. [Laughter] And then a week later, hard, fast, right over the center of the plate, Colin Powell up in Yankee Stadium. Sergeant Powell will be reporting—[laughter]—to Nome, Alaska.

> *Remarks at the presentation of a Points of Light Award*
> *to the U.S. Naval Academy/Benjamin Banneker Honors*
> *Mathematics and Science Society Partnership,*
> *at the U.S. Naval Academy Bancroft Hall,*
> *Annapolis, Maryland, April 23, 1991*

The last time, save one, that I was on this campus, I was not treated quite so hospitably. [Laughter] It was out at the baseball diamond, I think in 1948. Crowded along the first-base line—it was very hostile, the way it worked in Princeton—were a bunch of hyperventilating, celebrating alumni.

And I remember standing there at first base, and a gigantic tiger—I think his name was Neil Zundel—came to the plate. He lofted an easy fly towards Yale's first baseman, me. And as I reached for the ball, the guy just sheer bowled me over—[laughter]—to the cheers of the Princeton alumni. [Laughter]

I was hurt, my pride was hurt. But P. S., Yale won the ball game. [Laughter]

Remarks upon receiving an honorary degree
from Princeton University, at the Nassau Hall faculty room,
Princeton, New Jersey, May 10, 1991

The First Fan with Joe DiMaggio and Ted Williams . . .

I don't want to reminisce too much, but I was seventeen years old during their famous 1941 season, fifty years ago. And like many American kids in those days and today, I followed those box scores closely, watched the magnificent season unfurl. In those days I was, Joe, a Red Sox fan, and my brother, though, a Yankee fan. And fifty years later, that '41 season just remains a season of dreams.

Remarks on presenting Presidential Citations
to Joe DiMaggio and Ted Williams, Rose Garden,
July 9, 1991

CHAPTER FOUR

1992:
Finish This Job
in Style

Comedian Dana Carvey spreads some postelection holiday cheer
to the President and his staff in the White House East Room.
December 7, 1992.

The material presented in chapter 4 is not an attempt to convince anyone that 1992 was anything other than the worst political year of George Bush's life. He alluded to it at the time, particularly in his diary entries, and has said so many times since. The historical record on that is quite clear: 1992 was a dreadful year.

Nevertheless, between Pat Buchanan, Ross Perot, and Bill Clinton, it was also an extraordinary year—and whatever political angst President Bush felt in the privacy of the White House residence over the campaign, or the media, he faithfully discharged his duties throughout an otherwise seesaw year. Every time the administration seemed to take a step forward, something would seemingly set it, or the country, two steps back. For example, in early April, the President sent the FREEDOM Support Act to Congress to help the former Soviet republics nurture their nascent democracies; but in late April, Los Angeles broke out in riots. In the campaign, the polls closed to two points in late October; but five days before Election Day, the special prosecutor looking into the Iran-contra affair, Lawrence Walsh, indicted former Reagan defense secretary Caspar Weinberger. On the personal side, the Bushes' daughter, Doro, married Bobby Koch in June; but then in November, two weeks after the election, President Bush lost his beloved mother, Mum, as he called her.

Still, amid three presidential debates—and Ross Perot's on-again, off-again candidacy—President Bush hosted the second drug summit in San Antonio in February and the first U.S.-Russia Summit in June; launched a massive humanitarian relief mission in December spearheaded by the U.S. military to open supply lines and help end the Somali famine that had already claimed 250,000 innocent lives; and finally, in January 1993 he signed the START II agreement in Moscow with Boris Yeltsin. Together with *the START I, it legislated a 75 percent reduction of the nuclear arsenals held by the United States and Russia. "The world looks to us to consign the Cold War to history, to ratify our new relationship by reducing the weapons that concentrate the most destructive power known to man," the President said after signing the treaty.*

FAITH, FAMILY, AND FRIENDS:
The Fabric of Society

Sure we must change, but some values are timeless. I believe in families that stick together, and fathers who stick around. I happen to believe very deeply in the worth of each individual human being, born or unborn. I believe in teaching our kids the difference between what's wrong and what's right, teaching them respect for hard work and to love their neighbors. I believe that America will always have a special place in God's heart, as long as he has a special place in ours. Maybe that's why I have always believed that patriotism is not just another point of view.

Remarks accepting the presidential nomination
at the Republican National Convention, Astrodome,
Houston, Texas, August 20, 1992

Losing is never easy. Trust me, I know something about that. [Laughter] But if you have to lose, that's the way to do it: Fight with all you have. Give it your best shot. And win or lose, learn from it, and get on with life.

Remarks at the U.S. Military Academy, Washington Mess Hall,
West Point, New York, January 5, 1993

FAMILY

We are blessed with family, with kids that come home, and with the loyalty and strength that one gets when one is in public life from sons and a daughter. And so, I don't have to ask for any more there. But if I were, I would simply say, "Keep it strong, Lord, because we're going into a hell of a year over there." It's politics; it's politics from tomorrow on. And it isn't very pleasant.

Exchange with reporters at Scots College, Sydney, Australia,
January 1, 1992

It feels odd to hear myself referred to as the leader of the free world. I told Barbara somebody in Sydney said I was leader of the free world. She says, "Hurry up and get out of the bathroom; we're late. Run."

Remarks at a dinner hosted by Prime Minister Keating
of Australia, Parliament House/House of Representatives Chamber,
Canberra, January 2, 1992

Diary, January 9, the day after taking ill during a state dinner: "I remember breaking out in a cold sweat, water just pouring out of me, and then the next thing I knew, literally, I was on the floor. I woke up, and I had this euphoric feeling. . . . I realized I was lying flat on the floor, having thrown up all over Miyazawa . . ."

I understand that some of the journalists have had the flu. And people in our country have had it, so why isn't the President entitled to twenty-four hours? [Laughter]

The President's news conference with Prime Minister
Kiichi Miyazawa of Japan, Akasaka Palace, Tokyo,
January 9, 1992

Response when asked if it's hard to be a grandparent and President at the same time . . .

Barbara and I try very hard to be good grandparents, and we stay in touch. And she's on the phone a lot. But I think you can do both. I think you can keep your family together. Of course, I salute

Barbara Bush for what she does . . . encouraging them all the time. But you know you asked a very good question because there's a lot of times when you just wish you could do what everybody else does. But I wouldn't trade it because I've got a job to do, got a mission to fulfill, and I'm going to finish that. But then, I don't fear the future because after all that, I think we'll be better grandparents.

Remarks and a question-and-answer session
at Hollis/Brookline High School, Hollis, New Hampshire,
February 16, 1992

You may have read my tax returns, and you can tell who the breadwinner is in that family. The dog made five times as much as the President of the United States.

Remarks and a question-and-answer session
with the Mount Paran Christian School community in
the school gymnasium, Marietta, Georgia, May 27, 1992

Explaining life in the White House to students . . .

Q. What is your life like?
The President. . . . The same as—this may be difficult for you to understand—pretty much the same as what a lot of people are. We've got five kids, and we've got twelve grandchildren, one of them—how old are you? Nine. I'm not sure we've got a nine-year-old; I think we do. [Laughter]

I get a kick when they come to the White House. Have you seen pictures of the White House? The President has to work there all the time. Sometimes when it's quiet . . . my grandchildren—a couple of them—will come running in, or . . . one of my dogs, Millie or Ranger, will come in there. And you feel just like I did when I was a kid with the family, you know.

Some of it's personal like that, and then some of it is very serious, when world leaders and presidents and kings and mayors and governors come to see you. But it's not that different in how we actually live our lives with Barbara and I over there in the White House. We try to stay in touch a little and try to keep our family going, get on the phone and call the kids that live in Texas and Florida and all around the country. Even though it's very formal and complicated at times, you still have a feeling these are the values.

You know, when things are tough—my mother told me when I was a little guy, younger than you, "Do your best. Try your hardest." That advice is good for a kid, and it's good for the President of the United States.

Remarks and question-and-answer session with the Sheriff's Youth Athletic League at the Lynwood Youth Athletic Center, Los Angeles, California, May 29, 1992

Response when asked about Democratic opposition research investigating the Bush family for improper personal financial relationships . . .

I think they're going to drill a dry hole on that one because I have really tried my very, very best to keep the public trust. I told these friends who are in the Congress, I think I view as part of my responsibility keeping the public trust, the decency and the honor of the presidency.

Remarks at a meeting with the House Republican Conference on health care and an exchange with reporters, U.S. Capitol House Chamber, July 2, 1992

My granddad knew how America was blessed . . . he lived here in Columbus. His company, Buckeye Steel, made couplings for the railroads. My father was born here in Columbus, Ohio. He . . . lived over on East Broad Street for a while. He knew how this city loved the American spirit, how you lived it from one generation to the next.

Remarks on beginning a whistle-stop tour at the Old Mound Freight Yard, Columbus, Ohio, September 26, 1992

I remember something my dad told me. I was eighteen years old, going to Penn Station to go into the navy. He said, "Write your mother," which I faithfully did. He said, "Serve your country." My father was a honor, duty, and country man. And he said, "Tell the truth." And I've tried to do that in public life, all through it. That has said something about character.

Presidential debate at University of Richmond Robins Center,
Richmond, Virginia, October 15, 1992

A lighter moment from the Richmond debate, when asked when blacks and women candidates would be elected President . . .

I think if Barbara Bush were running this year, she'd be elected. [Laughter] But it's too late.

Presidential debate at University of Richmond Robins Center,
Richmond, Virginia, October 15, 1992

When I read stories impugning the honor and integrity of my sons, forget it. I get very moved by it because they're honest and they put up with a lot for their dad. They take a lot. They can dish it out, too. More so than I, my son—don't cross George down there, Texas Rangers man—he's a little "feisty" we call it.

Interview on CNN's Larry King Live,
Racine, Wisconsin, October 30, 1992

A week after Election Day, giving a family update . . .

Now she's [Barbara Bush] getting ready to shift gears. And my advice to those of you who are her friends, and I think you all are: give her a wide berth, which is what I'm trying to do around the White House there, because she's a bundle of energy, shifting gears from the present into the future. That's the way it ought to be.

Don't worry about the Bushes. We are looking ahead now. I didn't think we would about a week ago today, but we're doing it.

And we'll count our blessings when we get back to Houston on January 20 for all the friends who have supported us so much.

Remarks at a Senate Republican Leadership dinner honoring
the President, Union Station East Hall, November 10, 1992

FAMILY VALUES

On April 29, riots broke in Los Angeles after police officers who had been accused of and videotaped beating motorist Rodney King were acquitted by a jury. President Bush visited the area several different times in the aftermath . . .

To struggle against hard times, to overcome the devastation of poverty, of racism, or of riots, we need our family. We need our own family. We need our church family. And we must find ways to strengthen America as a family. Back to what the cardinal [Bishop Robert McMurray] said, we are embarrassed by interracial violence and prejudice. We're ashamed. We should take nothing but sorrow out of all that and do our level best to see that it's eliminated from the American Dream. A family that respects the law, a family that can lift others up.

Remarks at Mount Zion Missionary Baptist Church
in Los Angeles, California, May 7, 1992

I mentioned what government can do, but again, government cannot solve all the problems. We may be able to make good laws, but it's never been able to make men good. That doesn't come from Big Brother. It comes from your family. It comes from your mother and father. And I'm talking about the moral sense that must guide us all. In the simplest terms, I am talking about knowing what's wrong and doing what's right.

Remarks at a Bush-Quayle fund-raising luncheon
at the Duquesne University Union Building,
Pittsburgh, Pennsylvania, May 15, 1992

Diary, May 17: "In my speech at Notre Dame today, I talked about family values . . ."

It is in families that children learn the keys to personal economic success and self-discipline and personal responsibility. It is in families that children learn that moral restraint gives us true freedom. It is from their families that they learn honesty and self-respect and compassion and self-confidence.

Remarks at the University of Notre Dame commencement ceremony,
Joyce Athletic and Convocation Center, South Bend, Indiana,
May 17, 1992

On May 19, at the Commonwealth Club of San Francisco, Vice President Dan Quayle gave his famous *Murphy Brown* speech—also stressing the theme of family values. It set off a political firestorm. Here, the President addresses the issue . . .

The President. All right, this is the last *Murphy Brown* question.
Q. Maybe.
The President. This is the last *Murphy Brown* answer, put it that way. [Laughter]
   No, I believe that children should have the benefit of being born into families where the mother and a father will give them love and care and attention all their lives. I spoke on this family point in Notre Dame the other day. I've talked to Barbara about it a lot, and we both feel strongly that that is the best environment in which to raise kids. It's not always possible, but that's the best environment. I think it results in giving a kid the best shot at the American Dream, incidentally. . . . One of the things that concerns me deeply is the fact that there are an awful lot of broken families.

The President's news conference with Prime Minister
Brian Mulroney of Canada, White House South Lawn,
May 20, 1992

Commenting again on the L.A. riots . . .

I know I'm not particularly articulate on this, but I really feel strongly when we talk about family that anything you do with your kids in the outdoors does nothing but strengthen the relationship between parents and the kids. . . . Those kids that were coming out of that city in South Central, in L.A., they'd been denied that. And here, even though it wasn't with their parents, they were beginning to get that feeling of comradeship and of enjoyment and of . . . conversation, if you will, that strengthens . . . the American family. So it's hard to describe, but I feel it so strongly.

Remarks and a question-and-answer session
with outdoor groups at Red Butte Gardens,
Salt Lake City, Utah, July 18, 1992

I happen to believe that the family is still the fabric of society. And when a little kid is born to a thirteen-year-old mother, some way we've got to find a way to have that kid loved by the parent and teach values and respect. And it isn't happening.

Question-and-answer session at the Ohio Historical Society,
Columbus, Ohio, October 28, 1992

"GOD'S THERAPY"

I once asked one of my grandkids how he felt about prayer. And he said, "Just try getting through a math test without it."

Remarks at the annual convention
of the National Religious Broadcasters,
Sheraton Washington Hotel, January 27, 1992

We can say confidently, Americans won the Cold War. We won it by standing up for what's right. Tonight our children and grandchildren—and I take great joy in this—tonight our children and grandchildren will go to their beds untroubled by the fears of nuclear holocaust that haunted two generations of Americans. In our prayers we asked for God's help. I know our family did, and I expect all of you did. We asked for God's help. And now in this shining outcome, in this magnificent triumph of good over evil, we should thank God. We should give thanks.

By the way, I notice from your Washington newsletter that recently even *Time* magazine called the old Soviet Union an evil empire. Now they tell us. [Laughter]

Remarks to the National Association of Evangelicals at the Hyatt Regency O'Hare Hotel, Chicago, Illinois, March 3, 1992

I've been President for three and a half years now. More than ever, I believe with all my heart that one cannot be President of our great country without a belief in God, without the truth that comes on one's knees. For me, prayer has always been important but quite personal. You know us Episcopalians. [Laughter] And yet, it has sustained me at every point of my life: as a boy, when religious reading was part of our home life; as a teenager, when I memorized the Navy Hymn. Or how, forty-eight years ago, aboard the submarine *Finback* after being shot down in the war, I went up topside one night on the deck, on the conning tower, and stood watch and looked out at the dark. The sky was clear. The stars were brilliant like a blizzard of fireflies in the night. There was a calm inner peace. Halfway around the world in the war zone, there was a calm inner peace: God's therapy.

Remarks at a prayer breakfast, University of Houston, August 20, 1992

FRIENDS

Fresh from parting the Red Sea yet again on TV last night— [laughter]—our old friend Charlton Heston.

Remarks on signing the executive order on employee rights concerning union dues, Rose Garden, April 13, 1992

Arnold Palmer . . .

I had the pleasure of flying down here today from Pittsburgh with Winnie Palmer, and she said, "Well, I'm glad Arnold is not with us. He'd be trying to fly Air Force One."
*Remarks at a benefit for the United Negro College Fund
at the Greenspoint Club, Houston, Texas,
May 15, 1992*

Responding to questions about Ross Perot's suspension of his presidential candidacy . . .

I don't like to lose friends over politics. I never have. I've always turned the other cheek, and I've always tried to make new friends. And I don't think that's bad. I think that's a sign of character, not a sign of weakness.
*The President's news conference at the U.S. Air Force Seismic
Research Facility, Pinedale, Wyoming,
July 16, 1992*

This exchange touches on the persistent rumors throughout the summer of 1992 that Secretary of State Baker—who had helped run the 1976 Ford-Dole campaign, the 1980 Reagan-Bush campaign, and the 1988 Bush-Quayle effort—would leave Foggy Bottom to save the President's 1992 reelection drive. It also touches on a friendship unique in history, two longtime friends from Houston who helped change the world . . .

Q. Mr. President, you said you hadn't discussed with Secretary Baker the possibility of him coming over to your campaign.
The President. That's true.
Q. What besides fishing have you been talking to him about up to—
The President. Family. I had a son up here. The joy of fishing in a river in Wyoming, I'll tell you, it's hard to compare with any-

thing. And he has his son Jamie up here, and Susan Baker is here. Barbara's not here. She catches headaches at altitude, and so she didn't come. But we just fished, talking about fishing.

You know, when you're out in a river with a friend, it doesn't matter much what you talk about. And I've concluded, not just because of my own record, it doesn't matter whether you catch any fish or not. You're there, and you're in the outdoors, and you're away from all the hubbub of, I think, one of the ugliest political years I've ever seen. And I've been around the track a long time. You forget about your day-to-day cares. And it's been a total joy for me.

The President's news conference at the U.S. Air Force Seismic
Research Facility, Pinedale, Wyoming, July 16, 1992

Diary, November 10: "Bob Dole had called and asked me to come to a Senate Dinner. It's an annual event and the President goes with all the Republican Senators. . . . I dreaded going but then Bob made it fantastic. He choked up, he showed a warm side that many didn't feel he ever had. He was so generous in his comments and so thoughtful . . ."

It's well-known that he and I went head-to-head in tough primary days long ago. But the beautiful thing is—and I think . . . anyone that studies government can learn from all this. Here's a guy that took on this role of leader and working with a President with whom he had done combat in the past, but subsequently we became, again, fast friends. But he never put his own personal agenda ahead of the President, and that's the way it ought to work when you have the White House.

Remarks at a Senate Republican leadership dinner honoring
the President, Union Station East Hall,
November 10, 1992

"No Place like Texas"

I had many reasons for coming West, but the advice from one family friend tipped the balance. "What you need to do is head out to Texas," he told me. "That's the place for ambitious young people these days."

Now, this was just a few years, just a handful of years after World War II, what seems like a lifetime ago. My friend's advice was some of the best that I've ever had.

Remarks at the Southern Methodist University
commencement ceremony, Moody Coliseum, Dallas, Texas,
May 16, 1992

I am proud to be a Texan. Barbara and I raised our kids here. From 1948 on, we voted in every presidential election here. I coached Little League here, built my business here, worked in the party here. My presidential library will be here. My campaign started here. And when my work is over, I'll come back here. So it's great to be home. There is no place like Texas.

Remarks at the Texas State Republican Convention,
Dallas Convention Center, Dallas, Texas, June 20, 1992

I was not born in Texas, but in Texas . . . forty-four years ago, I came of age. The lessons that Barbara and I learned here are the lessons we have tried to live by. The friends that we made here and throughout our lives are the friends who are in this room, some from Texas, some elsewhere, every one of whom we owe a vote of gratitude to, the friends who have stood by us when times are great and when times are tough.

Remarks at the Republican National Committee Gala Luncheon
at the George R. Brown Convention Center, Houston,
August 19, 1992

Long before I was in the public sector, I worked for a living out in the oil fields of west Texas, built a company, and did what many here have in small or larger operations: I met a payroll. I took risks, and I made it work.

Remarks to the Chamber of Commerce at Warsaw Park Hall,
Ansonia, Connecticut, August 24, 1992

I learned this part in a very personal way thirty-five years ago when I started and headed a small drilling company. . . . But we sold our services in Japan, in Brunei, in the South Pacific, sold them over in the Middle East, sold them in Venezuela and Trinidad. And I learned something from that. I learned you don't have to be a big company to export.

Remarks to Findlay Machine and Tool employees
at Tall Timbers Industrial Park, Findlay, Ohio,
August 27, 1992

I remember when west Texas was dry. I remember picking the Lubbock tumbleweeds out of one of those evaporative air conditioners in our little house in Odessa. No more, I'll tell you. [Here's] one more reminiscence that some of you football fans, older ones, might remember. We had a touch football team in Midland. And we played against the Lubbock team made up of Glen Davis, Mel Kutnow, and Bobby Lane. Now, how do you like that for Lubbock excellence?

Remarks to Shallowater Co-op Gin Company employees
in Shallowater, Texas, September 2, 1992

Texas, that's where it all started for Barbara and me: forty-four years ago when we moved out to Texas . . . we voted in our first presidential election out there. Here in Houston, thirty years ago . . . I gave my very first speech on my own behalf. And tonight in Texas, I will give my last speech ever on my own behalf as a candidate for reelection as President of the United States. . . .

I got book learning back East, but I learned about life right here in Texas, first at Corpus Christi, where I got my navy wings—and yes, I am proud that I served my country in war—and then out west in the Permian Basin and later right here on the Gulf coast. . . .

I learned that the strength of our nation does not end up in the marble mausoleums along the Potomac but in the souls and hearts of the hardworking people in places like Tyler and Waco and Corpus and Houston.

Remarks at a rally at the Houston AstroArena,
Houston, Texas, November 2, 1992

THE VISION THING:
New Worlds Are Born

The future does not belong to the status quo.
Remarks to the Forum of the Americas,
Sheraton Washington Hotel, April 23, 1992

I will confess, there have been other greater speakers. But to me, real eloquence lies in action.
Remarks to the American Legislative Exchange Council
at the Broadmoor International Hotel,
Colorado Springs, Colorado, August 6, 1992

My friends, we stand today in the twilight of one millennium and the dawn of the next. Never before has mankind beheld such a view. Never before has our nation been pressured by such deep energies of change and growth reshaping America like the strong hands of a potter on wet clay.
Remarks to the community in Hamtramck, Michigan,
September 7, 1992

"TURN AN ENEMY INTO A FRIEND"

History teaches that peace is indivisible; political isolationism doesn't work.

Remarks to business and community leaders
at the World Congress Centre, Melbourne, Australia,
January 3, 1992

On the demise of the Soviet Union . . .

When citizens pulled down the hammer and sickle ten days ago and hauled up the new tricolor of freedom over the Kremlin, the Soviet Union ceased to exist, and the prospect of a new world opened before us. That act culminated a decade of liberation, a time in which we witnessed the death throes of totalitarianism and the triumph of systems of government devoted to individual liberty, democratic pluralism, free markets, and international engagement.

Remarks and a question-and-answer session
with the Singapore Lecture Group at the Westin Stamford Hotel,
January 4, 1992

Even as President, with the most fascinating possible vantage point, there were times when I was so busy managing progress and helping to lead change that I didn't always show the joy that was in my heart. But the biggest thing in the world that has happened in my life, in our lives, is this: by the grace of God, America won the Cold War.

Address before a joint session of Congress on the State of the Union,
U.S. Capitol House Chamber, January 28, 1992

With the passing of the Cold War, a new order has yet to take its place. The opportunities, tremendous; they're great. But so, too, are the dangers. And so, we stand at history's hinge point. A new world beckons while the ghost of history stands in the shadows. . . .

This is an article of the American creed: freedom is not the special preserve of one nation; it is the birthright of men and women everywhere. And we have always dreamed of the day democracy and freedom will triumph in every corner of the world, in every captive nation and closed society. And this may never happen in our lifetime, but it can happen now for the millions of people who for so long suffered under that totalitarian Soviet rule. . . .

Three times this century, America has been called on to help construct a lasting peace in Europe. Seventy-five years ago this month, the United States entered World War I to tip the balance against aggression. And yet, with the battle won, America withdrew across the ocean, and the "war to end all wars" produced a peace that did not last even a generation. Indeed, by the time I was born in 1924, the peace was already unraveling. Germany's economic chaos soon led to what, to fascist dictatorship. The seeds of another, more terrible war were sown.

And still, the isolationist impulse remained strong. Years later, as the Nazis began the march across the Continent, I can still remember the editorials here in the United States talking about "Europe's war," as if America could close itself off, as if we could isolate ourselves from the world beyond our shores. As a consequence, you know the answer, we fought the most costly war in the history of man, a war that claimed the lives of countless millions. At war's end, once again we saw the prospect of a new world on the horizon. But the great victory over fascism quickly gave way to the grim reality of a new Communist threat.

We are fortunate that our postwar leaders, Democrats and Republicans alike, did not forget the lessons of the past in building the peace of the next four decades. They shaped a coalition that kept America engaged, that kept the peace through the long twilight struggle against Soviet Communism. And they taught the lesson that we simply must heed today, that the noblest mission of the victor is to turn an enemy into a friend.

And now America faces a third opportunity to provide the kind of lasting peace that for so long eluded us. At this defining moment, I know where I stand. I stand for American engagement in support of a democratic peace, a peace that can secure for the next generation a world free from war, free from conflict.

After a half century of fear and mistrust, America, Russia, and the new nations of the former USSR must become partners in peace. After a half century of Cold War and harsh words, we must speak and act on common values. After a half century of armed and uneasy peace, we must move forward toward a new world of freedom, cooperation, reconciliation, and hope.

Remarks to the American Society of Newspaper Editors,
J. W. Marriott Hotel, April 9, 1992

It's astonishing to be here with the class of '92 as a graduate of the class of '42. I realize the world that I thought of as new, for you, well, it's history. But look now at the world you'll soon call your own, at the pace of change we've come to expect. Each day we see history played out in the headlines, literally. Old empires expire; new worlds are born. In the past six months alone, six months, we've seen the birth of eighteen new nations. Who knows how many there will be by the time you take your big geography final a few weeks from now.

But the challenges we face, the sheer complexity of our world, cannot obscure the basic values that guide this nation. Times change; but truths, fundamental truths, endure. I'm talking about the big issues that shape our world, about the values close to home. Everything I've tried to do and done to preserve and advance three precious legacies: strong families, good jobs, and a world at peace. These are my goals. They should be all of ours. Securing those legacies has been my mission as President, and it's going to be my mission today and every day as long as I'm President of the United States.

Remarks to the Lehigh Valley 2000 community,
Dieruff High School, Allentown, Pennsylvania,
April 16, 1992

Some say our victory in the Cold War allows us to pull back to our own water's edge. And I say, just as America's vigilance helped win that war, so a strong America can now help us win the peace.

Remarks on signing the proclamation commemorating
the fiftieth anniversary of World War II,
White House Roosevelt Room, June 4, 1992

Welcoming Russia's President Boris Yeltsin to the White House for the first U.S.-Russia Summit . . .

Today marks the beginning of a new era, a new kind of summit, not a meeting between two powers struggling for global supremacy but between two partners striving to build a democratic peace. From this summit we see a new horizon, a new world of peace and hope, a new world of cooperation and partnership between the American and Russian people. Our hope is that this partnership will end forever the old antagonisms that kept our people apart, that kept the world in confrontation and conflict.

Remarks at the arrival ceremony for President Boris Yeltsin
of Russia, White House South Lawn, June 16, 1992

Our work in the world did not end with our victory in the Cold War. Our task is to guard against the crises that haven't yet even caught fire, the wars that are waiting to happen, the threats that will come upon us with little or no warning.

Remarks to the American Legion National Convention
at the Sheraton Chicago Hotel, Chicago, Illinois, August 25, 1992

Securing democracy and securing the peace in the century ahead will be no simple task. Imperial Communism may have been vanquished, but that does not end the challenges of our age, challenges that must be overcome if we are finally to end the divisions between East and West, North and South, that fuel strife and strain and conflict and war. . . .

In the face of today's changes, with the loss of so much that was familiar and predictable, there is now a great temptation for people everywhere to turn inward and to build walls around themselves: walls against trade, walls against people, walls against ideas and investment, walls against anything that appears new and different. As the Berlin Wall fell, these walls, too, must fall. They must fall because we cannot separate our fate from that of others. Our peace is so interconnected, our security so intertwined, our prosperity so interdependent, that to turn inward and retreat from the world is to invite disaster and defeat.

Address to the UN General Assembly
at the UN General Assembly Hall, New York City,
September 21, 1992

———

Signing NAFTA to help foster a "zone of peace." It would fall to President Clinton to push this landmark agreement through Congress . . .

This year marks the five hundredth anniversary of a voyage of discovery to the New World. And let this also be a time of rediscovery for my country, the United States, of the importance of our own hemisphere. If we are to be equal to the challenges before us, we can build in the Americas the world's first completely democratic hemisphere. Just think about that. Think of the importance. Think of the significance. Think of the example for the rest of the world.

This hemisphere can be as well a zone of peace, where trade flows freely, prosperity is shared, the rule of law is respected, and the gifts of human knowledge are harnessed for all.

Remarks on signing the North American
Free Trade Agreement, Organization of American States,
December 17, 1992

"An Eagle, Not an Ostrich"

It's always been a hallmark of U.S. foreign policy, and I think of the heartbeat of this country, that if people are hurting—health reasons, famine, food reasons—that the United States is willing to help.

The President's news conference, White House Briefing Room,
January 22, 1992

We Americans don't hide from a good test of our abilities. We rise to the challenge. After all, our national bird is the eagle, not the ostrich. . . .

The glory of this century is America. And history will call this the American century because we fought the battle of freedom, and we won. And history will tell of a second American century when we led the world to new heights of achievement and liberty. This is our legacy. This is our challenge. And this is our destiny.

Remarks announcing the Bush-Quayle candidacies for reelection,
J. W. Marriott Hotel, February 12, 1992

I think the United States has a burden to bear. But we have worked effectively through multilateral organizations. The clearest example of that is what happened in the Gulf War. You see the United Nations trying to stay involved in the resolution of the Yugoslavian question. We have peacekeeping set up in Cambodia and other places that relieves some of the unilateral burden from the United States.

But we are the leaders, and we must continue to lead. We must continue to stay engaged. So, it isn't a clear-cut choice of either-or. For people that challenge our leadership around the world, they simply do not understand how the world looks to us for leadership.

The President's news conference, White House Briefing Room,
March 11, 1992

There is no distinction between how we fare abroad and how we live at home. Foreign and domestic policy are but two sides of the same coin. True, we will not be able to lead abroad if we are not strong and united at home. But it is no less true that we will be unable to build the society we seek here at home in a world where military and economic warfare is the norm.

Remarks at the Richard Nixon Dinner, Four Seasons Hotel,
March 11, 1992

If we are to remain the most hopeful and vibrant nation on earth, we must allow our diversity to bring us together, not drive us apart.

Address to the nation from the Oval Office on the civil disturbances
in Los Angeles, California, May 1, 1992

A great lesson of our age is that trade and enterprise can build jobs and certainly can preserve freedom.

Remarks at the Cinco de Mayo celebration,
Mexican Cultural Institute, May 5, 1992

Guaranteeing a hopeful future for the children of our cities is about a lot more than rebuilding burned-out buildings. It's about building a new American community.

Radio address to the nation from the Oval Office
on the President's visit to Los Angeles, California,
May 9, 1992

On countless small occasions, each of us is called to open our hearts; each of us is called to lead, to take responsibility, to show the power of faith in action. I have spoken today of our economic future, about free enterprise, personal liberty. But the freedoms we cherish mean nothing unless they're infused with the old virtues, the time-honored values: honor, honesty, thrift, faith, self-discipline, service to others.

I do not pretend to know the shape of the next century. The genius of a free people defies prediction. Certainly Barbara and I, when we loaded up that Studebaker for the trip to Odessa so long ago, could never have imagined the technological marvels that our grandchildren now take for granted, fax machines and VCRs, for example, not to mention the most amazing invention of 1992, the supermarket scanner. [Laughter] But I do know this: the next century will be your century. If you believe in freedom and if you hold fast to your values and if you remain faithful to our role in the world, it is sure to be yet another American century.

Remarks at the Southern Methodist University
commencement ceremony, Moody Coliseum, Dallas, Texas,
May 16, 1992

The American people have just completed the greatest mission in the lifetime of our country: the triumph of democratic capitalism over imperial Communism. Today, this year, for the first time since December of 1941, the United States is not engaged in a war, hot or cold. Throughout history, at the close of prolonged and costly wars, victors have confronted the problem of securing a new basis for peace and prosperity. The American people recognize that we stand at such a watershed.

We sense the epic changes at work in the world and in the economy, the uneasiness that stirs the democracies who served as our partners in the long struggle. We feel the uneasiness in our own homes, our own communities, and we see the difficulties of our neighbors and friends who have felt the change most directly. We know that while we face an era of great opportunity, we face great risks as well if we fail to make the right choices, if we fail to engage this new world wisely.

But America has always possessed unique powers, and foremost among them is the power of regeneration, to transform uncertainty into opportunity. Only in America do we have the people, the talents, the principles and ideals to fully embrace the world that opens before us.

Remarks and a question-and-answer session at Cobo Hall,
with the Economic Club of Detroit, Michigan,
September 10, 1992

The third and final time President Bush would commit American forces into harm's way, this time to end the starvation in Somalia . . .

The people of Somalia, especially the children of Somalia, need our help. We're able to ease their suffering. We must help them live. We must give them hope. America must act.

In taking this action, I want to emphasize that I understand that the United States alone cannot right the world's wrongs. But we also know that some crises in the world cannot be resolved without American involvement, that American action is often necessary as a catalyst for broader involvement of the community of nations. Only the United States has the global reach to place a large security force on the ground in such a distant place quickly and efficiently and thus save thousands of innocents from death. . . .

To the people of Somalia I promise this: We do not plan to dictate political outcomes. We respect your sovereignty and independence. Based on my conversations with other coalition leaders, I can state with confidence: We come to your country for one reason only, to enable the starving to be fed.

Address to the nation on the situation in Somalia,
Oval Office, December 4, 1992

Two final postelection thoughts on leadership: first at Texas A&M, the future site of his presidential library . . .

The challenge ahead, then, is as great as the one we faced at the end of the last great war. But the opportunity is vastly greater. Success will require American vision and resolve, an America secure in its military, moral, and economic strength. Success will require unity of purpose: a commitment on the part of all our people to the proposition that our nation's destiny lies in the hope of a better world, a new world made better, with our friends and allies, again by American leadership.

History is summoning us once again to lead. Proud of its past, America must once again look forward. And we must live up to the greatness of our forefathers' ideals and in doing so secure our grandchildren's futures. And that is the cause that much of my public life has been dedicated to serving.

Remarks at G. Rollie White Coliseum, Texas A&M University,
College Station, Texas, December 15, 1992

And second, at West Point . . .

Leadership, well, it takes many forms. It can be political or diplomatic. It can be economic or military. It can be moral or spiritual leadership. Leadership can take on any one of these forms, or it can be a combination of them.

Leadership should not be confused with either unilateralism or universalism. We need not respond by ourselves to each and every outrage of violence. The fact that America can act does not mean that it must. A nation's sense of idealism need not be at odds with its interests, not does principle displace prudence.

No, the United States should not seek to be the world's policeman. There is no support abroad or at home for us to play this role, nor should there be. We would exhaust ourselves in the process, wasting precious resources needed to address those problems at home and abroad that we cannot afford to ignore.

But in the wake of the Cold War, in a world where we are the only remaining superpower, it is the role of the United States to marshal its moral and material resources to promote a democratic peace. It is our responsibility, it is our opportunity, to lead. There is no one else.

Leadership cannot be simply asserted or demanded. It must

be demonstrated. Leadership requires formulating worthy goals, persuading others of their virtue, and contributing one's share of the common effort and then some. Leadership takes time. It takes patience. It takes work.

Remarks at Washington Mess Hall, U.S. Military Academy,
West Point, New York, January 5, 1993

"TESTED BY FIRE"

So often politicians do the easy things, the popular things. But it's the tough things that tell you about character and honor and leadership. Anyone can demagogue, but Presidents must make decisions. . . .

The presidency is not a popularity contest. I think you elect a President to say what America needs to hear, even when it's not what people want to hear. In the campaign you hear all kinds of quick fixes, all kinds of political rhetoric, but a President must make decisions and lead.

Remarks to the Home Builders Association of Greater Columbia
at the South Carolina State Fair Grounds, Columbia,
South Carolina, March 5, 1992

The pros and cons of the 1990 budget agreement . . .

It simply did not do what I thought, I hoped, it would do: control this, get this economy moving. There were some good things about it. So I can't say, shouldn't say, total mistake. But the spending caps were good. . . . Keeping the government going as opposed to shutting down for whatever number of days it would have taken, that was good. But when you have to weigh a decision in retrospect—have the benefit of hindsight—I think we can all agree that it has drawn a lot of fire.

The President's news conference, White House Briefing Room,
March 11, 1992

For more than forty-five years, the highest responsibility of nine American presidents, Democrats and Republicans, was to wage and win the Cold War. It was my privilege to work with Ronald Reagan on these broad programs and now to lead the American people in winning the peace by embracing the people so recently freed from tyranny to welcome them into the community of democratic nations.

The President's news conference on aid to the states
of the former Soviet Union, White House Briefing Room,
April 1, 1992

One of the great blessings of the presidency, obviously, is to live within the walls of this house, to roam its hallways, to absorb its history, and to be reminded at every turn of the noble men who have lived here and of their families. But a President can never, obviously, be more than a caretaker or a tenant in this house, for the White House belongs, as it has for two hundred years, to every American.

Remarks at the unveiling ceremony for the White House
commemorative stamp, Rose Garden, April 23, 1992

On the riots in Los Angeles . . .

As President, I pledge to this nation I will do what I can to heal the wounds. I will see that the law's enforced. . . . Society deserves a sense of order. But I will do my level best to heal the wounds and to bring people together in the aftermath of the ugliness that we witnessed last night. A President should do no less.

Remarks at a Bush-Quayle fund-raising dinner
at the Ohio State Fairgrounds Lausche Building, Columbus, Ohio,
April 30, 1992

Q. Do you think it's fun being President when people give you a hard time? [Laughter]

The President. That's a good question. . . . It's fun to be President. It's a challenge to be President. It's a great big job, and you kind of feel, well, I'm going to try to help people, or I'm going to try and keep the world at peace. And you meet interesting people. . . .

But I'll tell you this about the part that you asked about, about when people give you a hard time. You've got to learn something. . . . I learned this lesson from being President: When you lose something in sports, you can't get all upset about it. If somebody criticizes you because you do something that they don't like something, you just try to do better. You can't let it get you down. So there are easy times, and there are difficult times. It's in your life, and it's in my life as President of the United States.

So what I think I'd say is, I like my job, and I'm working hard in my job. And I'm doing my best in my job. But if you get a little criticism, you get a little grief out there, don't let it get you down. Just do better. Just do better.

Remarks and question-and-answer session with the Sheriff's Youth
Athletic League at the Lynwood Youth Athletic Center,
Los Angeles, California, May 29, 1992

The President's responsibilities are multifaceted. One of them is the national security of the United States. It is in this field that the President really has primacy, and I'm not going to neglect that. I'm not going to neglect it because of political criticism.

Remarks and question-and answer session
at the Simpson Vineyards with the agricultural community
in Fresno, California, May 30, 1992

The Bushes consider Larry King a good friend, but call-in shows were never President Bush's favorite format. Here, someone suggests it for the White House . . .

We have a comments line, but I just have a certain respect for the office, and I don't want to turn it into a call-in show place. I mean, I just think that I owe the people a certain respect for the office of the presidency.

But this isn't the first time we've done this [Q&A session]. As a matter of fact, we did it not too far away in the Valley, right here in California. I've been doing it. I did it up in the primaries up in New Hampshire, and I've been doing it ever since I ran for office.

It's a good thing to do, and you do learn. I learn from the questions and learn the anxieties of people. So we're going to keep on doing it. But I'm glad that you think that it makes some sense. I'll be honest with you, though. I think in a campaign year you've got to draw the line somewhere. I am not going to be out there, kind of being a teenybopper at sixty-eight; I just can't do it. [Laughter]

Question-and-answer session with employees of Evergreen Oil
at the Evergreen Environmental Services Oil Refinery,
Newark, California, June 18, 1992

By our willingness to stand up for freedom and stand against aggression and fight for what's right, we changed the world. And our mission for the next four years is to shape our new world, not just abroad but right here at home. It's a big job to set the course for the next forty years, and it means solving big problems with a level head, with tolerance and good judgment. Being President is a demanding job, and a President must be temperamentally suited for the job. I have been tested by fire. And I am the right man for that job. . . .

Since becoming your President, I have been to all fifty states in the country. I have felt the heartbeat of America. I felt it up close—farmers and ranchers and cities and city kids and teachers and truck drivers.

Remarks at the Texas State Republican Convention,
Dallas Convention Center, Dallas, Texas, June 20, 1992

I've found sometimes in this job as President, you have to do something that's unpopular. The person that's there must have a steady hand, must have the proper temperament, must have an experienced eye, and must have some vision, some knowledge of the waters ahead. The American people know that there's a flip side to change, and that is called trust.

Remarks at the College Republican Convention,
Omni Shoreham Hotel, June 25, 1992

Let me tell you a little what it's like to be President. In the Oval Office, you can't predict what kind of crisis is going to come up. You have to make tough calls. You can't be on one hand this way and one hand another. You can't take different positions on these difficult issues.

Then you need a philosophical—I'd call it a philosophical underpinning; mine for foreign affairs is democracy and freedom. Look at the dramatic changes around the world. The Cold War is over. The Soviet Union is no more, and we're working with a democratic country. Poland, Hungary, Czechoslovakia, and the Baltics are free. Take a look at the Middle East. We had to stand up against a tyrant. The United States came together as we haven't in many, many years. We kicked this man out of Kuwait. In the process, as a result of that will and that decision and that toughness, we now have ancient enemies talking peace in the Middle East. Nobody would have dreamed it possible.

I think the biggest dividend of making these tough calls is the fact that we are less afraid of nuclear war. Every parent out there has much less worry that their kids are going to be faced with nuclear holocaust. All this is good.

On the domestic side, what we must do is have change that empowers people, not change for the sake of change, tax and spend. We don't need to do that anymore. What we need to do is empower people. We need to invest and save. We need to do better in education. We need to do better in job retraining. We need to expand our exports, and they're going very, very well indeed. We need to strengthen the American family.

I hope as President that I've earned your trust. I've admitted it when I make a mistake, but then I go on and help try to solve the problems. I hope I've earned your trust, because a lot of being President is about trust and character.

Presidential debate at Washington University Field House,
St. Louis, Missouri, October 11, 1992

I am judged every day on my character. Every President must be judged on that.

Question-and-answer session at WSB-TV Studios,
Atlanta, Georgia, October 20, 1992

You cannot separate the leadership of the President from the character of the presidency.

Remarks at a rally at Veterans Memorial Park,
Ridgewood, New Jersey, October 22, 1992

Response when asked in the closing days of the campaign if he would personally lead the effort to pay down the national debt . . .

I've learned something: you don't blame somebody if it goes wrong, you take the blame as President. Once in a while you get a little credit, that's fine, as President. But I'm the captain of that ship. I'm the President of the United States, and I make the decisions. . . .

A foremost responsibility of the President is the national security of this country. And when the history of my presidency is written, hopefully five years from now, we'll have a library and everybody will go in there, and they'll see how my time was spent. My time, much more of it, has been spent on domestic matters. The problem is, and we keep getting the same question, I'm having to fight with a highly partisan Congress.

Question-and-answer session at the Ohio Historical Society,
Columbus, Ohio, October 28, 1992

Any President has several functions. He speaks for and to the nation. He must faithfully execute the law. And he must lead. But no function, none of the President's hats, in my view, is more important than his role as commander in chief. For it is as commander in chief that the President confronts and makes decisions that one way or another affect the lives of everyone in this country as well as many others around the world.

Remarks at the Washington Mess Hall, U.S. Military Academy, West Point, New York, January 5, 1993

LEGACY OF SERVICE:
Making a New American Destiny

Let me challenge all of you to find a place to serve in some capacity, definitely as models but also as mentors. Remember each of us has a contribution that only we can make. And let me remind you as you assume the mantles of tomorrow's leadership that children tend to shape their dreams in the images that they have seen. Show how a good education prepares one for a full, productive life. Show what it means to be a person of strong principle and integrity. Demonstrate how concerned individuals, by working in partnership, can transform our communities and nation.

Remarks at the University of Notre Dame commencement ceremony, Joyce Athletic and Convocation Center, South Bend, Indiana, May 17, 1992

"I WANT TO HELP"

We can only change things if we work in common purpose. We must call a cease-fire in the war of words that too often consumes us. Casting blame brings no solutions, nor will questioning each other's motives. We have got to focus every ounce of our energy to turn back this assault upon the American family and act as one nation to defend and strengthen it. As public servants, we must never forget that the best department of HHS, of health and human services, is, indeed, the family. In restoring the family, we restore to future generations the values, the sense of right and wrong, the will and confidence to succeed that only a family can provide a child. And in doing this, we will reinvigorate our cities and our communities as well.

Today, with family as the center, I've highlighted the role of government, both positive and negative, because we're men and women of government. But let's never forget the work of private Americans dedicating themselves to the voluntary service of others, who create an environment where families can flourish. Each is a Point of Light, offering service with no thought of reward, though the reward will be reaped by every single American.

And let me be very clear. When I talk about Points of Light, they are not a substitute for the good that government can do, but it's more this: we will simply not solve our most pressing problems without the dedication of those Points of Light, of those volunteers. And I urge all of you, when you return to your cities, to do all in your power to encourage these caring men and women, to make yours a community of light.

Remarks to the National League of Cities,
Washington Hilton Hotel, March 9, 1992

For all the good that government can do—and it can do some good—to solve our country's social problems, we need people. We need every individual to respond to the problems right around them. And when each American is no longer willing to accept that someone on their street or someone in their town is homeless or jobless or friendless, then that's when we will truly renew America, when everybody understands that they're going to help their neighbor.

Remarks at the Points of Light Awards Ceremony,
White House East Room, May 1, 1992

In a society that can sometimes be cold and impersonal, bring warmth and welcome. In a fragmented society, be a force for healing. In a society cut off from moral and spiritual roots, cultivate grace and truth. In the face of the uncertainties of the future, affirm your purpose and realize your promise. Together, we can lift our nation's spirit. Together we can give our material, political, and economic accomplishments a larger, more noble purpose, to build God's kingdom here on earth.

Remarks at the University of Notre Dame
commencement ceremony, Joyce Athletic and Convocation Center,
South Bend, Indiana, May 17, 1992

Foreshadowing how President Bush and his wife would spend part of their "retirement" years . . .

Government can certainly make good laws; it can't make men good. It can ban unfair acts; it can't banish unkind thoughts. And so it's up to each of us to reach out to those Americans disabled by ignorance or handicapped by prejudice and teach them a better way. Each American shares a responsibility for a kinder, gentler America, to follow the example that so many of you in this room have led with your lives.

I'm not sure I know exactly what I'll be doing a few months from now, but I want to say this: I want to stay involved. I want to help. I'll be a private citizen, not sitting at the head table, out of the government limelight, but I want to help. I want to stay involved in this kind of important work.

Remarks at a disability community tribute to the President,
Capitol Hilton, January 12, 1993

Barbara and I will soon be making our way back to Texas, but I'd like to leave you with one thought: If I could leave but one legacy to this country, it would not be found in policy papers or even in treaties signed or even wars won; it would be a return to the moral compass that must guide America through the next century, the changeless values that can and must guide change. And I'm talking about a respect for goodness that made this country great, a rekindling of that light lit from within to reveal America as it truly is, a country with strong families, a country of a million Points of Light.

Remarks at a celebration of the Points
of Light, White House East Room,
January 14, 1993

"Public Trust"

In '64, I ran with a spectacular lack of success for the United States Senate. In 1966, I started off to run for the Congress in Houston, Harris County. And it was then Richard Nixon, former Vice President, President-to-be, who came down there to kick off my little campaign. And I thought I was right on top of the world. And what he did in endorsing me and supporting me and many others like me that year resulted in our picking up forty-nine seats, I think it was, in the Congress and propelling me into a life that has been full and fascinating.

Remarks at the Richard Nixon Dinner, Four Seasons Hotel,
March 11, 1992

I know there are some who want to see a different future, people who want to sound retreat, run away from new realities, seek refuge in a dreamworld of economic isolationism or protectionism. Those voices have nothing to say to the nation. There is no turning back. There is no hiding from the new reality. We have no choice but to compete. The new reality of our new world economy is simply this: to succeed economically abroad, we must lead economically at home.

If we want to make a new American destiny our own, we've got to bridge the gap between the American people and the government that's meant to serve it. I know there's discontent. Travel around the country; you can't help but feel it, a deepening cynicism about the way things work or fail to work in Washington, a doubt about one person's ability to change, really change the system. To them, government has grown more distant. Too often, the government we get is not accountable. It is not effective. It is not efficient. And regrettably, it's not compassionate.

It's not that people are apathetic. It's that people are angry with government. Many of you recycle empty cans and plastic bottles because, when it comes to the environment, you believe that one individual's actions can make a difference. But when it comes to self-government, cynicism kicks in, and too many people have come to doubt the power of a single vote.

This didn't happen just overnight. It's the legacy of a theory of government grown too used to promising what government will do for the people. And this theory fails to see that people don't want government to make their decisions for them; they want government that gives them the freedom to choose. And they want government that spends within its means in the way families do. And they want welfare programs that provide opportunity, not the dead-end street of dependency. And they want to be free to choose the school that is best for their children—public, private, or religious.

And that message is getting through. Because in spite of the cynicism, we see positive signs, a new ethic of responsibility alive in America. The days of the no-fault lifestyle are coming to an end. We see it all around us: individuals taking responsibility, individuals taking action. In their private lives, people know actions have consequences. And what they want from government are policies and programs that hold people responsible for their actions. And that government is responsible to the people. And if you think about it, that's nothing more than a working definition of the word *democracy.*

We've got to bring the ethic of responsibility back into government. And when we do, we'll see the sense of public trust return to politics. And we'll see a government that reflects the real values of this great nation, proud, confident, caring, and strong. That's my mission as President. It's our challenge as a nation. And the way we do it is through reform.

Remarks at the Florida International University
commencement ceremony, Miami Beach Convention Center,
Miami Beach, Florida, April 27, 1992

I've been in politics a long time. I figured it out the other day because this one actually has some political significance: half my adult life has been in public life and half of it in the private sector. I think that's a pretty good mix, so you don't lose track of what the fundamental problems are in this country or how to go about solving them.

Remarks at Bush-Quayle headquarters, Washington, D.C.,
April 28, 1992

The federal government cannot teach values, but it can create an environment where they take root and grow.

Remarks to Town Hall of California, Biltmore Hotel "Bowl,"
Los Angeles, May 29, 1992

I think the two-party system has really given us the most stable political system in the world. And yes, we're going through an unusual period. But the two-party system has provided us fantastic historical stability. You look around the world and compare this system with any other democratic system. . . . I'm sure the Brits take great pride in their parliamentary system, but I think our two-party system has provided us with the stability that heretofore we've simply taken for granted.

The President's news conference, White House East Room,
June 4, 1992

Referring to the pardon of six former government officials for their conduct related to the Iran-contra matter . . .

Q. Mr. President, on the Christmas Eve pardons, does it give the appearance that government officials are above the law?

The President. No, it should not give any such appearance. Nobody is above the law. I believe that when people break the law, that's a bad thing. I've read some stupid commentary to the contrary. And of course, I feel that way. But the Constitution is quite clear on the powers of the President. And sometimes a President has to make a very difficult call, and that's what I've done.

But I'm glad you asked it, because I've read some rather frivolous reporting that I don't care about the law. I pride myself on twenty-five or more years of public service, of serving honorably, decently, and with my integrity intact. And certainly I wouldn't feel that way if I had a lack of respect for the law. And I don't think there is one single thing in my career that could lead anybody to look at my record and make a statement of that nature. So thank you for giving me the opportunity to clear that up.

Remarks on START II and the situation in Somalia
and an exchange with reporters, Rose Garden,
December 30, 1992

BROTHERS IN ARMS

Landing here in Reno this afternoon and being greeted by our very able lieutenant governor, Sue Wagner . . . I had an incredible treat. I was met by a Nevadan, a guy from Carson City named J. C. Crume, who has joined me here at the convention today. I met him—this is a little history—fifty years ago, 1942. I was eighteen years old. He was my first flight instructor at the naval air station there in Minneapolis, Minnesota. He took this scared eighteen-year-old kid and put me behind the stick of a navy plane. And

J.C.'s hair looked a little gray, but he told me that it wasn't age. It's the lingering effect of the terror he felt fifty years ago with this young kid sitting in the backseat. [Laughter]

But more seriously, I did learn something from him and from my other soul mates and comrades in arms in the navy. I learned about teamwork, and I learned about the importance of sticking together from Mr. Crume and all the other guys in the navy. I learned to depend on my wingman for friendship, for support, and even for survival.

As you know, some of you may know this history, but after I left basic training, J.C.'s great instruction, I was assigned to the Pacific. One day, my plane was shot down . . . and I parachuted into the water. When I was swimming in the middle of the Pacific, one of my wingmen pointed me to a life raft that had fallen from the plane, while another wingman then helped keep the enemy at bay. They [Japanese] put boats out from this island of Chi Chi Jima.

After the navy, I didn't wear my uniform every day, but believe me, friends have been part of every good fortune in my life.

Remarks to the Disabled American Veterans National Convention
at the Reno Hilton Hotel Goldwyn Ballroom, Reno,
Nevada, August 5, 1992

We honor the dead, not merely for their sake, but for our own sake as well. In commemoration and remembrance, we learn again that freedom, in the deepest sense, always hangs in the balance; that we earn it day by day in hot wars and cold; that its price, as Jefferson said, is eternal vigilance, an endlessly renewed dedication to keeping our great country strong, our defenses second to none, our leadership unquestioned and unchallenged.

Remarks at a ceremony at the Marine Corps War Memorial,
Arlington, Virginia commemorating the fiftieth anniversary
of the landing on Guadalcanal, August 7, 1992

This is a special place for me. I mention it because this is where I took that final flight training before I went overseas, at the old naval air station here. I was just a kid. I was nineteen at the time. Maybe that's why I've never forgotten the lessons that military service teaches. It shaped my character, and I hope that service to country has made me a better commander in chief, because I respect our military and the veterans.

Remarks to the community at Hollywood International Airport,
Fort Lauderdale, Florida, October 3, 1992

You are beginning your service to country, and I am nearing the end of mine. Exactly half a century ago, in June of 1942, as General [Howard] Graves [superintendent of the academy] mentioned, we were at war, and I was graduating from school. The speaker that day at Andover was the then secretary of war, Henry Stimson. And his message was one of public service, but with a twist—on the importance of finishing one's schooling before going off to fight for one's country. I listened closely to what he had to say, but I didn't take his advice. And that day was my eighteenth birthday. And when the commencement ceremony ended, I went on into Boston and enlisted in the navy as a seaman second class. And I never regretted it.

Remarks at the Washington Mess Hall, U.S. Military Academy,
West Point, New York, January 5, 1993

IN THE ARENA:
Heads Held High

My term is limited to two terms, and I want to serve both of them—[laughter].

Remarks at a Bush-Quayle fund-raising dinner
at the Ritz-Carlton Hotel, Dearborn, Michigan,
April 14, 1992

I think we're dealing in a funny time here, a time warp.
The President's news conference, White House East Room,
June 4, 1992

———————

I hope I can win you over. Maybe not. I'll put you down as
doubtful at this point.
Question-and-answer session at the Ohio Historical Society,
Columbus, Ohio, October 28, 1992

"FRAMED IN WASHINGTON
AND HUNG IN THE CAPITOL"

U.S. television carries Australian-rule football, and many Americans enjoy the rough-and-tumble of hard hitting with reckless abandon. We have something similar; we call it politics in the United States. [Laughter]
Remarks to the Australian Parliament, Parliament House,
Canberra, January 2, 1992

———————

Q. Mr. President, last weekend your commerce secretary, Bob Mosbacher, said that Japan was partly responsible for the recession in the United States. Was he reflecting official policy in saying that?

The President. Well, Mr. Mosbacher always reflects official views except when I disagree with him. [Laughter]
The President's news conference with Prime Minister
Paul J. Keating of Australia at the Parliament House
Main Committee Room, Canberra, January 2, 1992

———————

On the movie *JFK* and conspiracy theories . . .

There's all kinds of conspiratorial theories floating around on everything. Elvis Presley is rumored to be alive and well someplace—[laughter]—and I can't say that someone won't go out and make a movie about that. I have seen no evidence that gives me any reason to believe that the Warren Commission was wrong, none whatsoever.

The President's news conference with Prime Minister
Paul J. Keating of Australia at the Parliament House
Main Committee Room, Canberra, January 2, 1992

I have a rather technical question. What happens if you get the flu in space?

Question via teleconference to the crew of space shuttle Discovery,
referring to his illness at a state dinner in Japan earlier
in the month, Old Executive Office Building, Room 450,
January 24, 1992

We need a nation closer to *The Waltons* than *The Simpsons*.

Remarks at the annual convention of the National Religious
Broadcasters, Sheraton Washington Hotel, January 27, 1992

With the big buildup this address has had, I wanted to make sure it would be a big hit, but I couldn't convince Barbara to give it for me. [Laughter]

I see the Speaker and the Vice President are laughing. They saw what I did in Japan, and they're just happy they're sitting behind me.

Address before a joint session of Congress on the State of the Union,
U.S. Capitol House Chamber, January 28, 1992

I myself have sometimes thought the aging process could be delayed if it had to make its way through Congress.

Address before a joint session of Congress on the State of the Union,
U.S. Capitol House Chamber, January 28, 1992

I know that the eyes of sailing enthusiasts are again on San Diego this year with the America's Cup competition. And if you run low on wind—[laughter]—we've got surplus back in Washington, and we'd be glad to help out.

Remarks to the San Diego Rotary Club at the Sheraton Harbor
Island Hotel, San Diego, California, February 7, 1992

I read somewhere that at one time Mr. Sam [Walton] thought he wanted to be President of the United States. I have two thoughts on that one: One, I'm glad he's not running this year. [Laughter] And two, I've said he's a smart guy; not running proves it. [Laughter]

Remarks on presenting the Presidential Medal of Freedom
to Samuel M. Walton at Wal-Mart headquarters,
Bentonville, Arkansas, March 17, 1992

Referring to an earlier visit to Columbus to commemorate the five hundredth anniversary of Christopher Columbus's voyage . . .

I was here to commemorate a voyage five hundred years old; made me think of the Democrats. Most of their ideas are older than that.

Remarks at a Bush-Quayle fund-raising dinner at the Ohio State
Fairgrounds Lausche Building, Columbus, Ohio, April 30, 1992

Whenever you hear about someone being done in oil in this town, you can't be sure [whether] that means painting or boiling. [Laughter] But today it means honoring.

I will confess it took me a while to convince Bob that it's an honor to be framed in Washington and hung in the Capitol. [Laughter]

Remarks at the unveiling ceremony for the portrait of House Republican
Leader Robert Michel, U.S. Capitol Statuary Hall, May 4, 1992

Q. Mr. President, what's your comment on the criticism of the American position in Rio [UN Conference on the Environment and Development]?

The President. Hey, I get criticized at home. I don't have to go to Rio to get criticized. [Laughter]

Exchange with reporters prior to discussions with Prime Minister
Gro Harlem Brundtland of Norway, Oval Office,
June 5, 1992

You mentioned endangered species. We had a decision coming out of the Interior Department the other day where I caught hell on both sides; therefore I figured we did something right. [Laughter]

Remarks and a question-and-answer session with the Agriculture
Communicators Congress, Department of Agriculture,
June 30, 1992

In the line over there somebody asked if I wanted to comment on this week's big event, the one that captured the imagination of millions of TV viewers. And to be brutally honest, I thought the All-Star Game would be a lot closer than it was. [Laughter]

Remarks to the community, referring to the
Democratic National Convention, Jackson Hole Airport,
Jackson Hole, Wyoming, July 17, 1992

A participant asked about funding for education of handicapped children. Transcript of the question was not provided.

The President. Presidents are never supposed to say "I don't know." That's a very bad form. And Presidents are supposed to know absolutely everything and not be quite as omnipotent as the cardinal [Anthony Cardinal Bevilacqua, archbishop of Philadelphia] but nevertheless—[laughter]—know a lot. . . .

Lamar [Secretary of Education Lamar Alexander], do you know the answer on funding, what we are doing on special ed? Maybe you could grab the mike. And if you don't [know], pass it over to the cardinal. [Laughter]

Remarks at the Presidential Open Forum
on Educational Choice at Archbishop Ryan High School,
Philadelphia, Pennsylvania, July 21, 1992

I know that every speaker comes before you and says they identify with [Christopher] Columbus. But I really mean it. Think about it. The guy was faced with questions at home about whether his global efforts were worth a darn. Some critics even wanted him to cut his voyage short. He even faced the threat of mutiny. [Laughter] And yet Columbus persevered and won; not a bad analogy in my view. So I know this isn't political. [Laughter] Now, I admit, Columbus also had to worry at the time about a lack of wind. I don't have that problem with Congress. [Laughter]

. . . The Senate opens its meetings with a prayer. The House of Representatives opens its meetings with a prayer. Nobody doubts that they need it. [Laughter]

Remarks to the Knights of Columbus Supreme
Council Convention, Marriott Marquis Hotel,
New York City, August 5, 1992

I also want to bring you best wishes from a great friend and fan of yours named Barbara. She and I were talking about coolness under fire. I told her, the more I'm criticized, the more I turn it into humor. You know her; she said, "The rate you're going, you'll soon be funnier than Johnny Carson."

Remarks to the Disabled American Veterans National Convention,
at the Reno Hilton Hotel Goldwyn Ballroom, Reno, Nevada,
August 5, 1992

Breakfast speeches are always my favorite. I figure it's the one meal where broccoli is never served.

Remarks at a prayer breakfast, University of Houston,
August 20, 1992

Some of you may remember this. Four years ago, I met with you as Vice President: September 7, a day that will live in infamy. [Laughter] Okay, I wanted to say it before you did. What does it take to live something down with this crowd? [Laughter]

Remarks to the American Legion National Convention,
Sheraton Chicago Hotel, Chicago, Illinois,
August 25, 1992

I'm not saying these nice things about Ronald Reagan in case he decides to run for President again in 1996. Though I'll confess, if it weren't for a little something called the Twenty-second Amendment, he'd be well into the twelfth year of his presidency, and I'd be going to funerals halfway around the world.

Remarks at a welcome rally at Yorba Regional Park,
Anaheim, California, September 13, 1992

It's great to be back in Albuquerque, this beautiful city, and I understand that you'll host the International Hot Air Balloon Fiesta. I'll leave it to you to decide whether the presidential candidates should be invited. [Laughter]

Remarks to Sandia National Laboratories
employees in Albuquerque, New Mexico,
September 15, 1992

This is the first of several references to comedian Dana Carvey, formerly of *Saturday Night Live,* who impersonated President Bush in office. . . .

The last time I gave a speech on a college campus, one student came up to me afterwards and said, "That was the best imitation of Dana Carvey I've ever seen." [Laughter]
Remarks at Pennsylvania State University, Old Main Lawn,
State College, Pennsylvania, September 23, 1992

Diary, November 25: "I called Dana Carvey . . . a couple of nights ago and asked him to come to the White House for a farewell—he couldn't believe it. . . . Our boys are saying the guy is all out for Clinton and they asked, 'Why are you thinking of doing this?' Anyway, I think it'll be fun to get him to come to a meeting and say the President will be there and then have Dana walk in. . . . I think everybody will get a kick out of it . . ."

Don't dare move my hands—[laughter]—what I wanted to do—[laughter]. No, but I am very grateful to Dana and [his wife] Paula for being here. And Dana's given me a lot of laughs. He said to me on the phone, "Are you sure you really want me to come there?" [Laughter] And I said yes. And he said, "I hope I've never crossed the line." I knew exactly what he meant, and as far as I'm concerned, he never has. The fact that we can laugh at each other is a fundamental thing. I'm not sure on November 4 that the invitation would have gone out and then had the same enthusiasm. [Laughter] But we're shifting gears. I think he's given us a wonderful kickoff to what I hope will be a joyous, totally friendly, very happy, somewhat nostalgic but merry Christmas for everybody.
Remarks at a Christmas gathering for the White House staff,
White House East Room, December 7, 1992

Johnny [Carson], I don't care what you say, I still think Dana Carvey does a better impression of you than he does of me.
Remarks on presenting the Presidential Medal of Freedom,
White House East Room, December 11, 1992

Campaign '92

I'm also glad to visit this country where much of your beautiful land is called bush country. [Laughter] And now, if I can just get that description to apply to fifty states back home, all will be well. [Laughter]

Remarks to business and community leaders
at the World Congress Centre, Melbourne, Australia,
January 3, 1992

I know this is an election year. And I don't know about Damascus, but this primary season we're seeing a lot of conversions on the road to New Hampshire.

Remarks at the annual convention of the National Religious
Broadcasters, Sheraton Washington Hotel,
January 27, 1992

And yes, there's a big election here on Saturday. And I don't like to see this many people gathered together without mentioning it. [Laughter]

Remarks to the Home Builders Association of
Greater Columbia, at the South Carolina State Fair Grounds,
Columbia, South Carolina, March 5, 1992

I wonder if I have any Deke fraternity brothers out here. As I was driving—now, wait just a minute—as I was driving past the fraternity house, I heard him shouting: "Four more years!" And that's brotherhood for you, I thought. And then, Barbara said what they were really saying: "Four more beers!"

Remarks at Pete Maravich Arena, Louisiana State University,
Baton Rouge, Louisiana, March 6, 1992

On the balancing act between governing and campaigning . . .

I hope our presidency has been one of decency, a sense of honor, a sense of fair play, and I'm just going to continue to emphasize these themes.

I mean, I think Americans like a political battle, but I think they expect their President to express some of these fundamental values. And when I speak out against hatred, bigotry, anti-Semitism, racism, it's not aimed at anybody; it's aimed at values that this country really has, whatever side of the aisle you're on. And so, it's something that I just feel I must do. And it didn't just start with this campaign, if you'll go back and look at my speeches over the last few years.

So, it's really appealing to the better nature of the American people, and the American people are well-intentioned on these matters of fair play.

Exchange with reporters at the Pensacola Naval Air Station,
Pensacola, Florida, March 7, 1992

Somebody suggested that this visit has something to do with a primary election. True, I'm working to win that election. But if anyone thinks we've got political headaches here, they're nothing compared with the problems that free Poland is facing today, particularly Lech Walesa is facing. We have two major parties here in this country. But look at all the parties he has to contend with, close to twenty, twenty at the last count. Even the Polish Beer Drinkers' Party—[laughter]—true, they've split in two factions.

Remarks to the Polish National Alliance,
Polish National Alliance headquarters, Chicago, Illinois,
March 16, 1992

Q. How do you feel about running for President again?
The President. Good question to end on. [Laughter] You guys have to admit that there's been no politics in this up until now. And she said, "How do you feel about running for President again?"

I will only answer it that I've got a lot of work left to do, and I'm going to try to do what I said over here to this guy: do my best; try my hardest. I think things are getting better for some in this country, but nobody can relax until you try to help everybody.

So in some ways it's tough. You're going a lot. . . . But it's important, and I believe in this country. . . . I look around this room, and I am more confident than ever that the best days of our country lie ahead because you're a great part of our future.

Remarks and question-and-answer session
with the Sheriff's Youth Athletic League at the Lynwood
Youth Athletic Center, Los Angeles, California,
May 29, 1992

It's great to be back here in Chicago. I was half-tempted to call the mayor [Democrat Richard Daley] while I'm in town. My guess is he was pretty upset by his party's recent gathering in New York. He thought Chicago had the nickname "the Windy City."

Remarks at a fund-raising brunch for Rich Williamson,
Hyatt Regency Hotel, Rosemount, Illinois, August 2, 1992

If you're looking to restore America's moral fiber, why buy synthetic when you can buy real cotton? [Laughter]

Remarks to the Knights of Columbus
Supreme Council Convention, Marriott Marquis Hotel,
New York City, August 5, 1992

I admit I've been a little slow to fight back. My opponent has mentioned my name about once every five seconds, not always in the most flattering light. I still haven't said his name in full. I referred occasionally to my "opponent," "the other guy," and even "the governor of a certain state with a profitable chicken industry on the Mississippi River, located somewhere between Texas and Oklahoma." [Laughter]

Remarks to the American Legislative Exchange Council, at the
Broadmoor International Hotel, Colorado Springs, Colorado,
August 6, 1992

A "kinder and gentler" skewering of his opponent at the 1992 GOP National Convention in Houston . . .

If I had stood before you four years ago and described this as the world we would help build, you would have said, "George Bush, you must have been smoking something, and you must have inhaled."

. . . You don't hear much about this good news because the media tends to focus only on the bad. When the Berlin Wall fell, I half expected to see a headline, "Wall Falls, Three Border Guards Lose Jobs." [Laughter] And underneath, it probably says, "Clinton Blames Bush." [Laughter]

. . . You've heard of the separation of powers. Well, my opponent practices a different theory: the power of separations. Government has the power to separate you from your wallet.

Remarks accepting the presidential nomination
at the Republican National Convention, the Astrodome, Houston,
August 20, 1992

You cannot be on every side of every issue. He's [Bill Clinton] stuck riding the fence so hard he's got saddle sores. I might say "straddle sores." [Laughter]

Remarks to the community at Kapperman Farm, in Humboldt,
South Dakota, September 2, 1992

Response when asked "What can we do to help you fulfill your goals?"

Vote often.
> *Remarks and a question-and-answer session*
> *with employees of Uniform Tubes in Collegeville, Pennsylvania,*
> *September 9, 1992*

I'll debate Governor Clinton. I'm not a professional debater. I'm not an Oxford man—[laughter]—and I think he's good at that. I mean, he's got more statistics than there are problems. [Laughter]
> *Remarks and a question-and-answer session at Cobo Hall,*
> *with the Economic Club of Detroit, Michigan,*
> *September 10, 1992*

When it comes to crime, I wish that candidate Clinton, the Doberman pinscher, would meet Governor Clinton, the Chihuahua. [Laughter]
> *Remarks on arrival at Shreveport Regional Airport,*
> *Shreveport, Louisiana, September 22, 1992*

Our secretary of transportation was to be here, Andy Card. He's now secretary of transition—[laughter]—as well as secretary of transportation.
> *Remarks at the presentation ceremony*
> *for the President's Environment and Conservation Challenges*
> *Awards, White House East Room, December 2, 1992*

SPORTS

I've gotten so many compliments on that first pitch, I'm surprised you didn't ask about that. I thought there would be criticism. They could visualize the left-handed hitter standing there and the pitcher on the first pitch saying, "Outside and away, do not bring it in over the strike zone, and bring it in a little slower than normal because he's looking for the heat." And so, as one reporter pointed out, you give him the chill or the freeze.

And it was wonderful because it was a great comparison with my grandson, who had to get out there and arrogantly throw it right over the plate fast. So I've been surprised at the reaction from people. It's very understanding on that pitch.

Q. That's why you want to run for reelection, so you can throw out the first ball, right?

The President. Well, I think the American people seem to be sensitive. They see what the man is trying to do, keep it outside on the opening left-handed hitter. [Laughter] You notice how the third baseman came in on the very first pitch of the leadoff hitter. He was in for the bunt. Now, with my pitch, nobody could have bunted that thing. [Laughter]

Exchange with reporters while viewing the cherry blossoms
at the Tidal Basin, walking from the White House
to the Jefferson Memorial and back, April 8, 1992

Ed [Agriculture Secretary Madigan] was over here, for all you ardent golfers, showing me some golf tees made out of corn. I don't know that they'll help, but I'll try anything—[laughter].

Remarks and a question-and-answer session
with the Agriculture Communicators Congress, Department
of Agriculture, June 30, 1992

During the 1992 Democratic National Convention in New York, President Bush repeated his 1988 ritual and went fishing at Secretary Baker's ranch in Wyoming . . .

Q. How many fish did you catch, sir?

The President. It is an unimpressive record. However, here's my side of it. [Laughter] I caught two or three yesterday—three, and two today. But it's not—it's the hunt as well as catching the fish. It's trying to put the fly right where you think the action is and standing there in the beauty of this marvelous country of ours, standing in the middle of a stream. And it's very hard to describe. But for people that love the outdoors as I do, love this West as I do, why, they'll know what I mean. It's not catching the fish. It's being our there in nature with nature all around you.

Q. How's Jim Baker's cooking?

The President. Not near as good as his secretary-of-state-ship.

*The President's news conference at the U.S. Air Force Seismic
Research Facility, Pinedale, Wyoming, July 16, 1992*

MEDIA: THE GOOD, THE BAD, AND THE UGLY

My modus operandi is to be pleasant with you people when you ask me irritating questions.

*Statement on the death of Menachem Begin of Israel
and an exchange with reporters, March 9, 1992*

Throughout 1992, President Bush would revisit the subject of "leaks" . . .

One of the things I like least about this job is commenting on what advisers say, handlers say, in campaigns. They're normally referred to as handlers in the campaign season and advisers—has a nicer tone—in the noncampaign season. And I read all the time about some anonymous source who is known to feel strongly about the very questions you asked about, Jess. I read about ideas that I'm considering I haven't even heard of yet. I don't know. What I'd say to the American people is, please ask for a name to be placed next to the source so I can get mad at the guy who's doing this.

*The President's news conference, White House Briefing Room,
March 11, 1992*

I'm not unhappy about stories that are true. I read one today about my son George that isn't true. And so I'm glad to have that out there. It simply is not true. To suggest that Jim Baker and I were working to get George up here for a week is ridiculous. When George comes here, of course he goes to the campaign and talks to people here. But this isn't some manifestation of dissatisfaction. And if I were dissatisfied, you'd know about it loud and clear. I'm happy about it, and I know that many have to make their living by making these inside stories—inside, day-in, who's up, who's down, who's winning, who's losing. And it's ridiculous.

But the trouble is, nobody cares about it around the country, although we thrive on it inside the beltway. But John [Cochran of NBC News], you've asked about it. If you'd tell me the name of the author and which story you're referring to, I'll tell you whether it's true or not. If, by chance, you are talking about the one that was on the front page of the *New York Times* today, regrettably, it was not true.

> *The President's news conference, Rose Garden,*
> *April 10, 1992*

I find it extraordinarily difficult to find leakers. It's extraordinarily difficult. I'd like to find the leaker, and I'd like to see the leaker filed—fired. Filed would be all right. No, but the reason is it's very difficult to conduct government if somebody in his or her infinite wisdom can shape the decision by leaking documents. The debate and the discussion that should take place doesn't.

This was a very unhelpful leak. Bill Reilly [EPA administrator] was doing what he should, sending up here in confidence suggestions where we might be able to change the, I believe it was the biodiversity treaty, in order to have total harmony there. Some of the suggestions were, [it] turns out, were not ones that we could accept. But he did it right; he put a confidential memo in. Then for someone, who may or may not [have] been opposed to the treaty or any changes, to leak it, it's insidious.

I know many people in the press thrive on this. This is good journalism to find it out. All I'm saying is I would go after the leaker if I could because it's bad government. It's very difficult to conduct sound and sensible policy when the lowest common denominator in some office in the vast bureaucracy can release a document. But how you find it, how you find a person that is that low and that determined to disrupt, I don't know. It's real bad. It does not help conduct sound policy.

And I can't say there's any national security at stake on this; there's not. But it was just mischievous and bad, and I told Bill Reilly that. I said, "You did it right." And I apologized for lack of discipline wherever it was, whatever agency.

Q. Mr. Reilly said that he was not going to resign to give satisfaction to his enemies. This was leaked by somebody who is supposedly friendly to you.

The President. Well, help me find him, John [Cochran of NBC News]. Help me find him. He'd be gainfully unemployed.

The President's news conference with Prime Minister
John Major of the United Kingdom at Camp David,
June 7, 1992

Response when asked if his actions addressing Hurricane Andrew relief efforts were politically motivated . . .

Q. Sir, do you think your handling of this will be viewed in any way by the electorate down in Florida in a particular way?

The President. Look, may I tell you something? I am thinking about what is good for the people here. I don't even think about the politics of it. We're trying to help people.

I see a bunch of people running around interviewing people who have been thrown out of their homes by a natural disaster, saying how do the politics work. Good heavens, isn't there any honor here? Can't we help people without having somebody try to put a political interpretation on it?

Remarks and an exchange with reporters on disaster relief efforts,
White House Cabinet Room, August 29, 1992

Last week on one of the networks here there was a story asking why country music had become such a big part of national politics. I won't speak for any other politicians, but I love country music. Leave politics aside, I love it because country music loves America. I don't start listening just at election time. I listen to it every night of my life, and I love it. . . . It is wonderful.

Remarks to the community
at the Roy Acuff Theater, Nashville, Tennessee,
September 29, 1992

The last official transcript containing the words of George Bush as President, pondering his return to private life . . .

Q. Are you going to take a press pool to Houston?
The President. No. Oh, I forgot to tell you. On January 20 at noon, I'm through with press pools. We're shifting. It shifts over to the new President. And I'm going back to private life. And it's going to be low-key. . . . I'm trying to conduct myself with dignity and hopefully in a spirit of total cooperation with Governor Clinton. No bitterness in my heart. But look, January 20 when I walk out of that Capitol, I'm a private citizen; and I hope I'll be treated as a private citizen by my neighbors in Houston. And I'm not looking to sit at the head table. I'm not looking to have press conferences. I love you guys, especially the photo dogs. [Laughter] But we're not going to—we're going to really shift gears like that. It's going to be interesting. . . .
Q. I bet you won't be able to do it.
The President. I'm going to try. I'm going to sure try.

The President's news conference with Prime Minister
Brian Mulroney of Canada at Camp David,
January 16, 1993

"A Judgment I Honor"

Conceding defeat on election night, 1992 . . .

The people have spoken, and we respect the majesty of the democratic system. . . .

There is important work to be done, and America must always come first. So we will get behind this new President and wish him well. . . .

I remain absolutely convinced that we are a rising nation. We have been in an extraordinarily difficult period. But do not be deterred, kept away from public service by the smoke and fire of a campaign year or the ugliness of politics. As for me, I'm going to try and find ways to help people. But I plan to get very active in the grandchild business and in finding ways to help others. But I urge you, the young people of this country, to participate in the political process. It needs your idealism. It needs your drive. It needs your conviction.

Remarks in Houston on the results of the presidential election,
Westin Galleria Hotel, November 3, 1992

Diary, November 4, 12:15 A.M.: "The election is over—it's come and gone. It's hard to describe the emotion of something like this. . . . But it's hurt, hurt, hurt and I guess it's the pride, too. . . . On a competitive basis, I don't like to see the pollsters right at the end; I don't like to see the pundits right; I don't like to see all of those who have written me off right. I was absolutely convinced we would prove them wrong but I was wrong and they were right and that hurts a lot. . . . Now into bed, prepared to face tomorrow: Be strong, be kind, be generous of spirit, be understanding and let people know how grateful you are. Don't get even. Comfort the ones I've hurt and let down. Say your prayers and ask for God's understanding and strength. Finish with a smile and some gusto, and do what's right and finish strong . . ." (*ATB*, p. 572).

I can think of nothing other to say than let's finish this job in style. Let's get the job done, cooperate fully with the new administration. The government goes on, as well it should, and we will support the new President and give him every chance to lead this country into greater heights.

Remarks at a welcome home ceremony, White House South Lawn,
November 4, 1992

I admit, this is not the position I would have preferred, but it is a judgment I honor. Having known the sweet taste of popular favor, I can more readily accept the sour taste of defeat, because it is seasoned for me by my deep devotion to the political system under which this nation has thrived for two centuries.

I realize that defeat can be divisive. I want the Republican Party to be as constructive on the outside of executive power as it has been for twelve years on the inside. There must be no finger-pointing, no playing the blame game. New ideas flourish, and that is good. But as for what has passed, I can only say that it was my administration, my campaign. I captained the team, and I take full responsibility for the loss. No one else is responsible. I am responsible.

I hope history will record the Bush administration has served America well. I am proud of my cabinet and my staff. America has led the world through an age of global transition. We have made the world safer for our kids. And I believe the real fruits of our global victory are yet to be tasted.

I'm also proud of my campaign team. They put together a tenacious, spirited effort in a difficult year. When you win, your errors are obscured; when you lose, your errors are magnified. I suspect history will take the edge off both interpretations. One thing I know for sure: my supporters should go out with the heads held high.

One final thought. As I campaigned across this nation, I had the opportunity to talk to many people. I felt the anxiety that accompanies a time of change, but I could also see every day, in ways large and small, the resiliency of the American spirit.

Ours is a nation that has shed the blood of war and cried the tears of depression. We have stretched the limits of human imagination and seen the technologically miraculous become almost mundane. Always, always, our advantage has been our spirit, a constant confidence, a sense that in America the only things not yet accomplished are the things that have not yet been tried. President-elect Clinton needs all Americans to unite behind him so he can move our nation forward. But more than that, he will need to draw upon this unique American spirit.

There are no magic outside solutions to our problems. The real answers lie within us. We need more than a philosophy of entitlement. We need to all pitch in, lend a hand, and do our part to help forge a brighter future for this country.

On January 20, Barbara and I will head back to Texas. For us there will be no more elections, no more politics. But we will rededicate ourselves to serving others because, after all, that is the secret of this unique American spirit. With this spirit, we can realize the golden opportunities before us and make sure that our new day, like every American day, is filled with hope and promise.

Radio address to the nation on the results
of the presidential election, Camp David Laurel Lodge,
November 7, 1992

CHAPTER FIVE

Postpresidency:
DID IT WITH HONOR

After the rededication of the Ford Presidential Library
in Grand Rapids, Michigan. April 16, 1997.

At this writing, only a handful of men out of 280 million living Americans can describe with authority the personal experience of leaving behind the Oval Office and Air Force One and returning to private life. But one can imagine, even under the best of circumstances, it is a wrenching transition to make—to start anew after the splendor of the White House, to resume some sense of normalcy after bearing such eyewitness to the agony and ecstasy of history.

Unless, as George Bush testifies, you're married to Barbara Bush. In that case, you have no choice but to wake up January 21, make the coffee yourself, and get on with life.

It's been said that trying to keep up with the Bushes in retirement is like trying to get a sip of water from a fire hose. The numbers support the comparison. Since leaving office, President Bush has written two books; visited fifty-six foreign countries and most of the fifty states; helped to raise millions of dollars for a variety of charitable organizations; made two parachute jumps; had one hip replaced by surgery; welcomed two new grandchildren to the world; seen two sons elected governors of the second- and fourth-largest states—and one go on to become the forty-third President of the United States. In addition to that, President Bush was recently appointed chairman of the University Cancer Foundation Board of Visitors for the University of Texas M. D. Anderson Cancer Center in Houston, Texas, and is honorary chairman of the Points of Light Foundation.

But the centerpiece of George Bush's public life today is the George Bush School of Government and Public Service, located on the campus of Texas A&M University in College Station. Outside of his family, President Bush considers the work of the Bush School to be perhaps his most meaningful legacy. The former President spends increasing amounts of time there—preaching the *gospel of public service. He hopes to inculcate (his word) the concept of leadership with integrity into the students who pass through its doors. If so, they will inherit a mantle of service enriched by the forty-first President of the United States.*

FAITH, FAMILY, AND FRIENDS:
What Motivates Us

Now that my political days are over, I can honestly say that the three most rewarding titles I've held are the only three I have left—a husband, a father, and a granddad.

Remarks at the dedication of the George Bush Presidential Library, College Station, Texas, November 6, 1997

I tell a joke now . . . and people say, "I didn't know you had a sense of humor." People come up to me and say, "You're tall. I thought you were short." Who's the real George Bush? . . . I'm not sure if they knew the real George Bush, I would have been reelected President. But it's funny how such differences of opinion—maybe it's other public figures, too—but I am convinced that the American people didn't know my heartbeat. And I can't blame anybody but myself for that.

Interview with David Frost, "A President's Story," August 25, 1998

Life is not fair: Saddam Hussein still has a job, and I'm unemployed.

You know damn well it's not fair. [Laughter]

Panel discussion on the Gulf War tenth anniversary, College Station, Texas, February 23, 2001

BAR

Two months after leaving office, President Bush was invited back to receive the Forrestal Memorial Award from the National Security Industrial Association. Only his affection for the military and intelligence communities could lure him back to Washington so soon after the 1993 inaugural. Part of his opening remarks included an update on his wife's new mode of transportation . . .

We're doing all right. Barbara's doing great. She's way ahead of me. She went out and bought a car, and . . . we have an office on the ninth floor there on Memorial Drive in Houston, Texas, USA. And they said, "Barbara's coming over to the office." So I stood out there on the balcony . . . watching her drive in after twelve years of being chauffeured around. And she did very well. . . . She could go forward, and backwards, and we all cheered—reduced the overhead. [Laughter] So I'm delighted that she's doing that.

She's writing a book. Nice to be married to a rich wife after all these years. [Laughter]

Remarks on receiving the Forrestal Award, Washington, D.C.,
March 18, 1993

Camp David was the scene of numerous historic occasions during President Bush's four years in office. There, he learned that Manuel Noriega had been captured in Panama; discussed arms control with Mikhail Gorbachev; mapped out a strategy for German reunification with Chancellor Helmut Kohl; and relayed the still-secret battle plans for Operation Desert Storm to the new British prime minister, John Major. But as President Bush notes during one of the first interviews he granted after leaving office, another noteworthy event transpired at the mountain oasis . . .

I was riding down with Arnold Schwarzenegger on a toboggan, and we were yelling like a couple of little kids. We told Barbara it was very icy, and she went charging down. I remember yelling at her, "Bail out! Bail out!" She didn't, and she broke her leg. I was caught laughing, and that did not go over too well with Barbara. . . . She was a good sport about it. And then, I thought it was my obligation to stay with my guests—the Schwarzeneggers and others—continuing the sledding, and not go with her to the hospital down at the foot of the mountain. That was a huge mistake that I made. So I didn't handle that all too well, I don't think. I shouldn't have laughed, and I should have gone with her to the hospital.

Interview with Peter Roussel,
KUHT-TV's "A Conversation with George Bush,"
Houston, Texas, November 18, 1994

On January 6, we celebrated our fifty-first wedding anniversary. Last year, we celebrated a big fiftieth in Nashville at the Grand Ole Opry, where some of our country-music friends helped us in that wonderful celebration. This year, January 6, both of us forgot that it was our anniversary. [Laughter] I guess the moral of that story is, when you get older, you forget stuff.

Remarks at the Greater Washington
Society of Association Executives Foundation,
Washington, D.C., January 22, 1996

Referring to the recently released movie *Nixon*, directed by a noted conspiracy buff . . .

Perhaps the most significant thing to happen so far this year—and I know Barbara feels just as strongly about this because she came out very well on it—is our featured appearance on *The Simpsons*—[laughter]—that horrible television show. Who can wrestle with Homer in the basement? Some of you may have seen us with Bart and Homer. We loved it—sort of. [Laughter] The only thing missing was Oliver Stone as the director. [Laughter]

Remarks at the Greater Washington Society of Association
Executives Foundation, Washington, D.C., January 22, 1996

At a joint Q&A during their first joint appearance back in Washington since 1993, President and Mrs. Bush respond to the question "What do you disagree on?" with this exchange . . .

President Bush. She has some convictions on some of these social issues different from mine . . . [looking askance at his wife]—left-wing pinko. [Laughter]
Mrs. Bush. He better be careful, or I'll call for a vote. [Laughter]
President Bush. Sounds like a Geraldine Ferraro rally here. [Laughter] We gotta do something about this. No, I think we better leave it right there.

Remarks at the Greater Washington Society of Association
Executives Foundation, Washington, D.C., January 22, 1996

Recalling their first meeting at the Greenwich Country Club. Barbara Bush remembers that her future husband couldn't do the waltz, so they sat down. She also confesses to having another beau at the time, but she went to George Bush's senior prom at Andover—and they were soon in love. For his part . . .

I met Barbara at a dance in December, right after Pearl Harbor, December 1941. And she was the most beautiful girl, you can imagine. Never forget it—red and green dress. And I was a terrible dancer, something that has been maintained to this very day, but I decided to get up my nerve to dance with her.

Interview with David Frost, "A President's Story,"
August 25, 1998

An exchange on the subject of abortion devolves into a plea for sympathy and understanding . . .

President Bush. My point has been that it's not an issue that decides these elections. It's a divisive issue. It is a very divisive issue.

Q. Indeed, there's division on the subject within the Bush household.

President Bush. Probably. Couple of members of my family . . .

Q. Well, now, I mean you and Barbara have a different view, don't you?

President Bush. Well, she's a very difficult woman, David. [Laughter] She's an extraordinarily difficult woman. I'm working with her, to bring her along nicely. The trouble is, she seems to have 98 percent of the American people on her side, and I'm working with two. But I'm trying to build it up, and I think I can succeed. She's amazing, absolutely amazing. Every place I go—I was in Birmingham, England—they said, "We're very glad to see you. Where's Barbara?" And you go along to somebody else: "Where's Barbara?" And I told them, the fourteen thousand there at a Lions convention, "Don't ask me about that. I'm having an identity crisis." [Laughter] Hell, I used to be President of the United States of America, and now I'm known as Barbara's husband, or the father of the governor of Texas. What about me?

. . . I told Barbara once, I said, "Guess who I saw?" I'll make up a name here, but, "I just saw Phil Smith the other day." And she said, "Don't you remember what he said about you in 1960?" [Laughter] I mean, you know, she was a loyal fighter. But she's a forgiving person, too. She's got a very insightful judgment on people, but it's not a selfish thing for her. It was more "What's best for my husband?"

Interview with David Frost, "A President's Story,"
August 25, 1998

After leaving Yale—and both of their families—back East, the young couple and their oldest son set out for west Texas. They bought their first house for $8,500 in Midland and set down roots they haven't forgotten to this day . . .

We still feel it's home in a way. It's hard for people to believe that. And it's not necessarily the tumbleweeds and the dust storms, but it was the people out there—I mean, unfailingly polite, and warm and friendly. It's hard to describe to people who haven't been to west Texas.

Interview with David Frost, "A President's Story,"
August 25, 1998

Identifying the real counselor to the President in the family today . . .

The lady in the white hair here [BPB] is the one that gives advice to our son.

Panel discussion on the Gulf War tenth anniversary,
College Station, Texas, February 23, 2001

The "Kids"

President Bush allowed that the first of two postpresidential parachute jumps—in March of 1997—maybe have been "a Walter Mitty thing, but I loved every minute of it." Here, he relates how he broke the news to his daughter, Doro . . .

So I called her and told her, and she said, "Oh, Dad, do you have to do this?"
President Bush. "Yes, Dorothy, I'm going to do it. Now don't tell anyone."
Doro. "Do you think I'd tell anybody *this?*"

Interview with David Frost, "A President's Story," August 25, 1998

Another Doro story, this time her tearful reaction after then Congressman Bush lost his second Senate race—this time to Lloyd Bentsen in 1970 . . .

I asked, "What's the matter, Doro?" And she said, "I'm the only girl in class whose father doesn't have a job."
Texas A&M University Distinguished Lecture,
College Station, Texas, March 8, 1999

And then you leave out our other three kids, and we take the same pride in them, the same love for them, that we have in these two more high-profile kids. So I guess the bottom line is: What do you want? What do you aspire to? I think great happiness for all five of them, and our fourteen grandchildren. Because we've been there, we've done everything else in life. And so, on a personal basis, we want to see them go forward. I want to teach them to fly fish. I want to see them be happy.
Texas A&M University Distinguished Lecture,
College Station, Texas, March 8, 1999

The first of two remembrances of their second child, Pauline "Robin" Bush, who passed away in 1953 from leukemia . . .

We're very emotional in our family, and I've gotten over being a sissy about it. It's very personal. We hurt now.
Interview on CNN's Larry King Live,
Houston, Texas, November 2, 1999

We lost our daughter, and that was a tough experience. . . . Dear God, why does this child have to die? [She was] the epitome of innocence to us, beauty, everything else, and there was no explanation. But all these things contribute to your life, maybe your character, to what you stand for. And that was a very, very maturing happening. It hurt badly.

Interview with Hugh Sidey, "Time and the Presidency,"
Lafayette Square, April 11, 2000

Several observations on his office-seeking sons, George W. and Jeb . . .

My political days are over, so "on to the next event" would be on to taking great pleasure and pride in the fact that two of my sons did very well and campaigned with great honor and integrity for governor in two large states. One won, the other lost—but it's the way in which they conducted themselves, both George and Jeb. And I guess the next phase of my life in terms of politics that really interests me is seeing how George performs as governor of our state, and then seeing what Jeb does in what I am sure will be a bright political future. The rest of it, for me, I'll do my thing. I did forty events for other candidates this year, but my heart was in Texas and in Florida.

Interview with Peter Roussel, KUHT-TV's
"A Conversation with George Bush,"
Houston, Texas, November 18, 1994

Sometimes he [George W.] did a lot of heavy lifting, because he could go to people and save me the agony of having to break the bad news to people, and he did it, and that seasoned him. And he probably passed a test in there somewhere. The test being, you know, "Am I strong enough? Am I determined enough to get into this peculiar racket—this business that at times can be very ugly?" And I guess he concluded yes.

Interview with Jamie Gangel, NBC's Today show
Kennebunkport, Maine, April 25, 1997

The happiest day of my life—happier than when I was sworn in as President, or elected President—was when two of our sons were elected governor—one in our great state, and one in the state of Florida. . . . And should one of them go further and suffer through the ups and the downs of what everyone knows lies ahead, and should he be successful—and it could be one, or the other—Jeb is a very powerful, strong man who I am sure will be on the national political scene. He feels passionately; he's a kind guy; he believes in the quality of people. And I know that he will be heard from. But should one of them be successful in becoming President, that would be something . . . far more fulfilling and rewarding than I could ever adequately say. But it's a long enough shot [and] you don't count on it. But the very fact that they're both in there trying gives us enormous pleasure and satisfaction. It really is just so hard to quantify and describe to people.

Texas A&M University Distinguished Lecture,
College Station, Texas, March 8, 1999

I can't describe it. I'd say to any mother or father listening, leave aside politics. How would you feel if your son, or your daughter, might just be the next President of the United States? You'd be overwhelmed by it, and that's what it is for us. This isn't vindication. It's not "I want to see this particular issue come forth." It is pride in our able, proven, man-of-integrity son of ours. That's what it is. It is strength of family, and it's pride, and it's not legacy, and it's not handing something down. Great pride in our son.

Interview with Jamie Gangel, NBC's Today *show,*
September 28, 1999

I don't think it was really hard for me to the degree that I did follow in my dad's footsteps. . . . My father was totally honest, totally committed to service, per se. And that inspired me. Not just there, but in his whole life. So, if there's some parallel there, fine, but he'll [George W.] chart his own course. . . . We've never given anything to these myths of families that try to put out a lot of propaganda about themselves. I hope we're different. It's not a legacy—"I gotta do this because my dad did, and I gotta do this because of my granddad." That is not what motivates us.

Interview with Jamie Gangel, NBC's Today *show,*
September 28, 1999

My role is to stay out of his [George W.] way—be there if he needs me. Every once in a while we talk about some foreign policy situation around the globe, but he's got good people around him. And things change, and the best thing we can do as parents is to support him when there's a few bumps in the road and cheer for him when things are going well. He really doesn't need me picking up the phone and telling him what he's gonna do and how he's gonna do it. I always remember the Kennedy father, Ambassador Kennedy. Apparently he was saying, "You're gonna be doing this," "You're gonna be doing that," [and] to another boy, "Here's the way you ought to approach this problem," and we don't do that. It's just different.

Interview with Jamie Gangel, NBC's Today *show,*
September 28, 1999

Response when asked what advice he would give his son George W., who was a candidate for President at the time . . .

Give it your best shot, and I'll be there to help you if you get hurt.

Interview with C-SPAN's Brian Lamb,
College Station, Texas, November 25, 1999

The following exchange with Larry King took place at the 2000 Republican National Convention in Philadelphia, where George Bush's son accepted the GOP nomination for President. Here, the father is asked to guess what election night will be like . . .

President Bush. With George and Laura out there I will be a very, very nervous dad. And so will Barbara. That's what it's about. It's not about these issues, believe me. Everyone thinks it's a legacy thing, or entitlement, or—

Q. Adams family.

President Bush. Adams family. Which one? [Laughter]

Q. The Adams, the Kennedys, the Bushes—American dynasties.

President Bush. Yeah, I don't like that. I mean, I've got great respect for [those] families and all, but we don't feel entitlement. We don't feel the legacy thing.

Interview on CNN's Larry King Live
Philadelphia, Pennsylvania, August 1, 2000

And here, after the election was decided, two reflections shared with Fox News's Paula Zahn looking back on election night and the surreal aftermath . . .

It was an up-and-down night. Early on we were concerned for George—that he might not win. Then they started reworking some of the states, and Florida was called for George, and then the Vice President conceded—called George and congratulated him. So we went from concern to euphoria, emotional euphoria. Jeb hugging George, and BPB hugging both the boys, and me in there somewhere, and it's hard to describe the depths of the emotion.

And then, of course, it was taken back; and we had this feeling of not despair, but of gloom, and the joy wasn't there. The fact that our son had come that close at that juncture was in itself rewarding—but nothing like we thought it was going to be when we heard the concession.

So we—like the rest of the American people and people all around the world—then endured a thirty-seven-day period of agony. But it's worse when you're the father and mother. . . . You know very well that when your kid is called out on strikes, it's the umpire's fault. You know, you want to be with your son; you want to be at his side. That's what this was about for us. It wasn't politics. It wasn't left or right, or conservative or liberal, or even the good of the country versus any alternative. It was strictly about pride of a mother and a father in their oldest son—and I might say, as a result of that thirty-seven days, in their second-oldest son, who was so unfairly criticized by a lot of people for his role as governor of Florida. It just killed us as parents.

And then, it changed!

Q. Did you expect it to change?

President Bush. I think there was a period in there that I wasn't sure, I wasn't certain. But I'll tell you this, and it's not just revisionistic: I knew, and I think I told this to George and I know I talked to Barbara about it, that win or lose, he'd have a life. He was at peace. He got kinda teased—not teased, ridiculed— for being out at his ranch and not tuning into every little up or down in this long, long, arduous process. But he's at peace. He knows who he is. He did his best. He did all these old verities that you learn from your parents . . . do your best, give the other guy credit, try your hardest. I mean, he did those things.

But I must say, when it became clear that he was to be the President, then we had this huge emotional outburst. God, I don't even want to discuss it, it was so overwhelming. . . . And again not of vindication on an issue, but pride of a father in a noble son.

Q. When did the reality set in? Was it the night the Supreme Court decision came down?

President Bush. No, I think it was when he walked in and was introduced by Pete Laney, the Speaker of the Texas House, in the Texas House Chamber. I think that was really *the* most emotional moment for Barbara and me—realization that our son was the forty-third President. I'll never forget it.

Q. Did you watch it on TV?

President Bush. Yeah, we were alone. We didn't go over to Austin—we were tucked into our bed here in Houston, Texas. We watched, and we sobbed.

Q. What went through your mind when you saw your son sit down with President Clinton in the Oval Office for the first time?

President Bush. Well, I was trying to think what he [George W.] was thinking. You see, I didn't have that when I became President because I had been at Reagan's side for eight years. And so we didn't have the new guy coming in and the old guy bowing out—you know, outgoing President welcoming the new President. There wasn't this formality. So I didn't know how it would be personally.

I do remember vividly inviting President Clinton to the White House. I wanted to do it right, and I wanted to be sure he felt at home, and I wanted to be sure—as Barbara did— that Mrs. Clinton saw where they were going to live. And that was easy for me.

Q. That wasn't awkward for you?

President Bush. No, it was not. I had adjusted, by then, to the fact that I had lost. It took a while to be pleasant about that, but I had. And this guy beat me fair and square, and I told him right there, "You're not going to have me to worry about. I'm not going to be out there trying to make political hay out of the difficulties you might have." And I was pretty good about that for eight years. . . .

Then today I see our oldest son walk into the White House as the President, sitting next to a—very gracious to him— President Clinton. And I thought, this is amazing. This is absolutely amazing. I had just been on the phone with George from the Madison Hotel before this, talking about some other matters. And then I saw this, and there was another imprimatur of reality, another stamp of reality as he was greeted in that office he's going to serve in for the next four years.

Interview with Paula Zahn, Fox News Channel's The Edge,
Houston, Texas, December 20, 2000

———

Having a son as President of the United States changes some things, but not others . . .

George called me on Monday night—he was in Washington. He went to a Chinese restaurant, and he took his brother and his sister, who live in the area. Dorothy called in Tuesday morning, and I said, "Who bought the dinner?" And she said, "George did. He paid the check." And I said, "Were you all amazed?" And she said, "No, he made a big statement at the head of the table that when they come to this restaurant, he's going to do it like his dad did. He would buy the dinner." And they all fell over in a dead faint, 'cause George is not one to—well, he is generous, but they all tease him for not picking up all the checks around. So it was fun.

And they weren't overwhelmed that their brother was President. And yet, we all are in one sense, but not in a family sense. It's so hard to clarify. . . .

You know the way the kids are. That won't change. Publicly, it will. You'll hear my boys—Neil, Marvin, Doro, Jeb—calling him "Mr. President." But when you sit at that little Chinese restaurant or you sit around the table at Camp David, it's not going to be different. I'll tell you. The guy's gonna have to defend himself with his brothers and his sister on his case just as he had—and he's got to lead them—just as he has all his life.

Interview with Paula Zahn, Fox News Channel's The Edge,
Houston, Texas, December 20, 2000

I'm very careful these days about answering policy questions for the obvious reason: I don't want to get No. 43 mad at me. [Laughter]

*Panel discussion on the Gulf War tenth anniversary,
College Station, Texas, February 23, 2001*

More on the fallout from the Florida recount . . .

When a national leader accused Jeb and George of using Nazi tactics, and the media didn't really respond to that, I was outraged by that. But it was more than just the political outrage, it was the hurt of a father who has pride in two wonderful sons, who would never use Nazi tactics. So it was a period of anxiety, but if George had lost, it wouldn't have been the end of the world for us. We're very blessed, we're very close. We don't need to manifest that every single day because it's there. If somebody's sick, all of us care. If somebody wins a medal, all of us rejoice.

Interview with Mike Wright, KBTX-TV's
"An Evening with George Bush," College Station,
Texas, June 6, 2001

"THE GRANDCHILD BUSINESS"

I vowed that when I got out of the White House that I would catch up and be big into the grandchild business, and I like that. I love doing that.

Interview with Peter Roussel, KUHT-TV's
"A Conversation with George Bush," Houston, Texas,
November 18, 1994

———

There's a lot of living to do; and a lot of family to watch; and a lot of fish to catch; very few op-ed pages to write. And I want to be around for the future, and I want to see my grandsons and grand-daughters get married and achieve good things.

Interview with David Frost, "A President's Story,"
August 25, 1998

———

Some free grandfatherly advice to any student graduating from college . . .

[I was] interviewed by a couple of companies, one of them Proctor & Gamble, and they turned me down. I reminded the chairman of the board, when he came to see me in Washington when I was President. [Laughter] Not with any acrimony, but it's funny how life is. . . . I didn't know what I wanted to do, and I don't think there's anything wrong with not knowing the day you graduate from college what you want to be for the rest of your life. I was very happy, for obvious reasons, that I moved to Texas—and

Barbara feels the same way about it. But a lot of kids, including some of our own grandchildren, are not sure what they want to be. But there's so much challenge and there's so much opportunity, and I think you settle on something you feel comfortable with, but then if that means you have to change or do something different, so be it. But I would also say, gratuitously, learn something. Do well enough in your studies so you have the knowledge upon which to make a decision of taking a job or changing a job.

Texas A&M University Distinguished Lecture,
College Station, Texas, March 8, 1999

One day when we were in the Oval Office, and we were having a big, serious meeting about some big, serious problem . . . "Mr. President, you gotta see this." There was a kind of tap on the door off to my right that goes out into the Rose Garden. I look up, and there's Ranger, our dog—the squirrel's tail coming out of one side of his mouth—[laughter]—his head out of the other side. And Sam [LeBlond], our grandson: "Look at Ranger! Look at Ranger, Gampy! Look what he did!" He had caught this squirrel. Reagan used to feed the squirrels, and our dogs ate them. [Laughter]

But it just kind of changed the pace. And all the guys in the room understood when I stopped and said, "Look at this. Look at my grandson."

A conversation with Hugh Sidey, "Time and the Presidency,"
College Station, Texas, April 19, 2000

PARENTS

Response to the question "Who had the greatest influence on your life?" . . .

My dad was never there when I was President . . . I wish he had been. But I was blessed. You see, we were taught—we had the benefit of having somebody say grace at the meals, blessings. We had the benefit of having discipline—somebody to tell you, "You did this one real bad. Go to your room"—or worse, in the case of my dad. . . . We had love. When we got hurt, they were there to pick me up. If I did something wrong, they were there to straighten me out. And the advice my mother gave me, you know, every parent says it. Unfortunately, there are a lot of people who don't have parents to say it these days or care enough to say it: "Do your best. Try your hardest. Don't be a bragger. Be kind to people." These things [are] so, you know, amorphous, or so predictable I guess you might say, that they just seem like absurd truisms—but that's what motivated me. I was President of the United States, and I would remember that kind of advice: "Try your hardest. Don't be discouraged." That's why I would put my parents there.

Interview with Peter Roussel, KUHT-TV's "A Conversation with George Bush," Houston, Texas, November 18, 1994

My dad lived by example . . . [and] most of the time we learned from him by example. And then my mother's kindness, and discipline, and values inspired me all my life. We had, somehow, inculcated into us at an early age the idea of giving. Some used to use "noblesse oblige" when I was President. They said, "This man has led a life of privilege." . . . And, yes, I was privileged. If I got sick, my dad could pay a hospital bill. When a lot of kids weren't getting a good education, I was. So we were privileged in that sense, but we were far more privileged in the values we got from our parents—right and wrong, help others, kindness, don't be a braggadocio. All that kind of stuff.

Interview with Jamie Gangel, NBC's Today show, Kennebunkport, Maine, April 25, 1997

Recounting a near-death experience at the hands of his esteemed father . . .

Mother had gotten a call from a neighbor two miles away. I remember it well. And the phone call came in, and Mother said,

"Did you boys do this?" We said, "Yes." She told my brother and me, "Well, your father is going to have to handle this." We walked into our den in Grove Lane, and he picked up a squash racket, and I thought, "Oh, God, this is it. We've had it." And he threatened us with [it] and said, "Now you go over to the Williamses' house, you go over and apologize." And we got out of this, scared to death. Ran as we started, then the closer to the Williamses' we got, we got very terrified and slowed down. We had to knock on the door and say that we were very sorry that we had paid the beautiful daughter ten cents to run naked across the floor. We got out with our lives on that one, but you know, we were sixth-graders at the time—natural hormonic urges you get, I guess. But that was as close as we came to death.

Interview with David Frost, "A President's Story,"
August 25, 1998

Following his high school graduation ceremony in June of 1942, George Bush informed his father that he was going to fight in World War II as planned. After delivering the news, it was the only time he saw his father, himself a World War I veteran, cry . . .

I think he knew by then that I had made up my mind, and that I was gonna go right into the navy. It's hard for kids today to understand that the experience of Pearl Harbor was so monumental that everybody wanted to be in—everybody wanted a piece of the action. . . .

He put me on the train at Penn Station.

Interview with David Frost, "A President's Story,"
August 25, 1998

Lyndon Johnson was President when I was a member of Congress, and I've got to say that he was extraordinarily thoughtful to me and to Barbara—[as was] Lady Bird, who we love. My dad had served in the Senate with Lyndon—they never voted much alike—but my father told me that Lyndon Johnson was a great Senate majority leader because he kept his word. He said his word would be good for his own party mates, but his word would be good for the minority. And if he said that there was going to be a vote on an amendment at 5:03 on Tuesday, that's when it would be. And he earned the confidence as leader—not people agreeing on the issues—of my dad. And of course when I came to Congress as a lowly freshman, for some reason—I think it was a Texas reason—he and Lady Bird were very thoughtful to us. And it made a difference . . . in our lives.

Texas A&M University Distinguished Lecture,
College Station, Texas, March 8, 1999

President Bush was serving as the U.S. ambassador to the United Nations when his father was struck ill in the early 1970s and being treated in New York . . .

I remember one rather humorous incident where I went up and told my dad, who was very sick with lung cancer at Sloan-Kettering—and subsequently within a few days passed away—but I said, "Well, Dad, I had dinner with [Andrei] Gromyko." You may remember Gromyko, the foreign minister, and [Yakov] Malek—these were two very hard-line Soviets. We tried to do a lot of this. We tried to meet and, you know, kinda get things on a personal basis. So I told Dad, "Well, I had this wonderful dinner." My father was lying there, and he perked up enough to say, "Who picked up the check?" He hadn't changed much.

Texas A&M University Distinguished Lecture,
College Station, Texas, March 8, 1999

I don't think there's a man I've ever had more respect for than my own father. He was a great, big, strong, principled man. People wrote in those days that he was the epitome of what a senator ought to be in terms of civility and honor—terms that seem to escape us at times today. But in terms of influence on my life, it was all-encompassing.

Interview with C-SPAN's Brian Lamb,
College Station, Texas, November 25, 1999

Remembering some motherly advice received as President . . .

One time she said, "George, remember how President Reagan used to wait for Nancy as he got off the helicopter there on the White House lawn?"

I said, "Mother, are you sending me a message?"

"Well, I think it would be nice if you didn't walk ahead like Jack Kennedy used to do."

Interview with Hugh Sidey, "Time and the Presidency,"
Lafayette Sqaure, April 11, 2000

FRIENDS

I miss friends. I miss the people in the White House that were like family to us. I miss dealing with the military.

Interview with Jamie Gangel, NBC's Today show,
Kennebunkport, Maine, June 13, 1995

Though there are some strained relationships with the press— some individuals—I'm about an age where I want to make them all better. I really am—with no desire for publicity on my part. Hell, I've been there. . . . I don't like broken friendships. I don't like to have unfinished relationships.

Interview with David Frost, "A President's Story,"
August 25, 1998

In this day and age when partisanship seems to be rampant— although I don't think it's any worse than it ever was—you do make good friends on both sides of the aisle. One of my closest friends is a Democratic congressman from Mississippi [Sonny Montgomery]—he still is one of my closest friends. And that was important.

Texas A&M University Distinguished Lecture,
College Station, Texas, March 8, 1999

Two observations follow on Ronald Reagan. President Bush was also once overheard saying of his immediate predecessor, "He'd sooner fly to the moon than walk past a doorman without saying hello . . ."

One of the greatest things about Ronald Reagan is his sense of humor—absolutely the best storyteller I have ever heard. Professional, amateur, you name the kind of joke, he had it. But it was always with a twinkle, never hurtful or mean about somebody. He could diffuse some of the most difficult situations with humor.

Interview with David Frost, "A President's Story,"
August 25, 1998

On his regular weekly lunch with President Reagan . . .

No agenda. No paper. "Please, sir, this is a good opportunity to see my view on whatever it is"—none of that. It was more, I hope, for him a relaxing meeting that he would look forward to and not dread. We'd tell jokes. If there was something going on in a big way in the world, or on domestic policy, we'd talk about that. But it was totally relaxed. . . . I think he knew I wouldn't blindside him. I had people call me, "You're going to see the President tomorrow. Please tell him that we've got to do this on the airline strike," or something else like that. Well, I wouldn't do that—and he knew I wouldn't do it.

Interview with C-SPAN's Brian Lamb,
College Station, Texas, November 25, 1999

On what he learned during his four years in Congress . . .

I learned that—even though you're in your forties, as I was—you can still make friends. I kinda thought, well, maybe you make your fast friends in school, or in college, or—in my case—in the service. But I made a lot of friends, and I remember being somewhat frustrated being in the minority the whole time. But it trained me, I think, for being President, when I faced a Democratic majority in the House and Senate for all four years. . . . I loved being a member of the United States Congress. But it was hard to get something done—part of a huge, you know, 435 people, it was hard to get things done.

Interview with C-SPAN's Brian Lamb,
College Station, Texas, November 25, 1999

John Major . . .

The staunchest ally of the United States during Desert Storm and the run up to Desert Storm was John Major. He just came in as prime minister after Iraq had invaded Kuwait. He came to see me at Camp David. And I said to General [Brent] Scowcroft—the national security adviser . . . "General, do you think we ought to unload these plans on Major right now, or should we wait until he gets his cabinet set up and all that?" And he said, "No, we've got to tell him every detail," and so we did. He [Major] never flinched. He never said, "We gotta talk to somebody else about this." And of course the Brits, as the general [Norm Schwarzkopf] can tell you, were at our side, leaders in the fantastic coalition that set back aggression and simply made a moral profound statement that the army, the man with the fourth-largest army in the world, is not with impunity going to take over a member state of the UN. . . . We had no more loyal leader of the coalition.

Panel discussion on the Gulf War tenth anniversary,
College Station, Texas, February 23, 2001

FAITH

I have great convictions personally, but I was never very good as President at sharing these things with the American people. The night that the war [Desert Storm] was about to start, Billy Graham—who's our respected, beloved friend—came to the White House and, you know, we prayed. And there were other incidents that I don't particularly care to talk about where your faith sustains you.

Interview with Paula Zahn, CBS's Sunday Morning,
Labrador, Canada, August 4, 1996

Responding to a student's question regarding "the hope and message of Jesus Christ" . . .

Regarding my own religion, I am a Christian. I do believe in Jesus Christ. And I felt uncomfortable, very honestly, talking about the depth of my feeling about religion when I was President. I'm an Episcopalian. I'm kind of an inward kind of guy when it comes to religion. I felt it strongly. I think Lincoln was right: you can't be President without spending some time on your knees professing your faith and asking God for strength, and to save our nation. But I believe strongly in separation of church and state. I don't believe a President should be advocating a particular denomination, or particular religion. And yet, I can tell you in direct response to your inquiry that we, in our family, say our prayers every night—Barbara and I do, we say the blessing. And it's more than rote. The governor of Texas does exactly the same thing. We were there at Thanksgiving having lunch with him, and he got up—and I was down way below the salt now—[laughter]—but there you are. Our family is strengthened and united by our faith. But it's a very delicate subject. Having said all that, I don't worry, I don't believe that our country is moving away from our various, varied religious beliefs. I don't feel that. I still feel we're moving in the wrong direction in terms of strengthening family, and in terms of these things that are plaguing our society—teen pregnancies, drugs, all those things. But I don't feel that we're turning our back on religion, and I don't think we ever should.

Texas A&M 1996 fall semester lecture "Rhetoric and the Presidency,"
College Station, Texas, December 2, 1996

Barbara and I have never been comfortable talking about our faith, but I can tell you that I don't see how you could be President if you did not believe in a being greater than yourself. I don't see how you could get the strength that you need, in quiet moments—the tough moments.

Interview with David Frost, "A President's Story,"
August 25, 1998

During a Naples, Florida, speaking engagement on February 23, 2000, President Bush experienced a minor relapse of the atrial fibrillation that had hospitalized him as President in 1991. He gave a rare press conference upon his departure from the hospital the next day and was asked about his mortality ...

When you get to be seventy-five ... you do think about that, but not with fear. If you've got faith, you don't think of it with fear. But I've got a lot of living to do. I've got a lot of places to go, planes to jump out of, a lot of things that I want to do. And I'm going to do it.

Press conference on leaving Naples Community Hospital,
Naples, Florida, February 24, 2000

RETIREMENT

People say, "Well, isn't it a little intrusive when people want to come up and want an autograph over here at ... some of these places we eat up here?" And it's not. I mean, if it's overdone, it is—

or if people are up there to tell you "You got this all wrong"—
[laughter]—or try to give you a lecture. Why, you know, you don't
want that. But in terms of somebody just being polite, it's flattering in a sense. People are respectful. We don't feel put-upon at
all in that regard.

We went to the theater in New York one time—and . . . we
were going to have dinner over at the River Club on the East
Side—and here was a guy screaming wanting something, I think
it was an autograph. . . . There's a big industry that sells auto-
graphs, and you see 'em with FedEx envelopes. The minute you
sign, the guy rushes off, FedExes the envelope in, and picks up a
hundred bucks or something. So . . . I said, "I'm very sorry. I'm a
busy man." We went in and had dinner, got into the car, went to
see the *Lion King* or one of these plays on Broadway. And at halftime . . . here's this guy standing right next to my seat—[laugh-
ter]—you know, sixth row back on the aisle. And the agents saw
him coming. And he was not greeted so warmly. The guy had
waited to halftime, and then with the crowd swept in there.

So you have a few that do that kind of thing. But for the most
part, people are extraordinarily kind to us, and respectful to our
privacy.

Texas A&M University Distinguished Lecture,
College Station, Texas, March 8, 1999

**Another part of the exchange with reporters upon leaving
Naples Community Hospital . . .**

Q. What about retirement?

President Bush. Well, it's wonderful. I'll tell you this: we have
    never been happier in our lives, and a lot of it is because I'm
    not in politics. Maybe the reason I got a little tired or ended
    up here is I get nervous about politics now. When it's your son
    and not yourself that they're after, it's a little more difficult. But
    I have no political ambition. I don't do op-ed pages; I don't go
    to Washington . . . as I am sure some of you have noticed. But
    we're very happy; we're very happy in our lives.

Q. Mr. President, we heard you were a little feisty about having
to spend the night here.
President Bush. Feisty is not the word I would have used. [Laugh-
ter] *Irritated,* perhaps . . .

> *Press conference on leaving Naples Community Hospital,*
> *Naples, Florida, February 24, 2000*

THE VISION THING:
Eternal Vigilance

Q. How do you want to be remembered for all time?
**President Bush. I want to be remembered as the guy that did
it with honor—that did his best.**

> *Interview with Bernard Shaw, CNN's "After Desert Storm,"*
> *Houston, Texas, February 27, 1996*

I did feel the majesty of the office.

> *Interview with Hugh Sidey, "Time and the Presidency,"*
> *Lafayette Square, April 11, 2000*

LEADERSHIP

Before the Bush Presidential Library was completed in November of 1997, President Bush hosted two major conferences—the
first one on the end of the Cold War and the second focusing on
Asia. The panel for the Cold War discussion at the Broadmoor
Hotel included former Soviet leader Mikhail Gorbachev, former
Canadian prime minister Brian Mulroney, former British prime
minister Margaret Thatcher, and former French president
François Mitterrand (in his last public appearance before his
death). Here, President Bush offers a closing word . . .

I remain an optimist about the world. I am not a pessimist about
where we are going. I am going to make a statement that I hope

is not interpreted as pure chauvinism by President Gorbachev, or the former president of the French Republic, or the former prime minister of Canada. As I look at the world, I think we [United States] have a disproportionate responsibility to lead. We're blessed. We're blessed by geography; we're blessed by means; we're blessed by a history of democracy. All these things are a blessing, and with them go a responsibility. And I think we neglect broad strategic discussions with China at our own peril. I think we risk bad things ahead if we don't fully engage with Russia and try to help, if we can, with its evolution—the evolution started by President Gorbachev. I think if we ever turned inward and neglected Europe—to say nothing of our friendly neighbors to the north, which we would never do—we do it at our own peril. We're selfish if we do that, and I hope we come to our senses and have broad strategic dialogue with these countries, large and small— and never get so selfish that we say, "We've done our part. Come on home. Let somebody else solve the problems of security, or the problems of economy." So that would be my plea. And I conclude with great vote of gratitude to my collaborators. It makes me realize how much I miss it.

Bush Presidential Library Cold War Conference,
"A World Transformed," Colorado Springs, Colorado,
October 9, 1995

Here, President Bush explains why dumping Vice President Dan Quayle from the 1992 ticket, as some people urged him to do, was never an option for him . . .

Some things are more important than winning, and one of them is loyalty. . . . I don't believe in cutting and running.

Interview with Paula Zahn, CBS's Sunday Morning,
Labrador, Canada, August 4, 1996

Leadership around the world means keeping one's word. It means policy by conviction. It means never blaming others, or ducking, or dodging, or putting our troops under the United Nations command. Leadership means standing against the voices of isolation and protectionism. It means being able to make a tough decision even when the pollsters and the handlers say no.

Remarks at the 1996 Republican Party National Convention,
San Diego, California, August 12, 1996

Whether you're a President or a student or a businessman or a public servant—as I hope many of you will be—I hope you'll take an interest in serving our great country. Remember this: character matters. Words are important, but character is what remains.

Texas A&M 1996 fall semester lecture "Rhetoric and the Presidency,"
College Station, Texas, December 2, 1996

Response when asked why he asked President Ford to send him to China as ambassador . . .

I thought that was the future.

Interview with C-SPAN's Brian Lamb, College Station,
Texas, November 25, 1999

"The Majesty of the Office"

Two observations here from his first visit to Washington on the adjustment to his new life as a former President . . .

As I got up here, I was handed this. [Holds up a paper with a heart on it.] This says, "Memories of a wonderful President. To George Bush from Laura M. Baird, 9 years old. P. S. Nice try." [Laughter] Out of the mouths of babes, you know.

Things have changed a helluva of a lot. When I was last in this hotel room, I had speechwriters. I had a TelePrompTer. Now I have writing paper that says "Sam"—that's my grandson Sam out here where we're staying. There's a picture of a basketball, a baseball, a bat, a soccer ball, and a football. Things have gone to hell, I'll tell you, since I left here. [Laughter]

. . . Some suggested, in my presidency, that the only thing I gave a damn about was the national security and foreign affairs. Not so. I had a keen interest in domestic affairs. I was interested in education, and energy matters, environment, law enforcement, and certainly volunteerism, and problems facing the disabled. And believe it or not, I even had an interest in the economy. How 'bout the third-quarter economic growth at 3.2 percent— [applause]—and the fourth quarter at 4.8 [5.8] percent growth? I was President, I think, back then. But nevertheless, I'm not here to cry over spilt milk. This kid summed it up best—this nine-year-old—"Nice try." [Laughter] Okay, go on to the next event.

Remarks on accepting the Forrestal Award,
Washington, D.C., March 18, 1993

I'll never forget one year when I was President—I think it was maybe '90 or '91—I spoke at the dedication of a brand-new facility, hospital facility, on a beautiful, sunny day in Florida. And I was giving a great big speech—we'd launched a new health-care harangue out there. And in the middle of my speech, one of the old guys in the back who had been wheeled out into the middle of a sunlit porch was heard to say, "This is a bunch of bull. This is a bunch of bull. When's Ike coming?" [Laughter]

Remarks for the Greater Washington Society
of Association Executives Foundation, Washington, D.C.,
January 22, 1996

Another assessment of the 1992 defeat . . .

Right then I was hurt, probably, and "Oh, what did I do wrong? How could I not get clear, get through to the American people?" And all that stuff. So there was a period of that. But there was never really a period of self-pity, or thinking—on the other side of it—thinking you were entitled to a grand lifestyle. So we just went back to work and started answering mail, and doing some of the things you had to do when you were President—but with no decision-making. Go from one day making decisions—worried about getting a call that something was wrong—and next day, nothing. Nobody giving a damn about what I thought, or cared—and that was the way it ought to be. It has not been difficult. It has not been difficult at all. . . .

I wanted to win. I didn't. I accept the judgment of the American people. Let the historians define whether I was a good President or a lousy President.

Interview with Paula Zahn, CBS's Sunday Morning,
Labrador, Canada, August 4, 1996

Discussing the history behind the prized Scowcroft Award for Somnolent Excellence, named for his trusted National Security Advisor . . .

This is a powerful award that emerged fairly early on in my presidency actually. [Laughter] [Brent] Scowcroft is a modest fellow; and though he fell asleep fairly regularly in daytime meetings, he didn't feel that he was worthy for having the award named for him. But we all knew that that was modesty on his part, because he was terrific at falling asleep during meetings. And because it was such a successful award domestically, we got an international award. There's a ranking committee. It's a secret committee because people would try to corrupt it, but I was on the committee, and I would note at international meetings which international delegation might challenge for the international Scowcroft Award. And one time, a delegation from Iceland made a starring performance because they had three people sitting at the table at this CSCE meeting in Paris, I think. And all three of them were asleep at the same time. Even the guy that was speaking was asleep while he was speaking—[laughter]—and I know you will find this hard to believe. But it was a wonderful award, and people respected it. . . .

Part of the Scowcroft Award went for recovery, and Brent himself—[a] marvelous National Security Advisor and he did work all night long every night—he'd be sleeping in the middle of the meeting, and then he'd hear something subconscious—and he had a pad—and he immediately started writing, smiling, writing down what he hadn't heard. So recovery was a part of it.

The Japanese, they had a man who . . . was absolutely marvelous in the recovery department. He did exactly the same thing his American counterpart did: he'd fall soundly asleep when his own prime minister was talking, then he'd wake up and smile and write something down. Heroic.

Interview with David Frost, "A President's Story,"
Moscow, Russia, August 25, 1998

Perspectives on personal diplomacy first learned at the United Nations, which later became a trademark of his presidency . . .

Henry Kissinger, I don't think fundamentally believed in personal diplomacy. Actually, he was pretty good at it, but I don't think fundamentally he believed in it. And his point to me and to others was "You're not going to get somebody to change their vote, change their political philosophy, because they like you." The United Nations is a political forum. One day there's a vote on one question; another day there's a vote on another question. One day there's one alignment of nations voting one way; the other day some of those same nation nations may be voting another. I believe firmly that many of those ambassadors that came to the United Nations did not have instructions from their governments. They had enough standing at home that they could vote, they had flexibility on how they were going to vote on a lot of the questions—not some of the most important ones—and if you had a good relationship with them, I became convinced that they would indeed vote with you. And so we did a lot of things with some of the smaller-country ambassadors that nobody ever paid attention to.

When I became President, our chief of protocol would invite ambassadors from countries that never could see Jim Baker or Dick Cheney or Colin Powell—bring them to Blair House and let them have lunch . . . and then those ambassadors would go back and send a cable to their chief of state: "Today I saw Jim Baker and told him this and that." And it's a good thing to do. Those personal relations. And I would say to those that do want to go into the diplomatic field that personal contacts are very, very important.

Texas A&M University Distinguished Lecture,
College Station, Texas, March 8, 1999

On China then and now . . .

We went to China, because I really believed that a lot of the future of a peaceful world depends on the U.S.-China relationship. But I went there, as did Barbara, with some myths. For example, I think most Americans back then thought that because of the "down to the countryside" Cultural Revolution mentality, the family had been diminished. But as soon as we got there, we saw that the family was still terribly important in China. It still is. And you'll see three generations—sometimes four generations—on national days, people in the parks, holding the hands of the grandparents, or even great-grandparents. And there were little tiny things like that that suddenly brought China alive to us. And it made me to this day realize how important it is that we never get back to where we were before the Nixon opening, before the signing of the Shanghai Communiqué. We have a lot in common with China, and yet we have a very different system. But I don't think if Barbara and I hadn't lived there in 1974 and 1975 that when I became President that I would have this strong feeling that that relationship needs to be preserved. It must be preserved. There are problems today with allegations of illegal technology transfer. But somehow we have to get past these troubling things and keep that relationship strong. And I felt that way as President. When Tiananmen Square happened, it was terrible—they did horrible things. They did bad things, violated the international convention on human rights; but it is in our interest to keep open relations with that very, very important country. Now they were set back, but we didn't cut them off. We didn't cut off MFN [Most Favored Nation trade status]. We didn't bring home our ambassador, as some of the people in this country after Tiananmen Square were urging on me. And I might not have reacted the way I did as President if we hadn't had a feeling for the pulse, the real China, the pulse of the people in China.

Texas A&M University Distinguished Lecture,
College Station, Texas, March 8, 1999

On the presidency itself . . .

The thing that matters, at least to me, is not how a liberal views a conservative or vice versa—or Republican and Democrat—but did you serve and uphold the dignity of the office. And it's very important to me. Ronald Reagan taught me a lot just from watching him for twelve [eight] years, and the respect that he had for that place. And I held exactly the same feeling of respect. I have the same sense of awe. . . . I go up and stay at Jackson Place right across from the White House, there's a house where former Presidents can stay, and you walk around the White House—I have the same feeling of awe and respect that I did when I went in there as a tourist, as when I went in there for eight years with Reagan as President every single day . . . or when I was President for four years. I think the institution—I mentioned earlier that the institution has a resiliency to it—but I think it's important in one's life to try and do it so you can say to yourself, "Well, at least I conducted myself with integrity." But the historians will have to decide . . . where we might have done things better, or what we got right. But none of that is important to me now. What's important to me is this concept of service we're talking about at our little school [George Bush School of Government and Public Service] here. And you can't do that if you cut corners here or there.

Texas A&M University Distinguished Lecture,
College Station, Texas, March 8, 1999

People outside, who have never been there, are intrigued with Camp David because it's been properly isolated from people—and certainly the press. Once you landed, you would rip off the tie—total privacy. You could have guests there, and it would never appear in the paper who you had. You could have grandchildren there, and they could run through the woods and chase after whatever it was. And they had all kinds of facilities—skeet shooting, and golf where you could hit golf balls, and then they had a practice range, tennis, bowling—had everything. And still you could get a lot done.

Texas A&M University Distinguished Lecture,
College Station, Texas, March 8, 1999

After his second postpresidential book, *All the Best,* was published, President Bush sat down with Larry King and explained why he tried not to criticize his successor . . .

One, I told him he wasn't going to have a lot of grief out of me; and two, I had my chance and I know it's a tough and big job; and three, we've got loyal opposition spokesmen who've been elected. My sons can speak out and be critical. I've got plenty of differences, plenty of areas where if I didn't feel constrained, I would be critical. But I just don't think it's seemly for a former President to always be carping away at the President.

Interview on CNN's Larry King Live,
Houston, Texas, November 2, 1999

After his second atrial fibrillation, dispelling a myth surrounding one of the more unfortunate moments of his presidency . . .

I've had a history of this. It has nothing to do with when I threw up on the prime minister of Japan—[laughter]—I know that's what you guys were thinking about. No, that was food poisoning.

Press conference on leaving Naples Community Hospital,
Naples, Florida, February 24, 2000

Some historians have compared President Bush's advisers, particularly his national security team, to the Truman administration—which included James Forrestal, Dean Acheson, George Marshall, among other postwar giants. Here, President Bush talks about his philosophy on assembling a President's team . . .

The secret is to get good people and give credit to them and delegate, and not always be out there taking credit yourself. I think that was a value I got from my mother. I mentioned at a little dinner here about my mother was always against braggadocio. "Don't be a braggadocio, George. Nobody likes braggadocios." [Laughter] I thought how she would feel about our library over here, because it is a bit of an ego trip—all the pictures about me. [Laughter] I think what you do is get good people. . . . We had a compatible team. And I really think that makes a difference, because none of them was seeking aggrandizement to the detriment of the President. They knew I would back them up. That's another side of it. . . . I remember when Clarence Thomas . . . came down embattled in the nomination for being on the Supreme Court, and I walked with him around the South Lawn of the White House, and I put my arm around his shoulder. He was saying, "Well, maybe it would be easier for you if I didn't persevere." I said, "No, it would make it worse. You deserve to be on the Supreme Court, and we will back you." And I did the same thing with [defeated Defense Secretary nominee Senator John] Tower. If people see those things, then it gives confidence to your team that you're not gonna be looking for a scapegoat if something goes wrong. And we had plenty of things go wrong, but it was my duty, and training—value system—to say, "Wait a minute. This was my responsibility." So I think—not trying to be a big shot—but I think that attitude helped get the most loyalty. . . . You can't be everything yourself. You can't take credit and then jump sideways when something goes wrong. And so I think part of why we were blessed with few—yeah, we had some leaks, we had some things go wrong—but we had a clean administration, an honorable administration in terms of scandals and stuff. I think it's just getting good people, and having confidence, and letting them run with the ball.

A conversation with Hugh Sidey, "Time and the Presidency,"
College Station, Texas, April 19, 2000

During this exchange with *Time* magazine's Hugh Sidey about an important meeting during the Gulf crisis, President Bush recounts one White House holiday party where the Christmas cheer got the better of Saint Nick . . .

Q. You had just been with Santa Claus.

President Bush. A drunk Santa Claus. Our man in red . . . [Laughter]

Q. Had one too many, did he? He was jolly though. [Laughter]

President Bush. He said, "Hi there!" [Pretends to faint.] It was terrible. He was a plumber over at Fort Mead—[laughter]—no, it was Fort McNair. I used to go running there. And one day—this is the truth, where we met Santa. . . . What do you call those things in the middle of the street?—the manhole cover was off to the side. And this guy sticks his head up and says, "Hi, George!" And the military guys said, "Shut up. That's Mr. President to you!" [Laughter]

A conversation with Hugh Sidey, "Time and the Presidency,"
College Station, Texas, April 19, 2000

A little vignette of life in the Bush White House . . .

One of the best things we did was we had two horseshoe tournaments a year—the Sweet 16, and then the 32. The people that played were the groundskeepers, the helicopter pilots, the Air Force One pilots, the butlers, the cooks, the chefs, the gardeners, all had teams—and the plumbers. And it did lots for morale of the place. . . . I was kind of head of the ranking committee, so I put Marvin [Bush] and me seeded number one every year—which caused a little grumbling—"What are these guys doing?" But every noon when I was in the Oval Office, I'd hear them practicing, getting ready for the tournaments—the horseshoes clanging down by the southwest gate there.

It was just a lot of almost family things that just made it so very, very special. And it wasn't just service; it wasn't just somebody bringing you a drink, or offering you some marvelous dinner. It was so hard to describe. But it took this family of ours—every grandchild, every son, our daughter—all felt that they knew and loved everybody who worked there. It made it so much easier. It made it so very easy.

A conversation with Hugh Sidey, "Time and the Presidency,"
College Station, Texas, April 19, 2000

And an Oval Office view of the difference between foreign and domestic policy . . .

The budget fighting was much harder for me because I didn't feel as comfortable with it, and I recognized that I was going to have to compromise on taxes. I knew how horrible that was going to be politically. But we had half a million men overseas; we didn't want to shut the government down; and I was torn there because [of] my own political fortunes, and yet, having to compromise and do what eventually we did—which, ironically, didn't hurt the economy at all. Those decisions I found tougher than the war and peace decisions.

[Hosni] Mubarak, president of Egypt, told me, "Okay, now you're President. What you ought to do is pick the phone and call the leaders in the Gulf." And I said, "What about?" And he said, "It doesn't matter. Ask them how the weather is in Oman." [Laughter] But it was sound advice. Because then when I wanted a squadron of airplanes to land [in Oman during the Gulf War], U.S. fighters to be based out of Oman, Sultan

Qaboos—you know, I paid some attention to him. It wasn't just the mighty United States coming down on him.

A conversation with Hugh Sidey, "Time and the Presidency,"
College Station, Texas, April 19, 2000

Camp David was the best. . . . One day we took Gorbachev, Marshal [Sergei] Akromeyev [Soviet arms control adviser], [Soviet foreign minister Eduard] Shevardnadze, and I had Jimmy Baker and Scowcroft. We took off our coats—I can see it, feel it right now—right out there on the terrace of the President's house there. And we were talking real serious business—moving towards START II, and a lot of other big things. The atmosphere was such that you could really communicate. It was so different than some of the more formal settings—in the Kremlin, or even in the White House. And you felt you knew these guys well. You felt that there was no way that they would pull a fast one. We're just trying to work these problems out.

A conversation with Hugh Sidey, "Time and the Presidency,"
College Station, Texas, April 19, 2000

On the controversy that embroiled his successor . . .

I have been disturbed about some of the personal behavior, but only because I think it diminishes the office. But I also was there . . . the day Nixon left, and Jerry Ford was sworn in two hours apart—departure and the swearing in—and it's funny how resilient the office is. That scandal went out with that helicopter with Nixon, and decency and honor returned with Ford. So I think it still works. I think the same thing will happen whoever is elected in the fall of this year. And I believe that the White House is still the most respected building in the world. You see leaders come into the Oval Office, and there are many more splendid offices—in Prague, or in Germany, or in . . . France, the Élysée. But there's something special about the Oval Office, and the White House, where foreign leaders come there, [from] all different kinds of systems, with a certain high level of respect. I think it is certainly going to endure, and I don't think it will ever change, Hugh. It's there. It's strong.

*A conversation with Hugh Sidey, "*Time *and the Presidency,"*
College Station, Texas, April 19, 2000

Two days after the election of 2000—the outcome still very uncertain—President and Mrs. Bush attended a dinner celebrating the two hundredth anniversary of President John Adams's arrival at the White House. Following are several excerpts . . .

What a joy to see Lady Bird Johnson, and to be here with the distinguished men and women who have called this majestic building "home." It might be strange to think of the White House in those terms—but that's exactly what it is to those who have been called to serve here. In this most public of government buildings, amid the ecstasy and agony of history, exists a genuine family home.

Someone once likened living in the White House to living in a fishbowl—but thanks in no small measure to the dedicated professionalism of the White House staff, it is possible to have a very happy family life here. It is possible to protect one's privacy.

Speaking of interesting election outcomes . . . as this year's presidential contest wound down, much was made in the media of the potential historical parallel between the Adams and Bush families—and for once I am compelled to say the press are far more prescient than previously thought possible. The election of 2000, pitting the son of a President against a candidate from Tennessee, is destined to join the election of 1824, with the same personal dynamic—John Quincy Adams against Andrew Jackson—as one of the closest in our nation's history.

Whatever happens this time, my pride and Barbara's pride knows no bounds. Moreover, our democracy will go on—and the new President will become part of a continuum of service that sets our nation, and this building, apart.

Like the stonecutters who chiseled their "banker marks" into the stones that form this house, the forty-third President will have his chance to make his mark here. Together with the new First Lady, they will write the next chapter in the history of the White House—proving that the names and faces may change, but this house, like our beloved republic, endures.

Many years ago, Henry Longfellow foretold our country's storied destiny in confident terms with his epic poem "Ship of State" [*sic:* "The Building of the Ship"]—which, in my view, is an apt description for the White House. More often than not, it necessarily falls to this vessel of statecraft to set the pace and lead the way and push back the frontiers of progress and prosperity and peace.

For two hundred years and eight days, this old house has been buffeted by the winds of change and battered by the troubled waters of war. We have been favored by calm seas, too, but history tells us a democracy thrives when the gusts and gales of challenge and adversity fill its sails—and compel it into action.

And through it all—through trial and tribulation, as well as triumph—the White House has served as our nation's anchor to windward, a vision of constancy, a fortress of freedom, the repository of a billion American Dreams. Age and the elements occasionally wear her down; but this house is forever renewed by the ageless fidelity of its founders, and the boundless promise of its future heirs.

In the immortal words of Longfellow: "Sail on, O Ship of State! Sail on, O Union, strong and great!"

Remarks at the two hundredth anniversary celebration
of the White House, White House East Room, November 9, 2000

On one traditional duty of the President he doesn't miss . . .

I don't want to be there when they pardon the turkey. I've done that four years, and I am so thrilled that George will be out there following in the footsteps of every other President who sits in the Oval Office saying, "That #$%* turkey's coming in here again. Don't I have better things to do with my life?" [Laughter] "You ought to pardon him, sir." "Oh, funny one. Yeah, let's go out." Turkey's sitting out there flapping away—[laughter]—and you gotta go out there and pardon the turkey. I don't want to be around there for Thanksgiving. I want to be around when we give thanks, to God.

Interview with Paula Zahn, Fox News Channel's The Edge,
Houston, Texas, December 20, 2000

A President has to look at the vital national interests of this country. That means that you have to be quite selective in where you commit force, and when you commit force . . . that's the reality that a President faces.

Panel discussion on the Gulf War tenth anniversary,
College Station, Texas, February 23, 2001

WAR AND PEACE

After leaving office, President Bush accepted an invitation from the emir of Kuwait to visit his liberated country. Traveling with numerous family members and administration colleagues, one of the stops included addressing Kuwait's National Assembly . . .

We must remember that the price of freedom is eternal vigilance. Even the hope of a new world order cannot guarantee an era of perpetual peace.

Remarks before the Kuwaiti National Assembly,
Al Shaab Palace, Kuwait City, April 23, 1993

We had a three-point formula that we followed every time we committed American forces into harm's way. I might have stolen the formula from Colin Powell—I can't remember—but I was commander in chief, so it was the "Bush formula." [Laughter]

Remarks at the Greater Washington Society of Association Executives Foundation, Washington, D.C., January 22, 1996

President Bush granted two major interviews relating to the fifth anniversary of the Gulf War. The first was to British journalist Sir David Frost and included footage of a secret interview taped at Camp David on March 9, 1991, immediately after the coalition victory . . .

Q. Dan Quayle in his book [*Standing Firm*] said, "I believe the executive order prohibiting assassination of foreign leaders should be rescinded so the President has one more option in extraordinary circumstances." Do you agree with that?

President Bush. No. I didn't see that he said that, but having been the Director of Central Intelligence for one fascinating year, I don't believe that order should be rescinded. Now, if you want to put it into the context of the war, Saddam Hussein was the commander in chief of the Iraqi forces, and if his life had been snuffed out in a bombing attack or something— too bad, that's one of the prices of war. But I don't believe we should clandestinely target foreign leaders for assassination.

Interview with David Frost, "President Bush: Talking with David Frost," Houston, Texas, January 16, 1996

On ending the war . . .

There is a moral imperative here. I don't think the United States or the United Kingdom or France measure the extent of their victory by an increased body count. We could have massacred these people, fleeing up the "highway of death" in those broken-down, stolen vehicles. We could have killed another couple of hundred tanks and thus further diminished the capability of the Republican Guard to project their horror. . . . You know, war is immoral, but I don't think you measure the totality of its success by whether you can shoot down another, kill another fifty thousand fleeing soldiers—murderous though they had been in Kuwait.

Interview with David Frost, "President Bush: Talking
with David Frost," Houston, Texas, January 16, 1996

On Saddam Hussein, I guess I'd have to stop short of saying he's certifiably nuts.

Interview with David Frost, "President Bush: Talking
with David Frost," Houston, Texas, January 16, 1996

The presiding bishop of my church—I'm an Episcopalian, some might say Anglican—he felt that way [against using force]. He told me so. He came to the Oval Office and told me, "You must not use force." And I asked him to read the Amnesty International report. I said, "Please, sir, tell me after you read this, whether it would be right to use force—when you see the rape of these thirteen-year-old Kuwaiti girls, whose lives are ruined forever." And he wrote me back, and he said, "I read the report, and I wept, but I still don't think you should use force." That was pretty profound from the leader of my church as I was contemplating having to send young men and women into battle.

Interview with David Frost, "President Bush: Talking
with David Frost," Houston, Texas, January 16, 1996

In this second interview, given to CNN's Bernie Shaw, President Bush refers to the foiled Iraqi assassination attempt on him and his family during their 1993 visit to Kuwait . . .

Nobody likes to be the target of assassination.

Interview with Bernard Shaw, CNN's "After Desert Storm,"
Houston, Texas, February 27, 1996

Assessing the Iraqi commander in chief five years after the war . . .

He underestimated the courage of the American fighting force, the skill of our generals, and—frankly—he underestimated my fiber, because I was determined from day one that the aggression not stand.

Interview with Bernard Shaw, CNN's "After Desert Storm,"
Houston, Texas, February 27, 1996

We determined early on that we would not let the holding of hostages change our plans or, in any way, make us more reluctant to use force. I had that set in my mind, and I worried about it. . . . Some of the people that were captured—we were worried that he was going to stake them out next to some likely military target. I remember the time when Governor [John] Connally went over there with a man named Oscar Wyatt to kind of beg for the release of American hostages. And I was literally furious at that, because we didn't want Saddam Hussein to think that the hostages gave him a "hold card"—gave him some power over us. So I can tell you, and my colleagues in government will tell you, that I never wavered one bit.

Interview with Bernard Shaw, CNN's "After Desert Storm,"
Houston, Texas, February 27, 1996

In a war, you can't spare the innocent, but we tried to do that.

Interview with Bernard Shaw, CNN's "After Desert Storm,"
Houston, Texas, February 27, 1996

In terms of morality, what I loved was when the Iraqis came out of foxholes, their hands in the air, knowing they were going to be killed—the massive power of America [had] just swept over them, and the coalition forces with us. And they knew they were going to be killed. And some tough sergeant said, "We're not going to hurt you. We are American soldiers."

Interview with Bernard Shaw, CNN's "After Desert Storm,"
Houston, Texas, February 27, 1996

Reflections on Panama . . .

During Reagan's presidency, George Shultz and President Reagan had favored a deal to get Noriega to leave Panama peacefully. Indeed, the USA had tried to find asylum for him in Spain and elsewhere.

I will never forget the meeting in the lovely Yellow Room upstairs in the President's residence in May of 1988. This was the only time I differed in front of others with President Reagan. I told him, seconded by Jim Baker, that it would be very bad to cut a deal with Noriega, letting him get asylum and escape punishment for his drug activities.

Because I had been head of CIA many years before, and because Noriega had an "intelligence" relationship with us back then, people had already begun sniping at me for having had anything to do with Noriega. First, I thought it was just plain wrong to grant him immunity; and secondly, I knew that, if we did, I would be accused of making a deal with Noriega because he "had something on me."

In my view intervention was clearly in our vital national interest not just for the reasons cited above but because of the effect our nonaction would have on our standing in Latin America. I knew full well that, given our history of military intervention in this hemisphere, we would not get any overt support and would in all likelihood be vigorously criticized by Mexico and others. Nevertheless, I felt we had to act.

Remarks at the Fall Leadership Conference of the Center
for the Study of the Presidency at Texas A&M University,
October 23, 1999

Reflections on the fall of the Berlin Wall ten years later . . .

The emotions I felt as I watched Germans of all ages gathered at the Wall—and on it—are hard to describe. I had been to the Wall as Vice President and stood there with my friend Helmut Kohl and Mayor Richard von Weizsacker, as they pointed out where young East Germans had been shot while trying to cross to freedom.

In February of 1983, I had also been to the town of Moedel-reuth (with my dear, respected friend Manfred Woerner, whom we deeply miss). There, I saw a border fence that ran through the heart of the town—dividing the two Germanies.

But now, six years later, I was President of the United States—watching as the hopes and dreams of mankind, which for so long seemed so impossible, became a reality before my eyes. It was a surreal sight—as if Dalí himself had painted it. Then came the realization of what we were witnessing: the dam had been breached, and freedom was literally cascading over the Wall.

*Remarks commemorating the tenth anniversary
of the fall of the Berlin Wall, Reichstag in Berlin,
November 9, 1999*

On Desert Storm . . .

The evil against the good was so clear, it made it very easy for me. . . . It was an easy call for me on principle, not on execution.

*A conversation with Hugh Sidey, "Time and the Presidency,"
Lafayette Square, April 11, 2000*

The two kinds of intelligence . . .

I learned firsthand the limits of intelligence. I knew when they told me, "This is how many men he has in Kuwait today," I knew that would be 100 percent accurate. We call that "bean counting." *But,* if they said, "We think Saddam is going to move south," that would be "measuring intent"—not beans, not tanks, soldiers, and all that. Then I knew enough to know, well, this is the community decision—the intelligence community decision—but there might be room for error. So I think that experience helped me as the ultimate consumer of intelligence.

A conversation with Hugh Sidey, "Time and the Presidency," College Station, Texas, April 19, 2000

To mark the tenth anniversary of Desert Storm, President Bush and his Library Foundation hosted a panel discussion at Texas A&M with former British prime minister John Major, General Norman Schwarzkopf, former CIA director Robert Gates, and former White House spokesman Marlin Fitzwater . . .

As President, I remember an early meeting up at Camp David when Colin Powell and Dick Cheney . . . called together our military leaders and I had an opportunity to set out the objectives. I remember Vietnam, where political people kept calling the shots in the war. . . . The mission was originally clear but it got muddied up because it didn't quite give the military the full head to go ahead to fight and win the war. I remember meeting with General Schwarzkopf at Camp David with these others, and I immediately saw then what the whole world saw later—determination, leadership. . . .

We forget, because there were all these talks in the press about trenches of fire—fifty thousand body bags awaiting our young men and women that were going to be asked to fight under his [Schwarzkopf's] command and the coalition forces as well, and we forget all that because of the way that the military fought and won the war. . . .

I remember the agony, and I remember the worries about what the Russians [Soviets] were going to do, and I remember worrying about public opinion . . . but because of the way the war was fought and won, people are inclined to forget that.

Panel discussion on the Gulf War tenth anniversary, College Station, Texas, February 23, 2001

I'll tell you one of the ways where I was wrong: I honestly felt and so did every Arab leader—and I'm not going to put words in Prime Minister Major's mouth—but most of the coalition leaders felt that, given the pounding Saddam Hussein took, that he couldn't survive. He did. But he did through total brutality of his own people. Remember what he did to his own sons-in-law who went to Jordan. They came back and a couple of days later they were both dead. We underestimated the tyranny.

Panel discussion on the Gulf War tenth anniversary,
College Station, Texas, February 23, 2001

Danny Inouye, who's a Democratic senator [from Hawaii], came down to tell me before the war started—he's a war hero, he's a wonderful man, one of the top Democrats in longevity and, I think, in influence—and he came and he said, "Look, this is a difficult call. I can't be for you with the resolution, but if the troops are committed, I'll be with you." But he said, "You have to know that the feeling is so strong that if it doesn't go right, you're going to be impeached." I'll never forget his telling me that, and he didn't do it in a threatening way, he didn't do it in a "You better not do this because . . ." It helps you understand the depth of feeling. Many of the people who opposed us in the resolutions and opposed us in the run-up to the war had vivid recollections of the Vietnam War. And one of the good things . . . about the way the war was fought and won—it healed, it helped to heal a lot of the wounds of Vietnam. And I think a lot of the political opposition came from the fact that they had vivid recollections of a war that did not have as clear and concise a victory and conclusion.

Panel discussion on the Gulf War tenth anniversary,
College Station, Texas, February 23, 2001

Response when asked what he might have done differently . . .

I might have been able to do better in the buildup to it to get more support from the United States Congress. We tried. We tried very

hard on that, and perhaps we could have been more effective earlier on.

Panel discussion on the Gulf War tenth anniversary,
College Station, Texas, February 23, 2001

LEGACY OF SERVICE:
The Lord's Work

**It's a love of country and a willingness to serve your country.
It's a combination of those. It's pretty easy for me, because I
know that we are the most wonderful, freest, fairest, most giving country on the face of the earth. And to understand that
and appreciate it and count your blessings for that, that's like
a four-inch putt in golf—that's a gimme. It's pretty easy.**

Interview with Mike Wright, KBTX-TV's "An Evening
with George Bush," College Station, Texas, June 6, 2001

POINTS OF LIGHT

Along with the [Bush Presidential] Library, I'm trying to be what
I used to talk about in the White House as one of a Thousand
Points of Light—and that means helping others, that means
helping volunteer organizations. In my case, it's a great cancer hospital, M. D. Anderson, and AmeriCares, and Eisenhower
Exchange Fellows, and several others. And Barbara, her cause is literacy, and she's also on the Mayo's board. So we're trying to join
our neighbors in putting something back into the system, and it's
a wonderful life. . . .

I expect tomorrow as I look back or revel in the success and
ache about the trials of my sons, that these have been the best
years. You gotta always count your blessings, and mine are man-
ifold. I don't need anything else in life. I've been blessed with
everything. I've done more than I ever dreamed would come my
way. So, whatever I'm doing is the best in my life—right now. I
couldn't be happier, couldn't be luckier, and I hope I appreciate it

enough to try to continue to serve in some way—not politics—
but to serve mankind, do my little bit, as a tiny little Point of
Light. . . . Because I feel life has been great to me, and I have no
regrets. Made some mistakes, wish some things had been different. But the best years of my life, they probably lie ahead of me.

Interview with Peter Roussel, KUHT-TV's "A Conversation
with George Bush," Houston, Texas, November 18, 1994

President Bush joined Presidents Bill Clinton, Jimmy Carter, and
Gerald Ford—and honorary chairman General Colin Powell—
at Philadelphia's Marcus Foster Stadium to help kick off the Presidents' Summit for America's Future. Coconvened by the Points
of Light Foundation and the Corporation for National Service,
for three days it focused the country's attention on community
service.

You don't have to be a President to be a leader, and you don't have
to be a First Lady to touch the life of someone else.

Remarks at the Presidents' Summit for America's Future,
Philadelphia, Pennsylvania, April 27, 1997

PUBLIC SERVICE

I'd say get started early—it doesn't have to be running for office,
and it doesn't have to be in office. Get started early being of service to others. That's where you start. That could be in the community. I got more of a kick out of being one of the founders of
the YMCA in Midland, Texas, back in 1952 than almost anything
I've done. We did something and helped kids by doing it. So they
ought to start by working at some university—or when you first
get out of the university, in your community in one way or
another. And then, instead of sitting on the sidelines complaining
about politics, do something about it. Be in somebody's campaign
or write an op-ed letter or go get to know more about how the
Congress works. And then, don't be turned off by the ugliness of

the political climate. I mean, it is ugly—'92 was the most hurtful year that my family and I have ever been through, ever. But I would still say to a son or a daughter, if she ever decided, "Hey, do it. Get involved." If you don't, you leave it to people who may not be as well motivated as you are. . . . I just hope that young people do not turn their back on politics. And if they do, they get what they deserve: something lousy.

Interview with Peter Roussel, KUHT-TV's "A Conversation with George Bush," Houston, Texas, November 18, 1994

If good people don't get into the political arena, then you really forfeit the right to criticize, and you leave the arena to those who may be in it for some improper motive. I believe in public service, and I was kind of ridiculed as the elitist whose father before him served and, thus, service was the thing that mattered to George Bush. It did matter to me. Service fighting for my country as a scared nineteen-year-old pilot. Service in the political arena in the community—county chairman of Harris County, Texas. Service as President of the United States. It does matter. And I have great convictions on things, deep convictions. . . . I'm not cynical about our political system, and I think good people ought to serve. And I think I'm a good person, at least in that sense.

Interview with Bernard Shaw, CNN's "After Desert Storm," Houston, Texas, February 27, 1996

Advice to those who would seek public office . . .

I think it's a good thing for those that want to be in politics to have had some track record—in academia, in business, in something other than just the political arena. I think it broadens your dimensions—maybe the military—but something to give you something other than just aspiring for public office.

Texas A&M University Distinguished Lecture, College Station, Texas, March 8, 1999

On January 20, 1999–ten years to the day that he was sworn in as President, and "six years to the day that he was sworn out," as he put it—George Bush delivered the Senate Majority Leader's Lecture Series in the Old Senate Chamber Room. Once again, he found himself in unusual circumstances as the Senate trial of President Clinton was under way. Following are several excerpts from that speech . . .

Eighteen years ago today, Barbara and I were participating in another inauguration—one that brought us back to Washington, and back to Capitol Hill.

It's funny: I ran for the Senate twice—both times with a spectacular lack of success. But for eight years, and then four more after that, all the senators called me "Mr. President."

. . . I loved interacting with senators from both parties. Of course, it was easier for me, better, as Vice President. For one thing, with Howard Baker at the helm, my party controlled the Senate for my first six years here—and let's face it, that helped—[laughter]—when you're looking at it from a downtown perspective. But after I moved down the street to the White House, my dealings with the Senate seemed to involve more raw politics.

As president of the Senate, the primary constitutional role I served was breaking tie votes. I went to funerals—[laughter]—but I cast seven tie-breaking votes as VP—three times alone on the esoteric matter of nerve gas. Most unpopular, those tiebreakers were.

A myth arose from one of those votes that my mother bawled me out. Well, she didn't quite do that. She did give advice, however. After attending my first State of the Union address speech as Vice President, for example, she called: "Oh, George, this is wonderful. My own son, sitting there before the country . . ." "But, Mother, but you've seen me before." [She replied:] "But never before the country like that."

Then she said, "But I noticed something. I noticed that while Ronald Reagan was speaking, you were talking to Tip O'Neill." [Laughter] I said, "He started it." [Laughter] And it was true, O'Neill had started it.

She added, "And another thing, George, you should try smiling more."

I said, "Mother, the President was talking about nuclear annihilation, and I'm supposed to be smiling here like that." [Laughter]

———————

Since leaving office, I have stayed away from Washington—but that does not mean I lack interest in events here. I have refrained from commenting on the serious matter before the Senate—and will continue so to do—but like Howard Baker and others, I confess that the lack of civility in our political debate and official dealings with one another concerns me.

I worry, too, about sleaze—about excessive intrusion into private lives. I worry about once great news organizations reduced to tabloid journalism—giving us sensationalism at best, and smut at worst.

I have to be careful. I'm out there on this speaking circuit—with Colin [Powell] and others—and I got a huge standing ovation, fourteen thousand brilliant St. Louisans, after I knocked the hell out of the Washington press corps. I felt good about it. [Laughter] Then I got a letter from a friend who said, "You ought not do this. This is beneath you." So I joined Press Bashers Anonymous—[laughter]—and I've been clean for six months. And I hope my comments are not interpreted as my falling off the wagon.

But I think it's fair to note with seriousness that the times cry out for more accountability—and I think many people understand that.

All in all, it seems to me that, whereas the problems looming over this town dealt more with budget deficits in times past, today we are confronted with a deficit of decency—one that deepens by the day. Washington is a place for big ideas and doing big things; but it is also a small town in many respects, too small for the bitter rancor that sometimes divides us today.

———————

One last thought about the Senate. Fifty years ago, I was starting out in the oil business—out in the dusty fields of west Texas—in Odessa, and Midland, in the Permian Basin. In those days, and in that place, a man's word was his bond. So much so that much of our business was done on a handshake—no lawyers, no escrows, you just look a man in the eye, with a handshake, and you've got a deal.

There aren't too many places where you can still do business on a handshake, but you can still do it in the United States Senate.

Indeed, as we gather in this historic setting this evening, we not only marvel at how the universe outside these hallowed walls has changed over the last 189 years—but we also take comfort at how much the world inside these walls has remained the same—how a timeless code of duty and honor has endured. And we can thank Almighty God that it has.

In this light, perhaps it is fitting to close with the words that Aaron Burr used to close his career in the Senate. In his retirement address of 1805, Burr aptly noted: "It is here, in this exalted refuge; here, if anywhere, will resistance be made to the storms of political frenzy and the silent arts of corruption."

As long as there exists a Senate, there will exist a place of constancy, of Madisonian firmness—a place unlike any other, where the sacred principles of freedom and justice are eternally safeguarded. Like this magnificent setting, may we always be humbled before it—and cherish it ever more.

Remarks at the Senate Majority Leader's Lecture Series,
Washington, D.C., January 20, 1999

What he learned at the CIA . . .

I was only there one year, and it was perhaps the most fascinating individual year of my lifetime. I don't know that I left a mark, but they left a mark on me. The mark had to with the importance of intelligence. That mark had to do with dedicated, selfless, honorable public service. The mark had to do with my comprehending the fundamental importance as President of the best intelligence in the world.

Interview with C-SPAN's Brian Lamb,
College Station, Texas, November 25, 1999

Part of what's troubled me is there's a cynicism about public life. I think what I hope the legacy might be is that they served with honor—made plenty of mistakes, got some things right, bottom line: "served with honor."

Interview with Paula Zahn, Fox News Channel's The Edge,
Houston, Texas, December 20, 2000

I still believe politics is a noble calling. I don't believe a lot of the garbage I read in some of the sophisticated journals that tell us everybody's in politics to feather his own nest. And if we can inculcate into just one kid the idea that government service, public service, doing something for others, is important, then at this stage of my life that will be doing the Lord's work.

Interview with Mike Wright, KBTX-TV's "An Evening
with George Bush," College Station, Texas, June 6, 2001

MILITARY SERVICE

I'm pleased to receive this award, but did you know you were bestowing it on a pilot who took off two more times than he landed?

Remarks on receiving the Forrestal Award,
Washington, D.C., March 18, 1993

In these two excerpts from remarks delivered at a navy symposium in Pensacola, President Bush reflects first on the patriotic spirit that took hold as the country prepared for World War II . . .

The news about Pearl Harbor hit our campus like a ton of bricks. I was walking near our chapel with my roommate when I heard. We couldn't clearly see then how the attack on Pearl Harbor would affect our own lives, but we knew things would change dramatically.

The next day there was a student assembly. Our tough head-master saw all of us talking and straggling in sloppily. He called the meeting to order, and when "The Star-Spangled Banner" was fin-ished playing, he said, "Our country is now at war. That was 'The Star-Spangled Banner' that was just played. I never want to see any of you talking during that anthem. I want you to stand at atten-tion and show respect."

That lesson lasted me a lifetime.

And defends the navy against more recent attacks . . .

I hate the reckless attacks on the navy. It goes on and on and on. From Tailhook to the Academy—from wanton press attacks, to ugly books, to so-called "watchdog" members of Congress—they all seem to take delight in tearing down the navy.

When someone did something wrong, say in Tailhook, fine, clean it up. Censure the wrongdoer, but for God's sake don't con-demn the entire service, or don't knock down an entire brigade of midshipmen because one man does something dumb or even illegal.

Let the investigative reporters or some unhappy congressman or some liberal author in quest of a prize single out the things that might have gone wrong. Let them do it their negative way—judge the entire navy by the mistakes or misdeeds of the few.

For me, I'll forever judge the navy by the memory of those courageous pilots going up over Baghdad on missions fraught with danger. Doing that nobly, in the great tradition of the same navy that made a man out of me many years ago—the navy that I love and respect.

Remarks at the Naval Aviation Museum,
Pensacola, Florida, May 10, 1996

Explaining the rationale behind his first parachute jump since World War II . . .

It's not rediscovering my youth. It's not a thrill. That's not what this is about. It's a quiet inside thing that I am sure nobody will understand. [Laughter]

. . . It's about doing something right that I did imperfectly back in September of 1944. I made a parachute jump then. It had tragedy to it. My life was saved. And I didn't do it right. And I'm kind of a goal-oriented person—and I decided long ago, in my heart of hearts, I wanted to make a parachute jump.

Interview with Jim Nantz, CBS's Sunday Morning,
Yuma, Arizona, March 30, 1997

I even thought about going into the Royal Canadian Air Force [in World War II]—something I've never told anybody—because you could get in a little younger, get finished a little earlier.

Interview with Jim Nantz, CBS's Sunday Morning,
Yuma, Arizona, March 30, 1997

Lingering questions and memories from the day he was shot down in the Pacific, September 2, 1944 . . .

Made me count my blessings. Why me? Why was my life spared? Floating around in a life raft, knowing that the fleet was moving, going to go south in about four hours—it was a traumatic experience for a young guy, for anybody.

A conversation with Hugh Sidey, "Time *and the Presidency,"*
Lafayette Square, April 11, 2000

Commenting on why he wanted his second postpresidential book, *All the Best*, to be a book of letters already written . . .

There's no revisionism. There's no selective memory. Hugh [Sidey] asked me today about World War II. I could certify that I almost single-handedly won the war in the Pacific. [Laughter]

*A conversation with Hugh Sidey, "*Time *and the Presidency,"*
College Station, Texas, April 19, 2000

I learned a lot as a kid—just a young kid. Sworn in on my eighteenth birthday; in the service for three years; and I learned a lot about the spirit of America, about a country coming together. And it troubled me as I went along and saw the divisiveness of Vietnam particularly. People who served with honor in Vietnam coming home and spat upon—denied their respect for serving their country. So that little experience I had back when the country was united and watching it made a huge difference, and I think it made me a better commander in chief. Because when Powell and Schwarzkopf came to me in October after we had sent 250,000 to the Gulf, they said, you gotta double the force. And our guys were telling me, "Hey, Congress is gonna raise hell." And I said, "I don't give a damn what they say. This is something the President can do. We're doubling the force." And we sent that additional 250,000 people there. But my experience just in the navy, I think, I think made that decision easier for me.

*A conversation with Hugh Sidey, "*Time *and the Presidency,"*
College Station, Texas, April 19, 2000

IN THE ARENA:
Charging Forward

I think the bottom line is, as with the military, you give it your best shot, and you move on to something else. You count your blessings for friends, for family, and for the privilege of serving this great country.

Remarks on receiving the Forrestal Award,
Washington, D.C., March 18, 1993

As President, I defended freedom of the press; now I rejoice in freedom from the press.

Texas A&M 1996 fall semester lecture,
"Rhetoric and the Presidency,"
College Station, Texas, December 2, 1996

I don't know if my idol, Lou Gehrig, said it first; but I do know he said it best: Today I feel like that luckiest person in the world.

Remarks at the dedication of the George Bush Presidential
Library, College Station, Texas, November 6, 1997

MEDIA

But let me just say that this has been a wonderful occasion. I kind of dreaded coming back to Washington in a way, but this has been a happy occasion. I went to the reception, and everybody was so pleasant about our return. As for our life, we're going to stay out of the interview business. I've been in public service a long time, and there is a wonderful private life out there. . . .

I'm going to leave the spokesman role to others. I've been there. Perhaps someone more articulate might have handled it better. . . . I don't think anyone needs to hear some comments from the cheap seats down in Houston, so I'll stay out of all of that. And I'll wish our President well. I really do. I wish him all the best.

Remarks on receiving the Forrestal Award,
Washington, D.C., March 18, 1993

Anytime I felt sorry for myself in treatment I might have received, some editor would properly point out that Grover Cleveland had a helluva bad time, too—and that was no comfort to me— [laughter]—but I think it did put things in an inordinately proper context.

Texas A&M 1996 fall semester lecture,
"Rhetoric and the Presidency," College Station, Texas,
December 2, 1996

President Bush's first post–White House chief of staff was Rose Zamaria, who first worked for him in 1967 in Congress . . . (Editor's note: She *was* tough.)

Rose [Zamaria] was a tough, tough woman, who also worked for me in the White House. And one time she got a call from Lesley Stahl, and Lesley says, "We would like former President Bush to be on *60 Minutes.*" And Rose said, "No way, Lesley." Lesley said, "What do you mean, no way? Doesn't he realize that we have the largest audience for this kind of show anywhere in the entire world now?" And Rose thought for a minute and said, "Don't you realize he doesn't give a damn about that anymore?" [Laughter]

Texas A&M 1996 fall semester lecture,
"Rhetoric and the Presidency," College Station, Texas,
December 2, 1996

There are some times when you're President you can't be quite as frank as you want to be—you've got to be very careful dealing with various constituencies. But this one was one I felt strongly about,

David, and I had to speak out—and in the process, liberated many four-, five-, six-year-old kids all across this country who shared my hate for broccoli. The good news was the broccoli sales went up. . . . After I said, "My mother made me eat broccoli, I'm President, I'm not going to eat broccoli anymore," two huge broccoli trucks appeared on the South Lawn of the White House. [It attracted] the second-largest concentration of press for any event when I was President, and Barbara dramatically went out—because I refused, I thought it would be hypocritical to go out and greet these trucks. You couldn't expect that. So they asked, "What are you going to do with this broccoli?" And Barbara said, "We are going to give this to the homeless." And John Sununu leaned over to her and said, "Why do you think they left home in the first place?" [Laughter] . . . But, David, there's a terrible thing [that's] happened since I left the presidency. I came home unexpectedly for lunch in Houston—our little house there—opened the icebox door, and this whole waft, this horrible steamed broccoli. And I called upstairs, challenged Barbara on it, and her answer was "Well, I didn't expect you home for lunch, and I like steamed broccoli." What do you do?

Interview with David Frost, "A President's Story,"
August 25, 1998

They were very good, our speechwriters, but . . . I would go through a State of Union speech and say, "I can't do this high-falutin stuff." People know I'm no Thoreau, or Yeats, or something like this. I'm not a poet; I'm just a guy that's trying to do a job as President. And maybe, in retrospect, I could have done better if the words had soared a little more, and I hadn't kept crossing out intellectual quotes. Because I felt, well, this is being something I'm not—and maybe people might see through that. And yet, some of the best were speeches written by other people.

Interview with C-SPAN's Brian Lamb,
College Station, Texas, November 25, 1999

On the only letter to the editor he wrote as President . . .

I wrote one letter, to Punch Sulzberger [*New York Times*], when I was—I thought—smeared by an ugly story about being disconnected because . . . I never knew what a [grocery store] scanner was. [This was] brand-new technology, and most of the other media people reported it that way. It was in a convention unveiling new machinery—how you could take a crushed package for the first time in history and show the price on the package. And I said, "This is amazing." So some lazy little reporter from the *New York Times* sat in his office—wasn't even there—and wrote "There it is. He's out of touch. He doesn't know you can scan groceries." And the damn story lived on.

Interview with C-SPAN's Brian Lamb,
College Station, Texas, November 25, 1999

Explaining why, as of January 20, 2001, his media critiquing will be kept to a minimum . . .

What would happen if I told you . . . what I really feel about some of the reporting, and some of the reporters? There would be "This bitter old man is doing this." The pack would come together, climb all over me, and it would inure to the detriment of our son. So . . . we want to be off the stage. We don't want to be kinda "Wait a minute! I want to set the record straight on what that idiot said about our son, or what he said about me, or Barbara, or our family." It doesn't work that way. They got the last word; and besides, you might feel good for a moment, but it would be a loser. And these are people that have different political views—these editors and writers—and who am I to say they shouldn't say it the way they think it is? So I don't want to get into all that, and I don't plan to.

Interview with Paula Zahn, Fox News Channel's The Edge,
Houston, Texas, December 20, 2000

Correcting the record on one Florida recount story . . .

I read in the paper that I was the one that got Jim Baker to fly down to Florida, to lead this beautiful effort that he did. . . . His presence meant everything; and to me personally—as he's perhaps my closest friend, or certainly one of them—it meant everything. But I had nothing to do with that. I didn't know about it until I either heard it from Cheney, or from George W. And people don't believe that. But I'm telling you: that is the truth. I didn't know one, single thing about it. And then George might say, "What do you think about it?" And I'd say, "You couldn't have done better."

Interview with Paula Zahn,
Fox News Channel's The Edge,
Houston, Texas, December 20, 2000

In March 2001, President Bush hosted a discussion at his Presidential Conference Center on the subject of the media. Participating in the exchange were Tom DeFrank of the *New York Post*, Maureen Dowd of the *New York Times*, former Reagan/Bush White House press secretary Marlin Fitzwater, and former White House counsel C. Boyden Gray. The host offered several pointed comments, starting with this remark introducing his former spokesman . . .

He gave over 850 briefings to the White House press corps . . . you talk about cruel and unusual punishment . . .

The rest of the story behind the infamous "wimp" cover . . .

The one [story] that probably annoyed me the most was when a reporter from *Newsweek*—I was Vice President, running for President—endeared herself to me by saying, "We're going to do this broad-scale deal on you, the family." So she pled to see my mother—my mother was then ninety or eighty-nine years old, and we tried to keep her out of the interview business and give her a little privacy. And she endeared herself to my sister, and they went out for dinner. The next thing we know, we read *Newsweek* and here's the famous "wimp" cover—calling me a wimp. I didn't like the wimp cover. [Laughter] I didn't think it was fair. I didn't think it was right. I thought the reporter grossly misled us—the whole family—and I was furious about it.

And Tom [DeFrank] was doing a story—he was innocent of all this I might add—but he was doing a background political thing. Everybody was supposed to cooperate with him . . . and they wouldn't publish it until after the election. And this would be the "inside the election."

And I saw that wimp cover, and I said, "The hell with it. We're not going to cooperate. Now if *Newsweek* wants to ask a question at a press conference, fine. But I don't think I need to be subjected to that kind of unfair—at least I thought it was unfair—characterization." So the appeals process started and Kay Graham came out with some guy, big, tall guy from New York . . . I couldn't have cared less. I called Jimmy Baker, who tore 'em both up. [Laughter] Baker was sitting there. And Evan Thomas said, "I must take responsibility." Then the other guy said, "No, I did that, sir." And it burned me up.

Tom lost out, because I told our people, "Now I don't want you giving the other stuff. You answer questions about my vice presidency, our campaign, anything else—but they're not going to be singled out with favoritism." So you've touched a bit of a nerve . . . [Laughter]

The irony is, if they had reached that conclusion without kinda endearing themselves to my family—my sister, my mother, and all that stuff—I wouldn't have felt quite as strongly about it. It was to be the generic kind of a background—went to school here, did this there—and it turned out to be something very, very different. Some of the stories actually weren't so bad, but anyway enough about the wimp cover. But I can give you a few more examples, so stick around afterwards . . . [Laughter]

———

It's gotten too intrusive, the press coverage about private lives. In the old days, it didn't happen at all. You go back now, in retrospect, and look at the coverage and the allegations about President Kennedy, Bobby Kennedy, and all that, Lyndon Johnson—and it's changed. The ethic in the press corps has changed about these things.

On the other hand, when you have a legitimate interference with a person's job, or something that directly affects what he said, credibility, lying to people—then I think the press has an obligation to look into it. Hard to draw a distinct line on paper.

In the fall of last year, maybe the year before, when 43 [George W.] was running, they had a story in the *Wall Street Journal*, which is not hostile to Republicans—sometimes the news columnists are, sometimes in the editorials—but there are all the rumors that he's facing, and then they knocked them down. But we can't prove this one—the one about this picture out there of him dancing naked on the bar at the Deke fraternity house at Yale thirty years ago or whatever it was. Barbara Bush had the best answer. She said, "Well, I hope it's not a frontal shot." [Laughter]

The press thing's going to go on forever—love/hate. I went back in a fit of anger in 1992—when I thought I was grossly, unfairly treated—and looked at some of the things they were saying about Grover Cleveland . . . and it's ever thus.

I do think the press has changed. I do happen to believe the Washington press and New York press—that would largely be the *Times* and the *Washington Post*—are coming at it from a liberal bias. I believe that. . . . If you asked Al Gore whether he felt that way, he would probably argue the other way. In fact, I had a discussion with one of their people, who said, "I don't see how you can say that. Look what they did to our man, Al."

So it's all through the eyes of the beholder, I guess. We can't live without them in the political process. But now I'm a free spirit. I don't do press conferences. I don't write op-ed pieces. I sit in front of my television set and say, "I wish to hell those people would get out of the United States." [Laughter]

Bush Library Foundation Conference, "White House and the Media,"
College Station, Texas, March 29, 2001

POLITICS

Our family is not obsessed with politics. People think we are, I think, but we're not. But we like it, at times. We've got two sons that are so actively involved in it that Barbara and I are not totally removed, but I don't live and die politics every day of my life anymore—I used to.

Interview with Jamie Gangel, NBC's Today *show,*
Kennebunkport, Maine, June 13, 1995

No brutal dictator can remain in power, no matter how tight his security. So, yes, he's still there. I saw how he was elected late last year with 99.7 percent of the popular vote—to which I can only say it is good to see that democracy is alive and well in Iraq. [Laughter]

Ninety-nine point seven? That reminds me of last year's congressional elections. Whoops. I'm sorry. This is a nonpartisan event. As Dana Carvey would say, "Shouldna done it. Wasn't prudent. [Laughter] Wasn't prudent. Not gonna do it anymore." [Laughter] We made millions for that little guy. [Laughter]

Remarks at the Greater Washington Society
of Association Executives Foundation, Washington, D.C.,
January 22, 1996

The debates—that's a form of rhetoric—and I hated them, absolutely detested going into those debates. I know you had Paul Kirk and Frank Fahrenkopf here last year, so I hope they don't take it personally if I tell you I don't like those debates. It's show business. The press buildup to the debates was overdone—and subsequently the preparation, the hours, we spent rehearsing the answers: "No, wait a minute. Just a little more inflection in the last sentence, sir." And "Oh, that's brilliant, sir. You did that one just right!" [Laughter] Memorize this opening statement; memorize this closing statement; and then, off you go into the arena with the lions out there and the spin merchants—too much for me. Many in the press would like to see more debates, because confrontation and conflict seem to be in demand; but frankly I think they're overrated. I think there's a lot of showbiz now. "Well, now I've got to walk out into the crowd like Oprah Winfrey did and tell her, 'Yes, sir, I see your point on welfare reform,' or whatever it was. I wasn't good at that. I cannot say it was ineffective. I think President Clinton is good at that, and I think others can do it pretty darn well. But I can identify more with Admiral Stockdale [Ross Perot's 1992 running mate]: "Who am I? Why am I here?" [Laughter]

Texas A&M 1996 fall semester lecture "Rhetoric and the Presidency,"
College Station, Texas, December 2, 1996

Recalling a Watergate-era phone conversation with fellow Texan Robert Strauss . . .

"Another shoe has dropped," they kept saying in the press [about Watergate]. And Strauss—who was a friend of mine and happened to be chairman of the national Democratic Party, my counterpart with the Democrats—called me and said, "Your job reminds me of making love to a gorilla." And I said, "How come, Strauss?" And he said, "Because you can't stop until the gorilla wants to." [Laughter] And that's the way it was.

Interview with David Frost, "A President's Story,"
August 25, 1998

The minute I met Gorbachev—and I first met him at Chernenko's funeral—and the minute I met him, I said to myself—and it's confirmed in the cable to Ronald Reagan, my boss—this man is different. And you could tell he was different. And you could tell that he wanted a dialogue in a different way from the others. He was his own man. He was charismatic.

Interview with David Frost, "A President's Story,"
August 25, 1998

Visiting the LBJ Ranch . . .

We climbed into the white Lincoln, and President Johnson had the Secret Service guys instead of with him in the car, in another white Lincoln behind him—and you'd go tearing across this countryside down there in central Texas, the Hill County. I wanted to get the heck out there in a hurry, I'll tell you. [Laughter] He was still living, still living to the hilt—charging forward. It was marvelous.

Texas A&M University Distinguished Lecture,
College Station, Texas, March 8, 1999

There was no shortage of brouhahas—big and small—during his time as UN host ambassador . . .

There was an ambassador from Cypress. His name was Rosedes. He was mugged by Central Park. So that Rosedes—who was about seventy, he couldn't have chased anybody anywhere—to be sure he couldn't chase them, the muggers took off his shoes and threw them in the lake that was the water supply for New York City. So we got a protest from a delegation of ambassadors who wanted to see me: "How can we drink this water? Rosedes's shoes have been thrown in the water."

Which obviously taught him the craft of creative diplomacy . . .

Some of his [Rabbi Kahane] followers chained themselves in to one of the main meeting rooms over there in the UN. There they were, chained there, making some statement like that. The guy said, "So what are you going to do about these people, chained?" And I said, "Just leave them. Everybody at some point has to go to the bathroom." [Laughter] Sure enough, one by one, hour after hour, "May I please leave?" They took them out the side door. But it was one darn thing after another.

Texas A&M University Distinguished Lecture,
College Station, Texas, March 8, 1999

More on the UN days, including an incident where writer Dick Schaap put then Ambassador Bush on the list of the "10 Most Overrated New Yorkers." President Bush later said, "Schaap was too modest to include himself on the list—he should have been right up at the top . . ."

Sometimes those meetings got pretty boring, and I found that most ambassadors—including Yakov Malek, the hard-liner, the cold warrior from the Soviet Union—had a sense of humor. So I'd send him a little note—get the marvelous, beautiful woman that delivered messages—and I'd write it down looking very serious. "Take this to the Soviet ambassador." And he'd look over and smile. It'd be some humorous thing. It was fun. That part was fun. You could relax with people.

I gave a party for the Ten Most Overrated New Yorkers—my name was on the list. I thought that was a little unfair, but the guy that wrote the story felt I was worthy of the honor. And I invited a bunch of the diplomats, and I remember one of the ambassadors saying, "Vhat is dis Ten Most Overrated New Yorkers?" I got a letter from [New York senator] Jacob Javits, who said it was a little beneath the dignity of my office to do it, but it was fun. Bring all these people in, needle yourself—and them a little bit—and put a human face on diplomacy. Doesn't hurt.

Interview with C-SPAN's Brian Lamb,
College Station, Texas, November 25, 1999

The lessons of defeat . . .

It's a character-builder. I mean, I think I'm a better person because I've tasted defeat. Now, I worked like the dickens to see that I wouldn't be defeated in '64, and again '70, and again in 1992. It hurts a lot. But you learn. You learn that there's a life beyond your own personal defeat. You learn that you gotta be gracious in victory, and defeat. You learn that the pain of losing is not yours alone—in my case, the pain of a lot of volunteers and staff people that helped me every inch of the way. There's so many lessons that you can get out of a defeat, but there's a lot of lessons you can learn from a victory, too.

Interview with C-SPAN's Brian Lamb,
College Station, Texas, November 25, 1999

Moving from the UN to the RNC . . .

When he [Nixon] was reelected in '72, I'll never forget Haldeman [Nixon chief of staff H. R. "Bob" Haldeman] called the whole cabinet together: "We want everyone's resignation on the desk by the close of business today." It was not the kindest and gentlest approach to our service, but we all sent the letters in—and then were all summoned, at one time or another, to go to Camp David. One of the things he [Nixon] suggested to me was to be the deputy secretary of the treasury—George Shultz was then secretary—which would have been a high honor. But he said, "What I really want you to do is go be chairman of the [Republican] National Committee." And I believe, still, that when the President asks you to do something, you ought to try to do it if you think you can. . . . So I did, and, boy, was it a headache.

Interview with C-SPAN's Brian Lamb,
College Station, Texas, November 25, 1999

On Richard Nixon . . .

Oddly enough, when I became President, the President I got the most advice from was Richard Nixon. . . .

I think his presidency will always be sullied—and some could argue fatally so—by the ugliness and the finality of the lie of Watergate.

And Watergate . . .

Hell, I was head of the Republican Committee. They could steal all of my papers and they wouldn't have learned a damn thing. But then to have it covered up and then to get the FBI and kind of corrupt the process of government, that was the seriousness of Watergate.

Interview with C-SPAN's Brian Lamb,
College Station, Texas, November 25, 1999

Three observations here on the vice presidency; this first one on the speculation that President Ford would tap him for the number two spot . . .

The day that Ford announced his pick—he was going to walk into the East Room to announce who he wanted to be Vice President— my phone rang in Kennebunkport, and it was the President. He said, "I am going in right now"—we were watching—"I'm going in right now to announce Nelson Rockefeller, and I want you to know it was a hard call for me to make, George." And he couldn't have been nicer. Of course, Gerald Ford is one of the most consid- erate men I have ever met. And to take the time—I could see it on television, "The President is making one call" or "The President will be in here in a minute"—and here he was calling me because he didn't want hurt feelings. So there was speculation, flattering speculation, but I didn't expect that.

Interview with C-SPAN's Brian Lamb,
College Station, Texas, November 25, 1999

Until George Bush was elected President directly from the vice presidency in 1988, the most recent politician to accomplish that feat was Martin Van Buren in 1836. Here, President Bush comments on the "Van Buren curse"...

I didn't say, "Oh, gosh, the odds are stacked against me 'cause ol' Marty was the last guy to win"—Marty Van Buren, that would be. I didn't think about that, but the press speculated a lot. And a lot of it was: When you're Vice President, you're not your own man. Gotta get your own heartbeat and pulse out there—and to some degree that's true. You sublimate your own views to those of the President provided you want the vice presidency to mean anything, or if the vice presidency's going to mean anything to him. If I go out and start carving my own niche because over the hill I can see a chance to run for President, what's Ronald Reagan going to think? What kind of loyalty is that? What kind of use would he have for a Vice President? You'd sit up there, and it'd be like John Nance Garner said. [Garner famously said the vice presidency "wasn't worth a warm pitcher of spit."] Sit up in a Senate office—you wouldn't even have an office in the White House if the President didn't permit it.

Interview with C-SPAN's Brian Lamb,
College Station, Texas, November 25, 1999

Had I not been Vice President, I might well not have been President—because Reagan, at the last moment, put me on the ticket. He was so good to me in every single way. And so the pluses of the vice presidency far outweighed the confines.

A conversation with Hugh Sidey, "Time and the Presidency,"
Lafayette Square, April 11, 2000

SPORTS

The adrenaline factor in politics is identical to the adrenaline factor in sports. George Plimpton has written about what he calls the

"X Factor." There is an X Factor in politics, and there's an X Factor in sports. The extra last throw of a horseshoe where you need a ringer, or you're history. The time at the plate when either you produce, or you don't. There's a similar physical feeling in politics—on election eve, say, or when you're facing a debate situation, or a crisis in legislation—to the feeling in sports.

Interview with Peter Roussel, KUHT-TV's
"A Conversation with George Bush," Houston, Texas,
November 18, 1994

During a 1994 photo op in his first race for Texas governor, George W. shot a protected bird called a killdeer. Here, his father pokes a little good-natured fun at the new Texas governor-elect . . .

I love shooting. I'm not very much on the killdeer, but I'm very strong on shooting quail, for example.

Interview with Peter Roussel, KUHT-TV's
"A Conversation with George Bush," Houston, Texas,
November 18, 1994

Outside his family, fly-fishing is George Bush's first love these days . . .

It's totally mesmerizing, totally relaxing. You get your mind totally off everything as you try to put the fly where the swirl was. Time goes away. You could stay there forever. . . .

I am the past, a happy part of the past. I don't want to sit at the head table anymore. I want to go fishing.

Interview with Paula Zahn, CBS's Sunday Morning,
Labrador, Canada, August 4, 1996

A woman once asked me if I thought hunting was a humane pastime. I told her the way I shoot it is. But as we all know, other people feel strongly about this as well. I'll never forget the so-called demonstrations when I would go hunting in Beeville, Texas, as Vice President and then as President. There they'd be: ten or fifteen protesters out there with the Mercedes neatly parked along the roadside and signs showing. Frankly, I thought such a meager showing was beneath the office.

I was used to more militant demonstrators like the woman that charged my car in San Francisco. She was a rather unattractive lady yelling and bearing a sign that said, "Stay out of my womb." Hey, no problem!

Remarks for Safari Club International,
Las Vegas, Nevada, February 1, 1997

Remembering a main tennis nemesis from their stay in China . . .

President Bush. You know, I'm not a bragging kind of guy, but did you know that you are talking to the former men's doubles champion of the international community? Yes, indeed, sir.

Mrs. Bush. It almost broke up our marriage when we lost to the East German lady.

President Bush. You and I?

Mrs. Bush. You and I. You were furious. She played with a Pakistani and the East German lady who, I think, had triplets and looked like—

President Bush. I thought she had a sex change, I'll tell you. [Laughter] She had a serve like a bullet.

Interview with David Frost, "A President's Story,"
U.S. ambassador's residence, Beijing, China,
August 25, 1998

EPILOGUE

As the chief executive and chief diplomat of the U.S. government from 1989 to 1993, George Bush's values, his heartbeat, greatly influenced the rhythm of our national life and indeed the world. History will surely note that the breadth of his perspective, combined with the surety of his ideals, helped shape the dramatic times in which he led—when the tectonic plates of geopolitics shifted decisively in freedom's direction.

More important than history's verdict to him, undoubtedly, is the timeless legacy of values he inherited from his parents—and is today helping to pass down to his children's children. Not the kind of values that find their ultimate expression in the fleeting favor of electoral politics or the comfort of material wealth, mind you, but in the quiet, enduring strength of faith, family, and friends—and an occasional good joke or two.

In a letter written to his five children in 1998, George Bush confided, "Last year there was only a tiny sense of time left—of sand running through the glass. This year, I must confess, I am much more aware." But he fully grasped the imposing frailties of this world long before this 1998 letter implies. Indeed, if—as has been suggested—his heartbeat was tough for some to understand, it might very well be because few could appreciate the totality of experiences that dictated its pulse. He saw friends die in war as a teenager and nearly gave his own life. As young parents, his wife and he watched a precious little girl slip painfully away, taken by a cruel illness at an innocent age. And after a grueling climb to what he calls the "mountaintop of American politics," he then passed through the crucible of world leadership at a time of great risk—only to suffer an unlikely defeat at the polls eleven months hence. As much as any person, George Bush recognizes tomorrow is promised to no one.

Perhaps, just maybe, this explains why the man is always in a rush—always in a mode of "Come on, let's go, there's still so much to do." Perhaps this helps explain why, at age seventy-seven, he still works some Sundays—or, when he's suffering from jet lag in the wee hours, decides to go into the office and catch up on the mail. Perhaps this starts to account for his faith, his genuine patriotism, his fidelity to family. Perhaps it begins to explain why he's always saying "on to the next event"—if not in word, then certainly by his manner.

In sum, perhaps this helps us better understand the innate drive and decency—the heartbeat, you might say—of one of the great statesmen of the twentieth century.

INDEX

JIM MCGRATH has worked for George Bush since 1991, at the White House, as his post presidential spokesman, and currently as his speechwriter, for the past seven years. McGrath lives in Houston, Texas, where he is founding partner of CEO Communications. He studied journalism and government at the University of Maryland.